Eighty Odd Years in Hollywood

Eighty Odd Years in Hollywood

*Memoir of a Career in
Film and Television*

JOHN MEREDYTH LUCAS

with a foreword by Cari Beauchamp

McFarland & Company, Inc., Publishers
Jefferson, North Carolina, and London

LIBRARY OF CONGRESS CATALOGUING-IN-PUBLICATION DATA

Lucas, John Meredyth, 1919–2002.
    Eighty odd years in Hollywood : memoir of a career in film and television / John Meredyth Lucas ; with a foreword by Cari Beauchamp.
    p.   cm.
    Includes index.

    ISBN 978-0-7864-1838-1
    softcover : 50# alkaline paper ∞

    1. Lucas, John Meredyth, 1919–2002.   2. Television producers and directors—United States—Biography.   3. Motion picture producers and directors—United States—Biography.   4. Television writers—United States—Biography.   5. Screenwriters—United States—Biography.   I. Title: 80 odd years in Hollywood.   II. Title.
PN1992.4.L75A3   2004
791.4302'33'092—dc22   2004004451

British Library cataloguing data are available

©2004 John Meredyth Lucas. All rights reserved

No part of this book may be reproduced or transmitted in any form or by any means, electronic or mechanical, including photocopying or recording, or by any information storage and retrieval system, without permission in writing from the publisher.

On the cover: (left to right) mother Bess Meredyth, publicity photograph circa 1930; stepfather Michael Curtiz; John Meredyth Lucas, 1923

Manufactured in the United States of America

McFarland & Company, Inc., Publishers
   Box 611, Jefferson, North Carolina 28640
     www.mcfarlandpub.com

Contents

Foreword by Cari Beauchamp   1

1. A Hollywood Family   5
2. Cast of Characters   14
3. Home, School and Earthshaking Events   34
4. Life with Stepfather   48
5. Resisting Education and Other Pursuits   61
6. Coming Up for Air   75
7. Hungarian Goulash   91
8. Off Camera   113
9. In the Wings   134
10. Takeoffs and Landings   155
11. New Directions   166
12. Test Patterns   182
13. Foreign Accents   199
14. Finding Focus   218
15. Gains and Losses   234
16. Letters of Transit   255
17. Fade Out, Fade In   270

18	New Horizons	281
19	Full Circle	291

Epilogue   305
Index   307

Foreword
by Cari Beauchamp

Only in Hollywood… This extraordinary family of Michael Curtiz, Bess Meredyth, Wilfred Lucas and John Meredyth Lucas spans the history of filmed entertainment, from early silents through Technicolor and award-winning classics as diverse as *Casablanca* and *Yankee Doodle Dandy* on through television programs like *Star Trek*, still seen in syndication today. And now *Eighty Odd Years in Hollywood*, the memoir of John Meredyth Lucas, takes us behind the camera to give us this insider's history as it unfolded.

John was so much more than the proverbial fly on the wall; he was a high-perched witness and an active participant. Here is W.C. Fields juggling plates at the family dinner table, "Earl Flynt," as Mike called his *Robin Hood* star, playing a corpse in his U.S. film debut, *Case of the Curious Bride*, and a 12-year-old John Meredyth Lucas billing the family account at the studio to send his heartthrob Joan Crawford a basket full of baby ducks at Easter. Errol Flynn, Irving Thalberg, James Cagney, Hal Wallis, Bette Davis, Olivia de Havilland, William Powell, Ingrid Bergman, Humphrey Bogart—the list goes on of those who come to life in this incredible family tale. The combined talents of the Meredyth, Lucas and Curtiz family are more than enough to warrant a volume, but *Eighty Odd Years in Hollywood* is so much more than that; it is a first-hand, very personal account of these remarkable people. None suffered fools gladly or otherwise. They shared a real passion for filmmaking and each was as unique, enchanting and confounding in their real lives as any characters they ever put on the screen.

John's mother Bess Meredyth and stepfather Michael Curtiz both began making films in 1912; Michael was in his native Budapest working under his given name of Mihaly Kertesz and the ambitious redheaded Bess was in Los Angeles. Born Helen Elizabeth MacGlashan in Buffalo, Bess plucked Meredyth from the family tree when she began acting at Biograph. Leaving the career as a concert pianist that had brought her to California, she met up with Wilfred Lucas and together they wrote, directed and acted in films for Universal and a variety of other studios, including the serial she wrote and starred in, *Bess the Detectress*.

After they married, they packed up their cameras and infant son John and spent a year making feature films in Australia. When they returned to Hollywood in 1920, Bess put out a shingle as a screenwriter, becoming the only individual to be listed in the local directory as a scenario writer, and Wilfred returned to acting, primarily in Westerns. Bess was sent to Rome by MGM to "rescue" the script of *Ben Hur* and after she and the production had been brought back to Los Angeles, she and Wilfred decided to go their separate ways. Bess went to work writing one of the very first partial "talkies," *Don Juan*; it was at Warner Brothers that Bess met their most recent directorial import, the renamed Michael Curtiz. Michael and his "Besky" were married soon after and while Bess continued to write on her own, including *The Mark of Zorro* starring Tyrone Power, her friends knew her real energy was going into helping Michael behind the scenes on the films that would bring him fame such as *The Adventures of Robin Hood*, *Casablanca* and *Mildred Pierce*.

What talents they were and amazingly amicable, too; Wilfred was featured so often in Curtiz's films that he called Bess's ex-husband "my good luck charm." Her son John grew up on the sets, spending his teenage years as an extra in films like *Captain Blood* and as a "script boy" on many of Curtiz's films. John met his wife Joan Winfield (Jack Warner himself had dubbed her that after a character Bette Davis played in one of his films) on the set of *Gorilla Man* where John was the dialogue director and Joan one of the Gorilla's victims. The serendipitous anecdotes bring out layers of film history we would know no other way.

My first meeting with John ranks as one of my most embarrassing moments. I was researching my book on Frances Marion. Bess had been one of her closest friends and Wilfred had acted in many of Fred Thomson's films, so I was so pleased when John invited me to meet him at his home in Newport Beach. He charmed me with tales of his parents and reveled in showing me his mother's scripts and photographs as well as Frances' paintings on the walls. It turned out that Frances had played a key role in helping him marry his beloved wife Joan in the Catholic

Church; truly ironic since Frances was passionately irreligious, but her incredible network of friends included a very liberal and movie-loving cleric from New Orleans. So many gems just kept coming. Well, I had been being entertained and enlightened by John for over two hours when I finally looked up from my frantic note-taking to ask, "And what did you end up doing?"

An engaging, almost awkward smile crossed his lips as he paused; only afterwards did I realize it was because he didn't know where to begin. "Well," he finally answered, "I wrote, produced and directed *Ben Casey* ... and *Mannix* ... and *Star Trek* ... and *The Fugitive*." I must have turned crimson, but he couldn't have been more gracious, assuring me that I was so obsessed with the teens, '20s and '30s that obviously he was "after my time." I then learned John had also written and directed plays and several feature films, played a pivotal and longtime role in the groundbreaking series *Insight* and worked with Walt Disney in the early days of television on several projects, including my childhood favorite *Zorro*, starring Guy Williams. (Watch when they return to syndication; I swear, John's scripts are the most complex and satisfying.)

Of course now one of the wonderful things about *Eighty Odd Years in Hollywood* is that there will be no excuse for anyone repeating my ignorance. John not only forgave me, but was kind enough to continue to stay in touch, support me when *Without Lying Down* was published and invite me back to visit him and his wonderful wife Patricia, whom he had married after being a widower for several years. And when John told me he was working on his family's story, I couldn't have been more excited because I knew there were so many wonderful stories to share; who better to tell them than the man who not only experienced it, but was a consummate storyteller himself?

John passed away last year, shortly after completing this manuscript, but if there is a silver lining it is that it served to bring him even closer to his three incredible children, now artistic, accomplished adults: Elizabeth, an actress; Victoria, a film producer; and Michael, a photographer. John's gifts to us are many, but I am particularly grateful that he stayed with us long enough to finish and share this delightful, insightful and most illuminating memoir.

Los Angeles, 2004

1
A Hollywood Family

Like Adam's apple lady, whose bite got them thrown out of the Garden of Eden, her name was Eve. She was the wife of a famous movie columnist. She seduced me at a Hollywood party. I was 12.

It wasn't exactly a Hollywood party. We lived in Beverly Hills and the house was full of the same friends my family entertained almost weekly—when they weren't being entertained at the homes of those same friends. They were Aunt Virginia and Darryl Zanuck, Irma and Jack Warner, Louella Parsons, Louise and Hal Wallis, directors, stars, producers, just people like that. There were perhaps 20 that night.

Mother and Mike, my Hungarian stepfather, greeted them in the entrance hall with its paneled walls and checkerboard black-and-white marble floor. At their backs was the spectacular stained glass window lit from behind and consisting of two panels—one from St. Stephen's Cathedral and the other from the Hofburg Palace chapel—bought in Vienna on their last trip to Europe. These ecclesiastical and imperial mementos now graced the home of a man born to a poor but large Jewish family in a tiny house at 23 Sevetsigc Utza in Budapest in the Austro-Hungarian Empire—one of Emperor Franz Joseph's humblest subjects.

Mother divorced my father in 1925, when she came back from Rome and the making of *Ben Hur*. After the divorce, while working at Warner Brothers Studios writing John Barrymore pictures, she met this new director who had done spectacular Biblical pictures in Europe. The Warners, Jack and Harry, had gone to Europe and brought back Kertesz Kaminar Mihaly under contract. In 1929, he and my mother were married.

Mihaly was told, in this new country, that his name must be simplified. So Kertesz Kaminar Mihaly was transformed into Michael Curtiz (a name he pronounced Kurtehz and the rest of the world pronounced Curteez). Mike's pronunciation of his name was less bizarre than the rest of his speech, so this difference generally went unremarked. His European friends claimed he was unintelligible in five languages. This was not true—he made himself quite clear. What was remarkable was the way he did it. Curtiz malapropisms were quoted as often as Goldwynisms.

When the party guests arrived, the actual opening of the door was done by Collins, our chauffeur, butler and almost member of the family. Collins was, in the polite term of the time, colored. He would have regarded black or African-American as an insult. He had been with Mother forever. Everyone greeted Collins with affection. They joked with him and he joked back, successfully treading the tightrope that colored people walked in those days.

I, home from military school for the weekend, was favored with gems of conversational brilliance such as "Hey, Jack, look at you. You're all grown up."

Mother greeted her guests in the effusive manner of the industry, as though they hadn't seen each other for years, instead of only last week at the Academy Awards Dinner at the Embassy Club. Mother was a founding member of the Academy of Motion Picture Arts and Sciences, which gives out the Oscars.

When guests came to Mike, they were welcomed in a variety of languages. There were many Europeans in Hollywood in the early 30s. The specter of Hitler was just beginning to trouble those with wisdom to recognize the military threat and frighten those not purely Aryan. Some of Mike's fellow Hungarians cornered him with a copy of *Az Ember*, a Hungarian newspaper published in the United States. In a corner of the room they read from it excitedly in their odd language.

I was bored. The day hadn't started well. I'd had to eat my breakfast in the Hungarian breakfast room where I sulked amid the ethnic brilliance of Hungarian peasant furniture painted in shades of blue with the bright red of flowers and the yellow of wheat sheaves. I sulked because of Mrs. Radnoti, our Hungarian party cook.

Normally I took my morning repast in the kitchen at the servant's table, close to the butter, which I slathered generously on my toast and where I could con Coretta, our cook, into frying me another half dozen strips of bacon. But on party days, when Mrs. Radnoti commandeered the kitchen, she cast out not only me but also our colored servants.

A woman of gigantic girth, Mrs. Radnoti began her day by pounding the strudel dough until it seemed the massive kitchen table would break. She would then roll it, plunge the dough into ice water and begin the process again. For hours she would flatten, roll and flatten again, getting it thinner and thinner until a newspaper could be read through the translucent membrane.

Beyond the open door of the breakfast room I could watch Collins polishing silver in the butler's pantry. This was a job he usually hated but here, close to the kitchen, he could keep a wary eye on "that foreigner."

Coretta could be heard in her room, muttering loudly to herself. It was an affront that, at special parties, she, Coretta, the best cook in Beverly Hills "Ain't nobody don't like what I fix" was shoved aside and the guests fed "foreign food" prepared by that "*ofay.*" Ofay was a colored term for white folks—Foe, in the common colored usage of pig Latin.

The presence of Pearl, our maid, thin to the point of anorexia, was signaled by the whine of her vacuum. Her husband, James, an overly polite, despondent man who worked for us on special occasions and had permanent permission to share his wife's tiny room, was outside with his bucket and rags, slowly washing the windows. As far as I know, our parties provided James' only employment. Sometimes he would help Collins serve the table. Collins would generally remind him to bathe for such events: "You smell tired, boy. You can't serve the white folks smelling tired." Collins had been a waiter in a Pullman Car—even worked the Twentieth Century Limited—and knew about such things.

At that time there was no such thing as "race relations." The coloreds "kept their place" and the surface of the social pool was unruffled. Oh, there were some regrettable things happening in the South but that was almost a foreign country. "Down behind the sun," as Collins put it. However, beneath the surface stirred occasional signs of resentment, usually presented as humor. Collins' wife, who worked on and off as a maid—off when she drank, on when she promised never again—would say while making my bed, "We got to call them Miss Sheet and Mrs. Pillowcase, 'cause they're white." I thought she was real funny.

At parties, Collins, who could mix any drink known or invented on the spot, would tend bar—an illegal function, of course, Prohibition having not yet been abolished by the incoming president, Franklin D. Roosevelt.

Parties, in those days, required a great deal of drinking but Mike's Hungarians concentrated more on eating. In this they excelled. It was an art form to them, though quantity was also important. There would be great critiques of the meals, all in Hungarian and at full volume. Although he took part in such discussions, Mike himself ate sparingly.

After breakfast I had watched Collins make Mother's favorite punch. Cut-up fresh peaches that had been soaked overnight in brandy formed the base. Then in huge silver bowls they were drowned in equal parts of still white wine and champagne, all obtained from a reliable bootlegger who serviced most of the movie industry.

For the first time, when Collins was otherwise occupied, I tried it. Delicious. I am sure Collins knew what I was doing but elected not to see. Fathers might come and go but Collins was always there, filling the void between male parents. Collins brought me up.

Earlier, just before the party, I watched Mother's blond hair being done by the hairdresser while Pearl applied whitener to the freckled shoulders, which Mother deemed unseemly with her sleeveless beaded gown. "Put on your dress uniform, old man," she told me in the mirror. Most of the guests' children also went to military school. After considerable discussion, I managed, without an outright confrontation, to avoid the uniform. As a counter offer, I ran off and promptly returned in my blue suit and white shirt with starched wing collar and four-in-hand tie. I had seen a movie with the hero, an Austrian doctor, so attired and realized at once how mature and magnificent I would look in such garb. The shirt and collar had been secretly charged on my mother's account at Bullock's Wilshire, where I had been sent to get my birthday sport coat. Collins warned that the shirt would not be to Mother's taste. He was right. My handsome outfit was summarily rejected. After much meaningful discussion, I was allowed the blue civilian suit but forced to wear my school shirt and tie. I determined not to remove my coat and expose the shame of the shirt, which had epaulets. How could I have known I would remove much more that night?

When greeting the guests palled, I went to the dining room to explore the buffet. The sideboard and the huge Biedermeier dining table groaned with the weight of cakes, three kinds of Mrs. Radnoti's strudel: apple, poppy seed and red cabbage. These complimented the salads, sauces, Chicken Paprikas, bizarre pork and beef dishes, horse radish, breads of all kinds, fruit, cheeses and an Everest of whipped cream. Before I could make an appreciable dent, I was chased away by James. He had been relieved at the bar by Collins and now had nothing to do but remind me how Mother would want the table to look when the guests attacked it.

I moved on. Two of our great silver punch bowls had been placed beside the bar, which was part of the library overlooking the sunken garden with its fountain and the colonnades leading to the rear garden. The bowls contained Mother's favorite punch—the peaches, brandy and wine. When the guests were otherwise occupied, I again sampled the bowl's goodness unobserved by the adults. They were watching W.C. Fields, whose career had started in vaudeville, juggle four of Mother's best gold-bordered

Lennox plates. This diversion allowed me to sneak two generous punch samples before a plate shattered. Mr. Fields, who had fortified himself with gin beforehand, lest the party turn out to be Temperance, was in tears, inconsolable, not because of the loss of Mother's dish but at his own diminished juggling power, his intimation of mortality.

Mike moved to save the remaining plates but Mother intercepted him, assuring Fields she never liked the design. But despite that and Collins' instant removal of the fragments, the fun had been dampened.

Not for me, however. The punch had given wings to my tongue. I moved among the guests, discussing topics of interest with godlike rhetoric. It never occurred to me that I was expounding my ideas to important people. They were just friends of my parents and I never thought of my parents as special or that they or their friends were rich and working in a time when work, any work, was considered a blessing.

This year, 1931, was a terrible time in America and ultimately the world: the Great Depression had been triggered by the New York Stock Market Crash. The newspapers were full of the suicides of those who had lost everything in the crash and of the survivors, often reduced to standing in breadlines as there was no work to be had. Captains of industry were reduced to selling apples on the street corners.

There is a story of a child in a Beverly Hills school, assigned to write an essay on the Great Depression. The boy chose to describe a family poverty-stricken by financial ruin. "They are a very poor family," he wrote. "The father is poor. The mother is poor. Their cook, their maid and their butler are all poor."

I did not regard my lifestyle as unusual. I thought everyone lived the way I did, boarded at military school, and got passes to come home on weekends, barring some infraction of school law. That was just the way things were.

But parties were not the most fascinating part of my life. Real excitement involved riding in the car—going out with my parents to a prizefight at the Legion Stadium in Hollywood or to the Filmart Theater to see a foreign film. The Filmart on Vine Street ran movies from all over the world. Mike tried to see them all. He had worked at UFA, in Germany, at the cutting edge of film experimentation. I dozed through most of the pictures because they were not even subtitled. Fortunately, many were in German, which Mother was studying and in which I was to be tutored at the Berlitz School. As a subject of the Austro-Hungarian Empire, German was Mike's second language. His first, Hungarian, was impossible to learn.

We also drove to visit relatives; one branch lived in Glendale, another in Pasadena. Between our three groups, we alternated holidays. Uncle Bill and Aunt Vi had Thanksgiving in Glendale. We celebrated New Year's Day with Uncle Will in Pasadena. In Beverly Hills we had them all for Christmas and the Fourth of July.

Will's home was one of the lesser houses among the great mansions on Pasadena's South Orange Grove Boulevard. The Rose Parade passed by his door. New Year's Day was a large gathering of the family, among them two of Mother's elderly aunts, with whom she had boarded as a child. The aunts seemed not particularly interested in the themes of the floats or the flowers. With paper and pencil in hand, they would count the number of floats that passed and argue over their totals.

At one elaborate New Year's dinner, Mike, seated between Aunt Florence, the hostess, and Auntie Vi, said admiringly, "Goddamn, Florence, is wonderful salad." He turned to his right: "Better than you make, Vi." Then, as Aunt Florence repressed a satisfied smile, he added, "But not so good like we get at home." He contentedly went on eating, leaving Mother to soothe the two aunts.

Where we went, however, was not as important as riding in our car, being driven from place to place. My parents, naturally, rode in the back of the limousine, which was upholstered in ecru wool and had a fur lap rug. I sat in front with Collins. The front seat was black leather. I wore my white trench coat. For me, our car was a bulletproof limo. I was bodyguard for a family resembling Al Capone's. I would have preferred a Tommy gun but that, as everyone knows, requires a violin case. Instead, I jammed my hand into my coat, prepared to shoot from the pocket at the least sign of trouble from other mobs. My eyes, mere slits, followed the hostile motions of all cars we encountered. They'd better not mess with *us*!

"Jick." This was Mike's rendition of my name. "Is hot. Why hell you wear coat?" I would always think up some excuse but it did bother my concentration. I never discussed with Collins the vital and dangerous role I played. His response would have been his usual "Shit, boy!"

Collins was much in demand. Many of Mother's guests had tried to lure him away with offers of higher pay, lighter duties. He stayed. He drove Mother, never Mike. Mike had his own car, a Packard roadster. He had never driven in Europe and had mastered the Packard only as far as second gear. He drove everywhere with an angrily protesting engine until, years later, someone explained that it was necessary to pull the gearshift lever down one more time to achieve a smooth and silent ride. Reverse he never learned.

One morning he angrily called the house. "Colon [his version of Collins' name]. Am on the studio. Goddamn car don't work."

In front of the studio, Collins found police and a small crowd gathered in the middle of Sunset Boulevard. Blocking the streetcar and dismaying traffic was the Packard. A tire was flat. Collins managed to ease his way through annoyed police and all the civilian confusion. That night the car, all tires intact, was at the door of the sound stage for Mike to drive home.

Louella Parsons, columnist for the Hearst press and one of the most important voices in Hollywood (actors would do almost anything to gain a mention in her column), and Maggie Ettinger, Hollywood's foremost press agent, were double cousins as well as Mother's best friends. To this day I have never learned the meaning of double cousin but they made a great deal of it. Louella's byline was Louella O. Parsons. The O. was for Oettinger. Maggie dropped the O and was simply Margaret Ettinger. One summer they both shared a beach house in Venice with Mother. Louella was so impressed with Collins' cooking, bartending and general management of the household that, knowing the impossibility of getting him away from Mother, solved the problem by renaming her own chauffeur Collins. This man, whose original name is lost to history, adjusted to his new designation, showing resentment neither to Collins nor his employer.

Beside Collins, at the beach house, was Nat, cook and general handyman. Nat was young, slim, café-au-lait with what, to me, was a strangely funny manner. I stayed at the beach during summers when Mother, Louella and Maggie were at their offices. Nat was in charge of my safety and amusement. I had fallen asleep on the beach and gotten a third degree burn requiring brief hospitalization. On recovery I was made to wear a humiliating shirt under my swimsuit. This afforded amusement for the local children and ended the attraction of the water for me. After that, my amusement was to be found only at the Venice pier with its wide spectrum of rides and sideshows. There were the tame ones like Noah's Ark. That was for children and therefore uninteresting. Bumper Cars. Better. Nat would shriek pathetically when I rammed my car into his. But my real find was the roller coaster. This terrified Nat, so it became my favorite. He would try to distract me: "Come on, Sookie [his name for me], you like the baseballs, dunk the clown." I said I'd ride the roller coaster alone. Nat would protest that I couldn't and he was "absolutely not going near that thing." I reminded him that Mother expected him to take care of me. "Suppose I fall out?" Finally he would make the dreaded ride, eyes closed and screaming almost continuously.

Nat was an excellent cook but Mother finally fired him when she found that, on his days off, he'd been sneaking her expensive (and often yet unworn) dresses from her closet to wear to galas with his boyfriends.

At the time I knew nothing of crossdressing or the wide variety of sexual pursuits available. I thought Nat was just real funny.

But to return to the night of the party: After Mr. Fields' tragic loss of his juggling dexterity, I felt it necessary to make up for the guests' somber mood by telling a joke that was going around my current military school. I changed schools frequently. Institutional personnel tended to disagree with me on the value of discipline and formal education. For an only child, a boarding school with perhaps a hundred kids underfoot seemed an unconscionable invasion of privacy. Also, you were expected to make your own bed, clean the room and shine your shoes. I was being trained to become a servant. The school joke I told was mildly scatological and the guests did not respond as enthusiastically as I had hoped. Also, the sampled punch was making the room seem hot and unstable. Mother interrupted her playing of the piano to remind me it was way past my bedtime and I seemed overly tired. My tongue had difficulty forming a reply but I was saved by someone stopping to admire Mother's buglebeaded Bess Schlank dress. That respite got me out into the garden.

The air was fresh. I wandered to the garden house and was wondering whether to lie down or vomit when Eve came up. The events from that point are not quite clear. I realize now that she was as drunk as I was. But, at the time, it was like the most fabulous dream I'd ever dreamed. She grabbed me by the hair a little roughly but, before I could frame a protest, her lips were on mine.

Buzz Hammeras, briefly a roommate in one of my military schools, had smuggled a book back one weekend and read it under the covers with the aid of a flashlight. The reading was accompanied by a good deal of auxiliary action and panting. Next day, I got the book from beneath the dirty socks in his locker and read it in the toilet.

That chance encounter in the garden house was like the book, like the most delicious, most hoped-for wish I'd ever made. Briefly, I was annoyed at being undressed as though I was a child but I soon realized there was a significant difference. Despite the research I'd done in Hammeras' book, I was uncertain exactly what was expected. Encouragement like, "For Christ's sake, kid, come on, shape up!" did not totally reassure me. The garden house contained a croquet set, tables, garden chairs and a hammock. Unfortunately Eve chose the hammock, an unstable platform under the best of circumstances. I cannot, with any certainty, say how the affair was concluded. I have relived it in my mind a thousand times, adding countless variations. I like to think I supplied the racy excitement she could not find in a staid husband facing constant deadlines for his newspaper column. But perhaps we just passed out.

At any rate I returned to the party, disheveled but grinning widely. Aunt Virginia Zanuck, wife of the producer who was soon to leave Warners and set up Twentieth Century–Fox, noted the lipstick smeared on my face and informed Mother. They tried to ease me out of the room before Mike and the other guests noticed. Mother was not yet certain of the relationship between her unpredictable husband and the stepson he had inherited. She had pulled me as far as the kitchen door when Mike's voice cut through the hubbub of the room. "Besky, where hell you go?"

"Upstairs," Mother said quickly. "I'll be right back."

But Collins, ever vigilant, had taken over and led me away. Mother turned to find Mike laughing uproariously. "Jesus, Maria," he said. "The kid have the most fun on the whole party."

Collins put me to bed and, having a houseful of people awaiting drinks, had no time to listen to my triumph. "It's true, Collins," I sputtered happily. "She did it with me. Honest. She was really hot, Collins. Red hot!" Collins shook his head. "Shit, boy," he said gently and turned off the light.

2
Cast of Characters

In the morning, despite the awful pain of waking, the agony of dressing and Mother's studied silence when I performed the morning ritual of following her breakfast tray to her bedroom—despite all that, I sensed that I had successfully negotiated a rite of passage.

I refused the breakfast Coretta had prepared, ducking a tsunami of nausea at the sight of her usually welcomed bacon strips and hotcakes.

On the drive to school, Collins still displayed no interest in discussing the night's activities. Walking up the school steps, I was conscious of a thirst I had never known before. The steps were a huge sand dune in the Sahara and I had been long lost without water. I spent enough time at the drinking fountain to be late for class. Muttering an apology, I went unsteadily to my seat. The water must have dissolved the alcohol and brought back all the hazy splendor of the night. It also turned me green. As my face slumped to the desktop, the teacher asked what was wrong. When I could not explain coherently, I was sent to the nurse, and my home was called. Collins, waiting to drive Mother to the studio, had to pick me up first and drive me home. He was silent on the drive.

I tried to avoid Mother's eyes as I stumbled out of the car but I thought I detected the ghost of a smile as she climbed into the limousine, already late for a story conference at the studio.

It was to be over a year before I would again see my (perhaps) lover, Eve. Then she did not recognize me or, as I preferred to think, did not dare to in her husband's presence. It was at a Sunday afternoon gathering at the Zanucks' and Eve had been drinking heavily and arguing with her husband. The columnist, having taken a good deal of abuse from his wife, finally screamed at her to shut up.

"Don't raise your voice to your wife," Darryl said in mock outrage. "That," Eve retorted, "is about all he *can* raise for me."

Although I didn't quite understand the roar of laughter that followed, I pretended to laugh so as not to be thought stupid. I was quickly sent home with Collins to do my homework. The homework was never done but, by bedtime, I had figured out the meaning of the scene I had witnessed and conceived in my mind a dozen witty and wonderful replies I could have made to Eve's statement. I had thought of her a lot since our first encounter in the garden house.

On that fateful morning-after, when I had been sent home from school, I had spent the rest of that day in bed, sleeping fitfully. A fair amount of my childhood was spent in bed under what was called a croup tent, breathing fumes of foul medications supposed to ease my wheezing. I had asthma, so severe at times that the doctor had to come out and give me shots of adrenaline. The worst of my allergies continued well into my late teens. I went through hundreds of scratch tests and was found to be allergic to almost everything. To this day I avoid all animal danders, red wine, chocolate, shellfish, mangoes and honeydew melons. House dust and damp must are also no-nos.

But on the morning in question it was a simple hangover I suffered. I did read in bed, finding time so spent immeasurably superior to that wasted in school. By dinnertime, I put on my monogrammed green silk pajamas, a Christmas gift from Mother, made to measure at Machin's, and went in to make amends. In the hall mirror, just before her bedroom, I formed my face into a study of contrition but I never got as far as an apology because Mother told me, "If you're going to drink, old man, you'd better learn to hold your liquor." She revealed that, at an age half mine, she used to be given sips of my grandfather's whiskey. She and grandfather were inordinately proud of this accomplishment which was done out of sight of my grandmother, who was perpetually anxious about grandfather's too-free use of the bottle. That should have surprised no one familiar with the traditional rebellion of minister's sons.

My grandfather was Andrew Fuller MacGlashan. His father was a Scotch Presbyterian minister who shared a home with his brother, also a Scotch Presbyterian minister. All of Andy's youthful misdeeds (and they were legion) were punished, first by his father, then, with equal vehemence, by his uncle. Righteous Christian virtue was instilled with a heavy razor strop. These lessons in proper behavior were given in front of the parlor fireplace with Andy made to place his hands on the mantle and face the prime decoration of the room, a large print of the Roman coliseum where lions were making mincemeat of martyrs. This was, presumably,

Bess as a child with older sister Viola MacGlashan (at piano) and Mother Julia MacGlashan and aunt Agnes Woodard (circa 1884).

to display how light was his pain compared to the suffering of the founders of the church. Andy was not long faithful to the faith of his fathers. Grandmother, Julia Ginther, on the other hand, was Roman Catholic. Her name and her family came from Alsace-Lorraine sometime in the 1830s. Great-grandmother Ginther, along with many of the other passengers, died of cholera on shipboard during the crossing. The survivors moved to Canada where Julia's father married Lena, a woman of German extraction. They ultimately moved to Buffalo, New York, in the United States, where Julia was born. The move was unfortunate for great-grandfather. His allegiance to his new country caused him to enlist in a cavalry regiment and he died in the Battle of the Wilderness, fighting to preserve the Union.

Julia's brother, Jake, was a priest. But she, in the course of her marriage to my nominally Protestant grandfather, was disowned by her family as well as his church. Grandfather's family insisted Catholics "worshipped idols" and were going to hell. Grandmother's people told her that Presbyterians were "heretics" and would burn in everlasting flames. As both sides of this religious schism were equally intransigent, Grandmother simply abandoned religion altogether.

Mother was the third and last of Julia's children. Viola was 12 years older and Will (William Frederick MacGlashan) had a 14-year lead. Mother was obviously an afterthought and, probably, unexpected. Her birthplace was Buffalo and her relationship with her much older siblings was necessarily limited. She was left much to her own devices where play was concerned. That consisted, in the main, of reading and her imagination. Grandfather was, for a time, manager of a local vaudeville house. In his case, what "manager" meant is open to interpretation but Mother did get some exposure to a world of make believe more interesting than anything to be found at home. Her elder brother, Will, was, in the best American tradition, an inventor. He conducted his experiments with various chemical mixtures over the bathroom gaslight. Grandfather claimed the smell drove him to the corner saloon. For him this was neither a lengthy nor infrequent trip. His son, however, was later to develop Beaver Board, a type of pressed wood, cheap and very sturdy. This scientific breakthrough was widely used in World War I to build barracks, etc. For Uncle Will it built 14 plants in the United States and Canada and made him a multimillionaire. He constructed an elaborate mansion in the exclusive section of Buffalo and stocked it with Florence Brewer, a society deb from a wealthy Detroit family and there their only child, William Fredrick MacGlashan, Jr., was born—my cousin Sandy.

Florence, according to Mother, was somewhat embarrassed by and certainly displayed no fondness for her husband's relatives. After Will had taken the family to an elegant hotel lunch, Mother tells of crowding with her parents, Will and Florence into Will's chauffeur-driven Stanley Steamer. Will was let off at his office and Florence, announcing that she had shopping to do, also got out. She turned to the chauffeur. "Take these people home," she ordered and, without looking back, walked into a store.

It took Mother a quarter of a century to repay that insult. Meanwhile, her family remained lower middle class, that status due mostly to Grandfather's inability to keep steady employment. Will hired him as a supervisor at his local Beaver Board plant but Grandfather shared suds at the local saloons too generously with his workers and had to be let go. Grandfather did not like the work, anyway. Saloons were on every corner in those days and he was never far from one. Mother loved him, spoke of him constantly. Clearly she was his favorite, too. He must have been something in his younger years. I have his portrait, a handsome man with a high forehead and a stylish moustache. Unfortunately, my memory sees only an old man lying on a porch swing. I was taken to Grandfather's house and made to sing to him a French song I learned in kindergarten. I was four. He died a week later.

As a child, Mother evinced a serious interest in music. There being

Agnes Woodward and her Whistling Chorus. Viola MacGlashan top row, fourth from left.

no money for a piano or instructions, Grandfather arranged that Mother be sent to live with some aunts in Detroit who were deeply into that art form, taught it and would provide free piano instruction for Mother. She learned music but it was not the happiest period of her life. The aunts were an odd assortment. One taught whistling and later put together an all-female Whistling Chorus, which toured in its own bus. I have a yellowed photograph of the bus, an astounding sight with its bright banner (THE AGNES WOODWARD WHISTLING CHORUS) and the heads of the entire chorus smiling from the windows. After Mother had made a name in Hollywood, she scrunched down in her seat, stunned, when, at an Embassy Club luncheon, the Chorus appeared as the entertainment.

Aunt Mattie (Martha Woodward) was the stern elder ruler of the aunts' household. Mother always referred to her as the Virgin Aunt. Aunt Mattie had been engaged to a young West Point cadet with the unlikely name of Leander Hotchkis. Vows had been made, a wedding planned until the fatal night she came unexpectedly out on the veranda and caught him smoking. In Aunt Mattie's iron Calvinist eyes, this was a sin which could not be forgiven. The engagement was broken on the spot. She never saw Leander again but loved him all her life. His picture remained on her dresser and, night and morning, she turned it to the wall while she undressed. The sinful beloved face was turned back again when she was "decent."

The other member of the house was Lizzie, Aunt Mattie's younger sister, who was, in the term of the day, "feeble-minded." To her fell all the unpleasant tasks of the establishment: scrubbing floors, beating rugs, carrying slops. She deeply resented the lifestyle she had been assigned and, while never openly rebelling, muttered to Mother, "I hate that mean Miz Wooder," her rendition of her sister Martha's name, Woodward.

At the end of the year, Mother returned to Buffalo with a good grasp of the piano and many memories. She went back to school. In an English

Composition class, a teacher thought her stories showed a definite gift and that, with diligence, she might someday become an authoress "like Harriet Beecher Stowe."

Mother, still a child and not realizing how difficult, how near impossible such a dream was, went to the local newspaper with her work, spoke to the editor and began a daily fiction column. She was paid the sum of one dollar per story. Her output was phenomenal and unfailing. In high school she acquired the nickname of "Football." It is not certain if this came from a love of the game or for its players. After a football match, on a dare from a group of friends, she married one of the team, a boy called Burton Leslie. This was, at the time, a radical and unbelievably shocking act. Both were extremely young and the union lacked parental approval. It was annulled. Their alliance, while not achieving mention in the *Guinness Book of Records*, may have been the shortest marriage in history. Mother never spoke of their brief encounter until she received news of Burton's death. I was then already in my twenties.

Grandfather's acquaintance with the theater and the diligence of the Detroit aunts paid off in Mother's first stage work. She did Pianologues, playing while singing or reciting, an acceptable act in the innocent vaudeville of those days. I know very little of my mother's early professional life. There is a saying in theatrical circles that the worst three weeks of the year are Christmas, Easter and Buffalo. Mother's work in vaudeville did get her out of Buffalo and into New York, the big time. After endless interviews she did some stage work and toured in stock. Then she got into a brand new medium, not much respected by anyone—motion pictures.

In 1911 she signed with Biograph and worked with D.W. Griffith, first as an extra, then as a stock player. It, unfortunately, never seemed important that I learn Mother's early history. She never wrote it, only mentioned a few disconnected anecdotes. I never asked. By the time the questions were formed, the answers had died. But she did act in early East Coast silents before World War I. Then she was diagnosed with a possible case of tuberculosis. It was a time before there were wonder drugs. She traveled to the warm climate that was thought to be the only possible cure, to the place that was to become the home of the movies, California. Fortunately for me, the dreaded "white death" never developed.

She and Mary Pickford rode together on the same streetcar to work at the Biograph studios. She began to write and also direct films—usually one- or two-reelers. Then she went on to Universal to play leads and eventually become a star of that company. Extremely important to me was the picture she did called *The Desert's Sting*, playing the white woman with

Wilfred Lucas and Bess Meredyth (right, in a scene with Jeanie Macpherson) met on the set of *The Desert's Sting* (1914).

whom the white husband of an Indian girl fell in love. The Indian wife was played by Jeanie Macpherson, the husband by Wilfred Lucas. Both Mother and Jeanie Macpherson went on to become very successful screenwriters. Wilfred Lucas, already a great success, went on to become my father.

Mother acted, had her own series and wrote photoplays, many with Wilfred Lucas. Then they co-directed and, in 1917, married. By this time, Mother had written some 140 scenarios.

In 1918 she wrote a Tarzan script—*Tarzan's Romance*, starring Elmo Lincoln. Mother and my father were co-directing. In one scene, Lincoln protested that he could not make the required run barefoot across a patch of jagged rock. His flat refusal created a terrible impasse. It was the last shot of the day and the light was fading fast. There was no time to choose a new location with smoother ground. It was equally impossible for Tarzan of the Apes to wear shoes. Mother, smiling, came forward and assured Elmo there was nothing to it. "Watch!" She took off her shoes and, as the whole company watched, made the run. "See," she called back, "just don't press down hard." Then she whispered to my father to start the camera rolling and the scene was shot before her bleeding feet became apparent to the actor.

She also produced and starred in a comedy series, *Bess the Detectress*. There were no rules in films in those days, everything was new and challenging, chances were taken that could not have been afforded as films became longer and more expensive. The beginning is always a wonderful place to start. By this time, Mother had changed her name from Helen Elizabeth MacGlashan, which did not fit well on a marquee, to Bess Meredyth. Meredyth was a family name. Gen. Charles Meredyth, related to the Detroit aunts, was a surgeon in the Army of the Potomac during the Civil War.

There were no big studios then, only small units that made films and actors jumped from one to the other with lightning speed. There were a few great movie names. The foremost was D.W Griffith, the innovator. Then C.B. De Mille, who became famous for a new type of film.

His spectacles were mostly Biblical, which excused the sexiness pervading them as having some moral purpose, attacking the very thing that made them popular. Having changed Demille to the more aristocratic spelling, De Mille, he lived his life as a spectacle. An entourage surrounded him on the set. His movements in the studio were like a king's progress through his realm. Jeanie Macpherson, who had played with Mother and my father in *The Desert's Sting*, wrote many photoplays for him and their collaboration did not stop at the printed page. Their affair was common gossip, known even to De Mille's wife. He had many mistresses.

Mother told of having gone to his office to discuss a story she had in mind. The office, as elaborate as the rest of his image, featured a huge polar bear rug, which was rumored to have borne a lot of creative discussion. Mother started to tell him her story but he announced that he wished to defer discussion until they "got to know each other better." Glancing at the rug, he said that it was necessary for people working as closely together as writer and director to develop a "real relationship." Mother rose, politely rejecting the invitation and left with the story undiscussed, the bear rug unused.

I am not even sure how she met my father. He was 15 years older than Mother. Wilfred Lucas had been acting and directing since 1908 and had the Gold Seal Label, one of the top production units that made up Carl Laemmle's Universal Studios. A story has been told with many alleged directors as the recipient but Father swore to me it happened to him. Laemmle, determined to cut studio costs, brought in two relatives from New York to oversee the budgets. (Nepotism has a long history in Hollywood.) Father was about to shoot a film set in the Italian Alps. He wanted to use Yosemite National Park as the location and spoke lovingly of the beauty of the place, the grandeur of the great rock formations, the huge trees, hundreds of feet high. But Yosemite was hundreds of miles away and would have been an expensive location. Most mountain locations were shot in Griffith Park, a hill near the studio. The nephew budgeters shook their heads. "A tree is a tree, a rock is a rock," they told father. "Shoot it in Griffith Park."

I think it was at Universal that my parents worked together but I am not sure it was the first meeting. Mother wrote and my father directed a 15-episode epic called *Trey o' Hearts*. It was from a book by Louis Joseph Vance, a noted author of the period—which was 1914—and starred such forgotten luminaries as George Larkin and Cleo Madison.

In his foreword to the book, published by Grosset and Dunlap in October of 1914, Vance wrote about the film they made:

> If the written work is lacking in the quality known as characterization, the fault is the author's, if the picture is not, the merit is all the players'. But both would have gone for naught without the never-failing patience, ingenuity and intelligence of Mr. Wilfred Lucas, who directed the production of the pictures.
>
> The author would be guilty of high treason to his kind if he forgot the traditional feud between author and adapter long enough to give any credit whatsoever to Miss Bess Meredyth, the scenario writer, who

Bess Meredyth stars in an episode of her *Bess the Detectress* serial, "The Old Mill at Midnight" (1914).

minced the stories into such screen fodder as is most palatable to the reeling cameras.

Father was Canadian. His family had been Empire Loyalist during the American Revolution and had fled from New York to Toronto. He graduated from McGill University in Montreal, then had an extensive career on the stage and light opera before becoming involved in The Movies. His theatrical reviews proved him an actor far ahead of his time. In the era of grandiloquent gestures and overstated actions, he brought naturalness to his work that was unusual and effective. He and Mother worked together on several other pictures before their marriage in 1917 before a judge in Philadelphia. Why there, a whole continent away from Hollywood? I have no idea except that I have photographs from a film they did on an ice-choked river, which must have been in the East. It was a second marriage for both. My father had two sons born considerably earlier and living with their mother. I arrived in 1919, two years after my parent's nuptials when they were already in negotiations to make a film in Australia, Mother to write and share Father's directing, as he was also to star. The feature was called *The Man from Kangaroo*. It was an exciting experience for them but a bad career move for my father. It took him out of the mainstream of movie production, away from Hollywood at a time when things were changing rapidly and powerful new companies forming.

I luckily was born a year after 1918 when my parents had managed to survive the worst pandemic in human history—the Spanish Influenza in which friends and co-workers they had partied with the night before were dead the next day. World wide, the "flu" killed over 40,000,000 people—far more than the casualties of the Great War.

At the age of three months, I began my travels with my parents and my nurse, a Mrs. Mueller who, when I had achieved the age of speech, I called Numb. The retinue accompanying us to Australia included my grandparents, Julia and Andrew Fuller MacGlashan, Aunt Vi and Uncle

Wilfred Lucas, publicity photograph.

Bess and Wilfred with son John Meredyth Lucas (1921).

Bill Reynolds, all taken along for the prolonged outing. There were also cast members. We sailed on the steamship *Coronia* from San Francisco to Sydney Harbor. At all ports of call, doctors came aboard to check for symptoms of the deadly "flu" before passengers were allowed ashore. The entire trip was wasted on me. I remember nothing of it. I do, however, have pictures of myself being held by various relatives and actors in a variety of exotic ports.

Forty years later, I was to return to Australia with my wife, our housekeeper, Paula, and our three children to make a television series called *Whiplash*. Life is a circle.

When my parents returned from Australia, my father was not getting the offers he was used to. Mother was working with L.B. Mayer at the old Mission Road Studios, near the Seileg Zoo, home of Leo the lion, whose roar was to alert eight decades of moviegoers to an MGM picture. In 1924 Mother was in a story conference with Irving Thalberg on *The Red Lily*, which was to star Ramon Novarro and Enid Bennett. Fred Niblo was to direct. Thalberg excused himself, returning to announce that the merger of Metro, Goldwyn and Mayer was official. When L.B. Mayer,

under the aegis of Marcus Loew, took over the Metro Goldwyn Studio and make it Metro-Goldwyn-Mayer, *Ben Hur* had been shooting in Italy with what Mayer regarded as terrible results.

He inherited this production along with the studio and promptly fired the crew. Mother was assigned to rescue the script and Niblo to direct it. She boarded a train with Ramon Novarro, Enid Bennett, Mae McAvoy, Niblo and Carey Wilson, another writer. In New York they were joined by Marcus Loew and other executives of the new company. With some press people they sailed on the *Leviathan* for France and, thence, to Rome. From the ship, Mother wrote to Mayer, apprising him of the progress of the script she and Carey Wilson were reconstructing.

From Rome, she wrote, describing to Mayer what scenes the dismissed company had done. Jaffa Gate—fine. Desert scenes with Three Wise Men could have been done better in Palm Spring, California. The war galley scenes were impossible. She told him which sets worked and which didn't. She added, "Miss Mathis [June, the original writer] left today and we'll all breathe easier now." She and Carey had three-quarters of the script finished. Niblo had heard it and was enthusiastic. She told Mayer how well Niblo was handling the complex politics that had developed in the company with everyone pulling against everyone else. The job had been extremely difficult, as they had to build a studio from scratch. But they now had their own modeling plant, their own mill and a wonderful costume department. Mother praised the star's costumes from Germany. Then she asked Mayer for a favor. She said she "didn't know how to mention this but I wonder if you have anything you could use Luke in. Have a talk with him because he really is an awfully good actor but, for the past year the breaks have all been wrong."

This request did not seem to have been acted upon by Mayer and the need for asking did not bode well for Father's future or the future of the marriage.

But on a more upbeat note, Mother reported that everyone was confident that *Ben Hur* would be a great picture. Mr. Lowe was convinced enough to leave Rome and everybody was convinced they would be shooting within a few days. Interior scenes were filmed at the studio that had been built in Rome. Mussolini, fascinated by the cinema as a propaganda medium, was convinced that *Ben Hur* would display the glory of the Rome he was trying to revive. He was often on the set.

Opposite: **Louis B. Mayer and Bess Meredyth (far left) in the cast and crew photograph for** *One Clear Call* **(1922). Others include Henry Walthall, Irene Rich, J.M. Stahl, Shannon Day, Clair Windsor and cameraman Ernest G. Palmer.**

2—Cast of Characters

The star was Ramon Novarro as Ben Hur. Novarro was second only to Valentino as a heartthrob during the '20s. Francis X. Bushman played Massala, the evil Roman.

Mother had planned to take me but the doctors dissuaded her, arguing that the milk and general sanitary conditions in Italy were considered inadequate. Also, I probably would have been a great deal of trouble.

So, in 1925, while Mother was in Rome doing *Ben Hur*, I was in the care of my father and, I was much later given to understand, a young lady who helped fill his lonely hours. I also learned that I was in a car crash with them. I would have thought that so dramatic an episode would have left a strong memory. I have none. Mother heard of the incident in a friend's letters while she was in Rome. I imagine it did little to reassure Mother about the domestic tranquility awaiting her return.

In that period, my memory of my father is very spotty. There are a few disconnected incidents. I remember being spanked by him for I know not what infraction. The effect of the discipline was diluted, however, when he promptly took me out to buy me an ice cream cone.

But the very first thing I can recall was much earlier. I was taken in Uncle Bill's Buick touring car, sleeping in Auntie Vi's lap, out to some distant location. I was awakened by my father, who was directing a picture there. He told me to stay awake and watch the train. I then have a hazy memory of a line of tall trees. Suddenly a train, engulfed in flames, came rushing down the tracks and, blazing, vanished into trees on the other side. I would love to see that scene repeated on film, but I have never been able to discover what picture it was for.

Mother loved Italy and her Roman flat on Via Venato. L.B. Mayer, on the other hand, was displeased with the local cuisine, grumbling that he could not get a decent piece of apple pie.

Mother's time in Rome was exciting beyond the mere creation of what was to be billed as the greatest movie ever made. For years afterwards "Bigger Than *Ben Hur*" was used to sell tickets on epic pictures.

One rainy night, Novarro, riding in a horse-drawn carriage, met Mother and insisted on driving her home. During the leisurely, clip-clopping ride, he made feverish advances. At her reluctance, he sobbed that he had just confessed to a priest that he had sinned with her. Surprised, Mother asked how this sin might have been committed without her knowledge. Novarro said that he was a Catholic and the desire was as bad

Opposite: Cast and crew photograph of *Ben Hur*, taken at Cines Studio, Rome, on June 22, 1924. *From left:* #1 Bess Meredyth; #2 Ramon Novarro (Ben Hur); #3 June Mathis (co-screenwriter), #5 Marcus Lowe; #6 director Fred Niblo; #7 actress Enid Bennett; #8 Francis X. Bushman (Massala).

as the actual act. Before she could pursue this line of reasoning, he leaped from the carriage and ran off into the rain, leaving Mother to ride behind the grinning driver all the way home.

Either Novarro was drunk or she had caught him on an off night, as he was a devout homosexual.

Later, when I was perhaps seven or eight, he was at one of Mother's famous parties. Quite drunk, he smashed a glass, which cut his hand. There was a great fuss made over the bleeding and a bar towel was wrapped about the wounded member. Someone suggested that an antiseptic was needed, so I led the way to the guest bathroom and applied iodine liberally. This elicited a good deal of screaming and, undoubtedly, much pain. Frightened, I felt I had done something wrong and backed away. Instantly sympathetic, Novarro took me in his arms and reassured me that I had done the right thing. Then he stroked my hair and kissed me. I was embarrassed and also indignant at getting iodine stains on my face. Mother appeared and led me away after assuring herself that no permanent damage had been done to me or to the star. I went to bed and he went home safely from that party. Years later, however, his erotic orientation was to kill him. Long after his film career was forgotten, he picked up two brothers in a Ventura Boulevard bar and took them home for a night of fun. It was the time of his life for they robbed and murdered him.

But in 1925, at the start of his career, the sets for the interior and exterior of Ben Hur's palace had been constructed in Rome. Hur was a Jewish prince. Mother promptly named the set "The Hur House." Italians were greatly puzzled by the amusement this aroused among the American crew.

In the film, Ben Hur, denounced as a traitor by the Roman Massala, is condemned to serve as a galley slave and is chained to an oar during a huge naval battle. Great war galleys had been built with scrupulous attention to detail. Under the view of multiple cameras, they rammed each other, then grappled so that their armed men could board for hand-to-hand combat. Many of the extras in this sequence were Italian soldiers. As the ships collided, some sank and men spilled into the sea, their heavy Roman armor pulling them down.

It was a magnificent sequence but no one was sure whether anyone had been drowned. A head count was ordered by the police. The representative of the Fascist government then ordered the confiscation of the film to see what carelessness had been responsible.

Hastily, with stealth worthy of Mata Hari, Mother sneaked the film cans, hidden in her hatbox, aboard the Rome-Paris express and got the precious scenes out of the hands of the police and into a French laboratory. Fortunately both the film and the extras survived.

The climax of the picture, the great chariot race, was to have been filmed in Rome. A replica of the Circus of Antioch had been built in Cinecitta but was rained out and destroyed. The scenes had to be shot in a reconstructed Circus in Culver City near the MGM studio.

When Mother came home from Italy, my father was shooting a picture in Mexico. They had been separated for a year and, when she returned, Mother was prepared to make the separation final.

I have an indistinct memory, or perhaps I simply heard of the incident from Mother, of sleeping on the floor of the limousine when we went to pick him up at the train station. We were late. As we approached the front of the station, Mother saw him standing outside with his luggage, looking impatient. She told Collins to turn around and go home.

After their divorce, my father went East and worked on the stage, a return to his roots. He came back to the West Coast a couple of times briefly and saw me even more briefly. In the meanwhile, amid his stage work, he kept in touch with me by sending me stories, which were read to me by my nurse. They were small, hand-made booklets with illustrations cut out of magazines, the pictures pasted onto paper and the stories typewritten around them. The stories had to be tailored to the illustrations available and obviously required a good deal of work. They were silly stories—one concerned a boy whose dog had hydrophobia, inspired, no doubt, by a magazine illustration of a dog jumping out of a bathtub in which a boy sits, scrubbing. I say the stories were silly but the target of this literature was a six-year-old boy. I do not recall my reaction at the time but later, when I was a mature nine or ten, I remember being embarrassed by them. I still have several of the stories today. It would have been much simpler for him to write a letter and he clearly went to considerable effort to provide amusement for a child. The problem was that I always hated being a child.

Even though her feelings for my father had obviously taken an unfavorable turn, Mother insisted I keep up a relationship. This was not a simple matter as we were a continent apart. I had little memory of him and, consequently, very little interest in the task. I was, however, required to write him letters every week, under the supervision of my nurse. I sweated, thinking of things I might say. "Just tell him what you're doing," I was told. My suggestion that the nurse write the letter did not meet with her approval. "It has to be your letter." So I faced the task reluctantly. I have one letter that so impressed Father that he showed it to me when I was an adult. Strangely scrawled, it reads:

Dear Daddy,
   Saturday I went to the Sircus to see animals. My cat, Persia, just died. Auntie Vi's goldfish kicked the bucket. How are you feeling?
           Love
           Jack

When I was in my late teens, father moved back to Hollywood for good. He brought his new wife, an exquisite woman of Swedish extraction who played the piano well and, as had my mother, accompanied him when he sang for company after dinner. She bore a marked resemblance to Queen Nefertiti, mother-in-law of King Tut, whose elaborate golden tomb had been opened in 1922. Nefertiti was the wife of Akhenaten, the Pharaoh who briefly brought monotheism to the Egyptians in 1379 B.C. Nefertiti's statue was much in the news at the time—Charlie Chaplain having declared he was in love with it. It was the most beautiful face he had ever seen.

My stepmother's name had been Mabel but Father loved, and often sang, "Who Is Sylvia," a song adapted from Shakespeare's *Two Gentlemen of Verona*. Father changed Mabel's name to Sylvia. I never heard her views on this arrangement.

I saw a lot of him in this period. My father had been a motorist before most people had seen an automobile. I have pictures of him sitting in several strange-looking open "machines." Paved roads, when my parents were married, were not common. Blowouts were frequent. Motoring took skill and perseverance and the ability to fix things on the spot. Also, there was a sort of camaraderie of the road. Motorists helped each other—but not always. Mother tells of coming home one night when the headlights picked up a body lying beside the road. Father stopped and had started across the front of the car to help the victim when Mother screamed at him. Two men had emerged from the concealment of roadside bushes, one with a knife. It was an ambush. Father spun back, grabbed a tire iron from the car and held them off while Mother slid into the driver's seat and got the car in motion. Father, brandishing the tire iron, shouted threateningly at the two, then jumped on the running board and they sped away, chased a short distance by the two attackers and the "victim." Father had played the hero in too many pictures to be outsmarted by a mere three thugs.

When he came back to Hollywood, and I was in my teens, he was driving a Franklin—then an old car. A Franklin, he explained, had an air-cooled engine, such as airplanes had had in the First World War. You didn't have to trouble about constantly filling a radiator. This surprised me as I was driving at the time and had never had to fill a radiator. I was either very lucky or the chauffeur took care of the problem. There were, by then, very few Franklins left. Father was proud of his.

Unfortunately, I only knew my father as a grown-up, as an acquaintance, a friend rather than a parent. He had been away too long. Worse, he had been away from the motion picture business too long. Hollywood has a short memory. Work was now hard to come by. He got small roles, then, finally, was down to bit parts. A couple of times he directed stage plays in Los Angeles for the WPA, which Franklin Roosevelt had instituted as an artistic version of the Civilian Conservation Corps, to give useful work to millions of unemployed during the Great Depression. But his name no longer mattered in the industry. As Mike often said, "Goddamn, the picture is a cruel business."

But there were parties at my father's house. I remember them as fun. He would have opera stars, actors, cameramen—all sorts of people—and, after dinner, Sylvia would play and my father, or one of his guests, would entertain. He made a few attempts to coach me but I could never manage to sing in any one single key.

When he sang for guests there was always a request for "Danny Deever"—done from one of Kipling's poems. He sang with the proper lower-class British accent and I still hear the closing lines:

> For they've done with Danny Deever,
> You can hear the quick step play.
> The regiment's in column
> And they're marching us away
> Ho, the young recruits are shaking
> And they'll need their beer today,
> After hanging Danny Deever in the morning.

There was always the same dramatic delivery and the same applause. My father had a very good voice. Sylvia never seemed to tire of playing for him as, obviously, Mother had.

Mike used my father in a big Western he was making, *Santa Fe Trail*, starring, among others, Errol Flynn and our to-be-president, Ronald Reagan. After that, Luke was cast in almost everything Mike did. Not big parts but long running ones. I think Father became a sort of good luck charm to Mike. My father died just before America's entrance into World War II.

3
Home, School and Earthshaking Events

Warners' new director, renamed Michael Curtiz in a language strange to him and hired because of the scope of his great Biblical spectacles, was given as his first assignment, a truly American picture which made his confusion complete. *The Third Degree* dealt with crime and the American criminal system. Oddly enough, most of Mike's early films were American. With the exception of *Captain Blood*, *The Charge of the Light Brigade*, *The Adventures of Robin Hood* and, of course, *Casablanca*, most of his films were set in America. Mike became solid Red, White and Blue—an oddly accented *Yankee Doodle Dandy*, a film with Jimmy Cagney he directed.

As his first assignment, *The Third Degree* dealt with the complexities of police practices and the American underworld. Mike, having no knowledge of the subject, had the then-sheriff, Eugene Biscailuz, lock him in jail over a weekend. For well over a hundred features, this kind of dedicated research continued until his death.

Mother had written *The Third Degree* but had not yet met its new Hungarian director. Later, when Mother was writing *Don Juan* for John Barrymore, she and Mike were introduced. Mother was working closely with Alan Crosland, who was directing Barrymore in *Don Juan*. Barrymore, a famous stage star, a matinee idol, was billed as the Great Profile. Women did not scream and swoon in those days, as was to become fashionable a couple of decades later with Sinatra—but Barrymore was thought to be the world's greatest lover, the fulfillment of every woman's dream. Don Juan was ideal casting for him.

Mother followed with more Barrymore pictures—*The Sea Beast*, then *Manon Lescaut*, retitled for a far less sophisticated audience *When a Man Loves*. *The Sea Beast* had begun as *Moby Dick*, the Melville classic account of Capt. Ahab's search for vengeance on the white whale that had taken his leg. This, however, was not deemed romantic enough for a Barrymore picture. A love interest was needed for audiences who flocked to see the Great Profile. Although Mother argued that Melville had created a book that had terrified and delighted generations, she surrendered to the studio's request.

During the filming of *Don Juan*, Barrymore was having a tempestuous affair with Mary Astor, his leading lady.

There was endless discussion for the role of the love interest for *The Sea Beast* and an actress had been tentatively cast as the lady who takes Ahab's mind temporarily off the white whale. It was thought that Barrymore would object to the casting and insist it be played by Mary Astor. Instead, he spotted a very young girl, Dolores Costello, on the lot, fell instantly in love and insisted she play the romantic lead. This pleased neither the studio (the girl was inexperienced, having played a small part in only one picture) nor Dolores' father, Maurice Costello. The elder Costello had been a Warner star; a romantic lead in many pictures, he was Barrymore's age, knew Barrymore's reputation and wanted no part of the Great Profile for his young daughter. But Barrymore insisted. Dolores played the part, went on to star with him in Mother's *Manon Lescaut*, and then eventually became Mrs. Barrymore, one of many.

More or less resigned to losing the part in *The Sea Beast*, Mary Astor, who assumed she still held Barrymore's heart, came upon Barrymore and his new discovery in an intimate off-scene relationship on the set. It was not a pleasant discovery. But Barrymore's heart was never his most stable organ.

He became a great family friend, dropping in at all hours of the day and night. Mother had cold potatoes kept in the icebox for him. He loved cold potatoes when he was drinking—which was almost all the time. I, not realizing he was drunk, thought he was the funniest man in the world.

The public didn't know his other side, his brooding, his long bouts of almost insensible drunkenness. They didn't know about his pet monkey, Clementine, who had run of the house and used Barrymore's bed and the great man himself as a toilet while he lay with his bottle, happily unaware of his condition.

Much of *The Sea Beast* was shot off Santa Cruz Island. Mother was there to handle whatever rewriting was necessary and to help the director. Living conditions on the island were primitive and there was little to do after the cameras stopped rolling. As a joke, Mother wrote a song mocking the popular lyrics of the day with lines like:

> Down beside the sounding sea
> With Bacardi flowing free.
> Santa Cruz Nights, Oh Santa Cruz nights.
> Things are tame, don't seem the same
> Since Santa Cruz nights.

That song used to delight me. I was not impressed with the really creative work Mother did, the scripts she wrote—that was routine, everyday stuff—but the song stayed with me.

One night on the island, when the day's shooting was wrapped, Barrymore was extremely morose all through dinner. The booze that night had not produced the elation for which it had been taken.

He got up from the table and insisted that Mother go with him in a small boat, saying he needed the quiet of the night, the stars, the hiss of water under the keel.

Mother managed the small outboard motor while Barrymore sat in the bow, brooding. Suddenly he came aft, shut off the motor and kissed Mother passionately.

She drew back, surprised. "Jack, why?"

"That, my dear, should be obvious." His speech was only slightly slurred.

She smiled. "How long have we known each other?"

"Quite long enough," he murmured in the husky tones that had made millions of women question their marriages. He threw cushions in the bottom of the boat.

"Look, Jack." Mother took a reasonable tone, "I know you're the Great Lover. The whole world knows you're the Great Lover. You don't have to prove it—certainly not to me."

He looked offended, then thoughtful. After a moment he straightened up and laughed. "Damn right," he said. "We're friends, which is a hell of a lot better." He kissed her forehead. "Bess, I love you." He went back to the bow, stretched out and, with a sigh of contentment, stared happily up at the stars.

Mother restarted the engine. "Goddamn it," she said, "you don't have to be *that* relieved."

I continued attending various military academies, employing my usual inattention to the learning process while Mike went through a succession of ever more important pictures at Warner Brothers and Mother returned to MGM, writing Joan Crawford's first pictures, vehicles for Greta Garbo, Clark Gable and Jean Harlow. Mother went back partly because of her prior relationship with Mayer, partly because of her friendship with Frances Marion, Anita Loos and June Mathis. This was the heyday of women writers in film, a situation not to be approached again until the '80s and '90s. Mainly Mother came to Metro because of her admiration for Irving Thalberg, the *wunderkind* Mayer had stolen from Carl Laemmle's Universal. Uncle Carl had brought Thalberg out from New York as a low-paid assistant. He had risen in almost no time from Laemmle's secretary, with some of the world's fastest shorthand, to studio manager.

While Mayer was still at the Seilig Zoo, he lured him away from Laemmle to oversee production. Thalberg was to handle the artistic side of the studio, managing writers, directors and actors while Mayer oversaw the business aspect of the operation. Thalberg's name was never on a picture—his own decision. Mayer, on the other hand, could never get too much public recognition.

When Mayer took over the old Metro studio and made it MGM, things started well with the arrangement of dual control. MGM became the studio where there were, the ads read, "More Stars Than There Are in Heaven." But with two steel wills, it was inevitable that friction developed between this new boy genius and MGM's grand old man. Mother always described herself as "a Thalberg man."

Warners was a profit-oriented organization. The brothers, having come from the family of a poor butcher, tended to squeeze every ounce of work from their employees. Mike, hired as a sort of European De Mille, directed, during 1927, *The Third Degree*, *A Million Bid*, *Desired Woman*, and *Good Time Charley*. None of the above titles would lead anyone into a theater expecting to see an historical spectacle. Mother had been out with Mike several times but it was not an exclusive attachment.

The year 1928 started for Mike in the same vein with *Tenderloin*. Finally came *Noah's Ark*, a vast Biblical spectacle by Darryl Zanuck. Zanuck was someone I could sympathize with. He had, as a child, been sent to military school. He was, however, able to break out of Page Military Academy and, by lying about his age, had at 14 been given a real uniform for World War I. In France, as an ambulance driver, he had written a few articles for *Stars and Stripes*, the Army newspaper, and, when returned to civil life, refused to return to school. His formal education had been slightly shorter than mine but equally incomplete. He got sporadic work writing gags for Chaplin and the Keystone Cops. But he wanted to break into movies as a serious writer. He had amassed a bunch

Mike's first big film in the U.S. was *Noah's Ark*, with Darryl F. Zanuck (1929).

of short stories and somehow met a man who had invented a new hair tonic. Zanuck wrote a story about the happy discovery and his prose lavishly praised the virtues of the tonic, which, he insisted, the world must learn about. As a result, the flattered man paid to have his story published. Zanuck included his other short stories in the volume and was now a published author and worthy of notice. With these credentials, he got a job at Warners. There he met Mal St. Clair, a director who had done many of the Keystone Cops comedies for Mack Sennett. Together they came up with *Rin Tin Tin*, the *Lassie* of the silents. There were endless sequels, all moneymakers. But now Zanuck had graduated from dog stories and was starting a career that would ultimately make him the top producer at Warners and, finally, studio head.

He is credited with writing *Noah's Ark*, a mixed bag of biblical scenes, taking something from D.W. Griffith's *Intolerance* and other prior epics. Mike gave it great production, nearly drowning many extras in the flood scenes. He was finally doing what he had been hired for in the first place.

This film and the indomitable personality in his small body gave

3—Home, School and Earthshaking Events

Michael Curtiz and John Meredyth Lucas on the set of *Noah's Ark* (1929).

Darryl the leg up and he took over as head of production at Warners. Warner, though never a man to give up authority, allowed him reasonably free rein and he produced a lot of profit. But, in 1933, the Bank Holiday, a closedown and reorganization of the nation's banking system, which ushered in Roosevelt's New Deal, made money temporarily unavailable. The studio heads saw an opportunity to cut salaries. At MGM, L.B. Mayer, amid a flood of tears, announced to his employees that a 50 percent cut was necessary if their beloved studio was to survive. Warner also issued a notice to all employees, cutting their salaries in half. Since the banks were closed and no money could be had, all must share the burden. Salaries of the upper echelon of production, however, were not cut. Among studio heads there was discussion about making the cuts permanent.

Darryl, whether genuinely angry over this blatant injustice or simply using it as an excuse, broke with the Brothers Warner to found his own Twentieth Century Productions with Joe Schenck, brother of Nick Schenck. They rented space at the Samuel Goldwyn studios.

Despite his long years of close personal friendship with Darryl, Mike remained at Warners but Mother went to Twentieth Century.

The Warners never left Mike idle. He had turned out *Glad Rag Doll*,

Madonna of Avenue A, *Hearts in Exile* and *The Gamblers*, slipping back into the Warners' original pattern of low-budget pictures.

Then, movies having found their voice, Mike did *Mammy* with Al Jolson. In 1930, he shot *Under a Texas Moon* and *A Soldier's Plaything*.

For me, school was, from start to finish, a cross I bore clumsily, falling often. In my formative years, Mother lived on Crescent Heights Boulevard, at the Hollywood end of the Sunset Strip. Kindergarten was less that a block from home. I have few memories of kindergarten, but nearby was a vacant lot full of cut palm tree branches. I fell and ran a palm thorn through my leg. It was painfully extricated and dressed.

The memory of my convalescence concerns the daily change of wound dressing performed by the nurse who was hired both to tend me and to securely confine me to bed. There were huge peppertrees in the backyard and the branches of one was very close to my window. I frequently climbed out with what seemed to me to be Tarzan-like agility. That tree, however, was quite high and several times I had to be rescued with a ladder brought out by Nellie, our laundress, who came on Saturdays by bus from the colored district to do our washing and ironing. Once, I had climbed so far out and so high that Collins had to drive the Lincoln under the tree and get me down on its roof.

The neighborhood kids would gather in my upstairs bedroom to observe the daily ceremony of cleaning and re-bandaging the wound and be allowed to look briefly at the world through the hole in my leg. I was something of a wonder to my peers. I had also been offered a valuable lesson—No Pain, No Gain. Had I absorbed this lesson, my life might have run a different course.

The painful visit to Dr. McCalister had brought back my memories of Christian Science. Mother had gotten interested in Mrs. Baker's methods at an earlier time—perhaps during the flu pandemic of 1918-19. I recall her saying that she was in the hospital, about to deliver me, and asked the practitioner to come to her bedside. The hospital, however, was St. Vincent's, a Catholic institution, and the practitioner said he couldn't work against the Catholics' negative thinking. Mother promptly lost interest in that religion but, later, her interest must have revived briefly because, at an early age, I was sent to Christian Science Sunday school and taught the virtues of Divine Healing. Mother obviously did not place complete confidence in this creed because, at the age of four or five, I was sent to the hospital to have my tonsils removed.

I have sketchy memories of being in the operating room, having an ether cone shoved over my face and, in an indignant but muffled voice, demanding why God couldn't heal my throat. The rest of my protest was lost as the ether dripped onto the cone and I breathed the fumes, sinking into an ever-steeping spiral, a sickening whirlpool of strange sounds and light, screaming, swirling, almost reaching the bottom before utter darkness engulfed me.

During this period I was forced to take naps in the afternoon, a practice most distasteful to me for two reasons. The first was that it made me seem like a baby. No matter how tired I was, I always protested that I wasn't sleepy. The second, and paramount, reason was that, at nap time, I had all sorts of nursery stories read to me. From one book, a beautifully illustrated edition of German children's tales, came a particular terror. In harsh Teutonic fashion the story concerned a girl who was a crybaby. Despite her parents' warning that she would someday cry her eyes out, the problem continued. Sure enough, one day she wept so much that her eyes fell out. The illustration showed the unfortunate child holding her eyes in her hands, and above them was her horrified face with its dark empty eye sockets. It terrified me and I always asked that some other book be read. That alone did not resolve the problem. Two things conspired against me. First, I had to take my nap in the playroom at the top of the stairs instead of my bedroom. I was never sure why. The second was that I knew exactly where in the bookshelf that evil book was waiting. I would try hard never to look at it directly. When put down for my nap, I was always in an ecstasy of uncertainty about the safest position to keep my body in. If my face was turned toward the bookcase, I might see it. If I turned away, the girl might sneak up on me with her sightless eyes. I would squirm for what seemed hours before I fell asleep.

I started my schooling in the first grade at Urban Military Academy. My roommate was Dean Riesner, son of a director and friend of Mother's at Metro. Dean became my lifelong friend despite having often to sleep with me beside him under a croup tent with the school nurse ministering to my asthma. From Urban, cadets got to come home every weekend after dress parade. Non-working parents came to watch this military display of five- and six-year-olds marching in their resplendent uniforms like militant dwarfs.

One Friday, Collins brought me home and I found our regular maid gone and Eda in her place. Eda was a large, powerfully built woman, fairly light-skinned. She felt superior to the other servants because of her lightness and said that in her teens she had "passed"—had been taken for white. Age had darkened her slightly and she was now colored. She was the first mean colored person I had ever met and I have yet to know why she disliked me. But when Mother was out at parties or otherwise absent from the house, Eda would constantly find fault with me and on several occasions

Bess and John, in his military school uniform (1925).

beat me soundly. I was warned never to tell Mother or "it'll be a whole lot worse next time." I must have believed her because it was years later before I mentioned it to Mother. Fortunately for me, Eda was not with us very long. One Friday she picked me up at school for my weekend at home. She was driving the new Stutz Mother had just bought as a second car.

3—Home, School and Earthshaking Events

The door no sooner closed that the insults started, more vicious than ever. Then, in angrily swinging a right turn, she smashed into another car. Whether it was damage to the car or, as I later heard from our laundress, "I spotted that girl was a drinker first time I saw her," we got a new maid—one that I liked.

Near this time, another frightening thing happened. Behind our house was a line of buildings: the garage, then a storeroom, then the stables where my pony, Babe, was kept on her frequent reappearance from the top of Laurel Canyon where she went whenever she ran away. In the rear of all these buildings was a vast mound of empty bottles. Liquor being forbidden in this Prohibition era, there was apparently nowhere else to hide them and Mother gave lavish parties almost weekly. All the neighborhood kids were aware of the forbidden pile but one day one of them, having found some fault with me, threatened to have his parents call the police. This terrified me. I was sure my whole family, which included our servants, would go to jail.

Since I had been involved in the argument that caused the threat, this pending family tragedy was my fault.

When Mother got home from the studio I, in an agony of contrition, sobbed out my fearful news, expecting her wrath. She laughed, explaining that the police were always invited to her parties. They made some extra money and kept things in order, handling any guests who got too drunk for their own safety or that of others. In Hollywood, the Eighteenth Amendment, the Volstead Act, outlawing liquor, was especially honored in the breech.

Those old buildings behind our house, however, held an even more sinister memory—if memory is what it was. Hazily I see a group of us catching a mouse and, in the garage, tacking it to a cross—a crucifixion ritual. I agonized over the pain of the tortured animal and remember it still across over nine-tenths of a century. But I have never been able to decide if it was a dream or something that really happened. If true, where would the neighborhood kids have gotten such an idea? If a dream, where would I, who had been exposed only to Christian Science, which does not go in for such symbols as a dead man on a cross, have found it in my subconscious? That and the picture of the sightless crybaby troubled many of my childhood nights.

Although Mother seemed to have lost personal interest or faith in Christian Science, I was still sent to Christian Science services. Mrs. Baker did not dispel my fears of either of my problems because I was too ashamed to mention them to anyone.

Later, when Southwestern Military Academy in San Marino became my place of learning, there was a brief attendance at the nearby Christian Science Sunday school. Then there was no more mention of it until years later when Mrs. Meyers, Marlon Brando's grandmother, a Christian Science practitioner, came into our lives. Mama Meyers was a wonderful, friendly woman who could have made devil worship attractive to the Religious Right. Mother was enchanted with her and, thereafter, daily readings from *Science and Health* accompanied her trips to the doctor and continued until Mama Meyer's death.

I had not yet declared myself an atheist but my contempt for religion was unconsciously growing. Later, when I discovered Darwin, I would feel that I had found a reason, an explanation and a weapon against the stupidity of believers. I felt that evolution was almost *my* discovery.

The monotony of school was broken occasionally by visits to the set of whatever picture my parents were working on, Mike at Warners, Mother at MGM. At the latter studio, I fell madly in love with Joan Crawford. She would allow me to sit in her chair in minor ecstasy while she did her scenes. Her stand-in was at my side, watching that I did not leave the chair or make any noise during the take. A stand-in is like an extra who is hired to watch the rehearsal of a scene and then go exactly where the star went, standing while the lights are adjusted and everything is made ready for the shot. This saves the star much exhaustion. Generally stars have favorite stand-ins and use them from picture to picture. I cannot remember her name but this one was a rather plain-looking girl with Joan's height and build and the same skin coloring—all-important assets to aid the cameramen when adjusting the lights. She seemed to worship Joan as much as I did.

I discussed with Mother taking up a course of jujitsu offered at my current military academy so that I could best Joan's current husband, Douglas Fairbanks, Jr., in fair combat. When this idea was rejected, I settled for sending her a dozen varicolored baby chicks, brilliantly dyed for Easter and charged to Mother's account at the local florist. I received an effusive letter of thanks signed, "Love, Joan."

I carried this token of my lady next to my heart until my shirt was laundered or some other tragedy befell it.

It was in this period that I, for the first time, experienced that special California treat—an earthquake. Late on a Friday afternoon, Collins had picked me up at school after dress parade and taken me to the studio to get Mother. Her office was in a wooden building above the MGM Publicity Department. There were more elegant offices open to her but she preferred this. It had a small outer office for her secretary, Mrs. Jackman. The inner office held Mother's desk, a bookcase, a comfortable chintz

3—Home, School and Earthshaking Events

couch and chair. It was a warm place, cozy. Mother, Mrs. Jackman told us, was on the sound stage with a new scene she had just written and given to the director, Clarence Brown. I think it was a Greta Garbo picture. It was late afternoon and Collins, in the outer office, and I, on the couch, settled down to wait. I was nearly asleep when I heard the noise, a deep rumble like thunder. Then it felt as though someone was shaking the couch. I opened my eyes to see the chandelier swing wildly and heard the terrified scream of Mrs. Jackman. The whole wood frame building was shaking and we, being on the second story, were doing a fantastic dance. From the corridor we heard an ominous crash as the Sparkletts water cooler fell and its huge glass container smashed. By now there were many screams and cries of "Earthquake!" The lights went out. I leapt toward the door of the outer office. There, Collins and I were wedged in the doorway, trying to reach the outside stairs and trapping Mrs. Jackman behind us. I forget who broke free first but I remember the rollercoaster feel as I ran down the wooden stairs to the street. Lights were out all over the studio and people were running in all directions. We stood in the middle of the street until the earth's motion subsided. Collins and I looked at each other. Wow!

Fire alarms were sounding from all directions. Collapsing roofs had set them off. That brought up a new worry. Where was Mother? Mrs. Jackman didn't know what stage the company was shooting on and there was no one calm enough to tell us. I started down the street, looking for her. The ground started to shake again. More screams. But this quake was gentler then the first. Also, since I was in movement myself, I felt it less.

I wandered for quite a while through masses of people and felt more aftershocks. Finally, Mother appeared. She seemed as happy to see me alive as I was to see her.

On the drive home, she told us she had been reading the scene to the director and the cast when the quake struck. The whole stage went dark and in pitch blackness they could hear the lights from the scaffolding above the set falling. One electrician sustained a direct hit. I think he later died. Several more of the crew were hurt. Mother said all she could do was stand still and hope that nothing breakable had her name on it. In the dark, they were all trying to make jokes.

Mike was not shooting and had been playing polo with Darryl and the rest of the team on a field near the Warner studio. They had finished and were in the showers when the earthquake struck. Forgetting dignity and propriety, all four rushed naked from the building.

When Mother and I got home, she sent Collins to his house to be sure his family was safe. Coretta, the cook, served our dinner. Lights had come back on and there were still occasional aftershocks, milder now. The epicenter was in Long Beach, some 30 or 40 miles to the south. Coretta, terrified, brought in the dinner with shaking hands. As she was returning to the kitchen, Mother winked at us and jumped to her feet, screaming, "Earthquake!" Coretta started to run in the large felt slippers she always wore. She slipped on the tile of the Hungarian breakfast room and fell on her amply padded bottom. Mother was convulsed with laughter.

All night I lay in my bed listening to the local radio station in Long Beach, where the damage had been disastrous. The announcer would give an account of casualties as they were reported to him and at one point said, "Sorry, I have to move the microphone, the east wall just collapsed." From this new vantage point he was able to describe the ruined sight of the city, a few scattered fires. Shortly after each aftershock he would describe, I felt the bed shake—much gentler at this distance. It was after two o'clock before I finally fell asleep.

The next morning, Mother went to the studio. Her office still stood unharmed and, crews having worked thought the night to repair the damage, shooting of her picture resumed on the same sound stage.

As the years rolled on, I continued my disinterested tour of schools in the Southern California area, Urban Military Academy, Southwestern Military Academy, Pacific Military Academy, etc., etc., etc. For one brief, shining moment there seemed a way out of all this. On my birthdays, my father's cameraman used to come to Armagh Farms—the name Father had given the Verdugo Hills home into which I was born—to photograph the happy occasions. I have seen this footage of myself, clumsily cutting my cake, riding in my wicker pony cart with Otie, the son of our cook, driving. Otie was a mature nine. For the camera I blew out the candles on my cake with an assist from Mother and my father.

On another birthday, a few years later, L. B. Mayer was shown this footage. He took a close look at me and decided that my face, with brick-red hair topping my mass of freckles, would appeal to an audience. He wanted to do a screen test with the aim of making me a child star. Mother, being well acquainted with the life and probable fate of movie tots, gracefully refused his offer. Jackie Cooper, who had been in Hal Roach's Our Gang Comedies and would have undoubtedly made it big anyway,

John Meredyth Lucas, 1923.

3—Home, School and Earthshaking Events 47

went on to become the hit of the studio's younger generation. Then there was Mickey Rooney to further lessen my chances. Yet without Mother's refusal and luck beyond all reason, all that glory might have been mine. Alas, I was put back in uniform and sent off to yet another school.

4
Life with Stepfather

When home from school on weekend passes, I was aware that Mother was seeing a tall handsome man, athletically built, who habitually wore a black ankle-length overcoat. The garment had a strange, ominous look, interesting to me. Beneath it, he dressed well but Mother was constantly trying to hide the coat before going out with him. I thought the coat fascinating but Mother felt otherwise and, whatever the weather, she invariably remarked on the warmth of the night. The man spoke in an almost indistinguishable tongue. I was not so far removed from baby talk as to be critical of his syntax but I simply couldn't understand him.

If all else failed when they were going out to a party or whatever, Mother would have Collins turn on the heat in the rear of the limousine. (Mother always had Lincolns—usually sand colored.) The warmth was intended to force the doffing of the offending coat and, hopefully, it would be left in the car when they got wherever they were going. The coat eventually vanished. I am not sure how she finally accomplished that objective because I was never home for long, continuing my seemingly endless succession of military schools, bad grades, confrontations regarding study habits, lack of application, etc.

There were two breaks in this sorry interval—I was in the movies, though certainly not as a star. At one military school—probably Urban—a group of us were selected to grace a W.C. Fields picture with Mae West. I believe it was shot at Paramount. We cadets were extras, appearing in our school uniforms and in all probability the butt of one of Fields' famous anti-children jokes.

Later, at Pacific Military Academy, I was among those picked for a scene in a Warners movie, *Gold Diggers of 1933*. Very early in the morning we were bussed to the studio where Mike worked, taken to Wardrobe and outfitted in World War I uniforms. There was much talking among ourselves. Cast, not in our school uniforms but as real soldiers, we proudly inspected ourselves in the wardrobe mirrors. The rest of the day we spent marching on a raised treadmill with rain pouring down on us from overhead pipes. This was for Busby Berkeley's "Forgotten Man" number. The lyrics of the song were a woman's lament of the treatment of her ex-soldier lover during the Great Depression. Our moment of glory on the screen came in later under the lyrics that poetically described a huge number of boots tramping through hell. The camera photographed only our feet. This long-in-preparation and complicated shot was to be used for a few seconds. After all the proud preparation in real soldier uniforms, all they photographed was our feet. We came to realize that motion picture work was not as rewarding as one might think. I continued my round of military schools. Only the uniforms changed.

But at home, many things were changing. Mother sold the house on Crescent Heights Boulevard, near the future Schwab's Drug Store, and we moved to a suite at the Roosevelt Hotel, across Hollywood Boulevard from Grauman's Chinese Theater. It was Suite Number 101 and consisted of two bedrooms, a large living room, a library, dining room and kitchen. The suite ran along the entire front of the hotel.

We still had Collins and his wife, Irene. She was not drinking and now worked full-time. The other servants were not necessary because the hotel staff provided most services.

While still at the Crescent Heights house, in 1927, I learned of Lindbergh's transatlantic flight. It was constantly on the front page, on the radio and on everyone's lips. I dreamed of being an aero hero. So did all the kids in the neighborhood. We were not quite sure what, exactly, he had done or where Paris was but it was exciting.

Songs were written, records rushed to the market. I remember winding up our Victrola countless times to listen to the "Lucky Lindy" song. There were other songs of, I imagine, similar caliber. They all seemed wonderful at the time. The neighborhood kids talked of little else. But after the ticker tape parades, visible in the newsreels on Saturdays at our matinee along with the cowboy serials, interest gradually faded.

Then we moved to a succession of houses in Beverly Hills, Palm Drive, then Alpine and, finally, to a very elegant one on North Roxbury, where my encounter with Eve took place.

It was also here that Mother was able to repay Aunt Florence, Uncle Will's society wife, for her insult to the family by telling her chauffeur to "Take these people home." Mother bought an incredible amount of clothes, possibly because of all the parties she threw or attended. On holidays, when the entire family came over, she would go through her closets and give away clothes she had barely worn. Auntie Vi, Grandmother and Aunt Florence would watch and sometimes argue over who got what. It must have been really humiliating to Florence, who had come from wealth, married a multi-millionaire who lost it all and who now was reduced to taking favors from a woman who had succeeded in a business that her class would have looked down on.

We were living in Beverly Hills when the trial of Bruno Hauptmann took place. Hauptmann was the evil German who was tried and condemned to death for the kidnapping of the Lindbergh baby. There was a wave of panic in the movie community. There had been several kidnappings and attempts at kidnappings of movie children. Mother, as did many of her friends, hired a guard. Ours was Andy. He had been a policeman and carried a gun and talked of shoot-outs and crimes solved but mostly he napped during the night in Collins' room that was attached to the garage.

Andy's police training was called into play only once when a mysterious package was delivered to the house. There had been some mail bombs, Andy said. He knew all manner of criminal things. We hefted the package in our hands, trying to guess its weight and listened for ticking—an alarm clock being a classic method for triggering a time bomb explosion. Although there was no sound, Andy warned, "There's maybe a hundred ways to explode one." Just to be on the safe side, he got a bucket of water. "Water soaks the gunpowder," he explained, "so it can't go off."

With great care, we carried the package to the exact center of the back lawn, far from the house. The servants were warned to stand well clear of the windows to avoid flying glass in the event of an unexpected detonation. Carefully the package was submerged. This happened late morning when Mother and Mike were at their studios. The package remained in the bucket all day so as to get good and soaked. In the late afternoon, sending me off a safe distance, Andy bravely fished it out. I remember the tension as I watched him carefully cut the string, cautiously peel back the wrapping paper and open it.

It was a large, leather-covered dictionary Mother had ordered from the publisher. When dry, its India paper pages were twisted into bizarre shapes, warped and, in places, illegible.

But this all took place long after we had left the Crescent Heights house, moved to the Roosevelt Hotel and then on to Beverly Hills.

At the Roosevelt, I, like the fabled Eloise in the New York Plaza, rode the elevators constantly, making myself an intense pain to the elevator operators who were forced to smile politely at hotel guests of whatever

Bess Meredyth and Michael Curtiz (1929).

age and annoyance. I ran through the lobby. I ran through the shops that lined the lobby. I ran on Hollywood Boulevard. It was safe for a young boy to run on Hollywood Boulevard in those days.

Then came the wedding. I had probably been informed that it was pending but it had made no impression on me until, suddenly, the hotel suite was filled with flowers and people drinking and celebrating. Mother and Mike arrived late from the civil ceremony. I am told that I passed among the guests confiding that the marriage would last three months at the most. I was off by 33 years.

When I was an adult, Mother told me of the marriage proposal. Mike had a small apartment about a mile from the Crescent Heights house. Mother would occasionally stay there or he would stay at our place. After a while of this, Mother said, "It would probably be simpler if we were married."

"Bessky," he said, nodding sadly, "I like very much we should be marry but—" He looked away.

"But?" Mother asked.

His voice was very low. "I am Jew," he told her.

"I know," Mother said. "I have no idea what I am."

Mike looked incredulous. "Is not matter?"

So they got a judge who was a friend of Mother's.

I don't think I had any personal antipathy toward Mike. My childhood memories of my father were so sketchy that I am sure I did not resent Mike as an interloper. Perhaps I resented the time he took away from my relationship with Mother but that was, at best, minimal. When I wasn't away at school, she was at the studio all day, and at night there were dinners and parties. My most constant contacts were with the servants, particularly with Collins. Most likely I was simply being a brat at the wedding and had no motive beyond an attempt to shock.

While still living at the Crescent Heights house, I had created a letter to Mother when Mike was going on an extended location trip. I literally *created* it, getting a stamp and spending endless time copying a postmark from another envelope. The letter warned, "Don't let your friend go. There are other women at the location." I had signed it, "A friend."

It was well into the second day before Mother confronted me and asked if I had written it. I confessed, pleased that it had taken her so long to figure it out. Her pleasure did not match mine although I like to think she secretly applauded my ingenuity.

This was my period of pranks. After we moved to the hotel, I regaled my grandmother, Julia, with stories of meeting gangsters and having witnessed a murder in one of the rooms. Grandmother called Mother in horror.

Mother called me in. "Why?"

"I wondered how long it would take to get back to you," I said.

Mother could not suppress a grin but suggested, in future, it would be well not to upset relatives.

She could hardly be angry, as the game was probably genetic. We had an Italian marble statue of Cupid and Psyche, both nude, in the classical manner. It stood at the edge of a fishpond, which reflected the white perfection of the duo, the infant Cupid at Psyche's knee, staring lovingly up into her face.

When Grandmother first saw it, Mother could see that its nudity embarrassed her so she told Grandmother that she and I had posed for it.

"Naked!" Julia gasped, shocked "With little Jadie? Bessie, whatever made you do such a thing?"

Grandmother thereafter referred to the statue as "The Image." "That image, "she would say as it followed us from house to house. "There's that awful Image again." In its presence, she always averted her eyes.

During that first summer at the Roosevelt Hotel, Mike made an effort to establish a family relationship. I saw less of him than I did of Mother because directors tended to shoot late and I was usually in bed by the time he got home. But, on nights when he had a picture in preparation and, thus, worked less lengthy hours, he took me along with Mother to dinners at Musso & Frank's, a lovely old restaurant on Hollywood Boulevard, which still stands. Mike invariably ordered bouillabaisse. At dinner there one night, Mother said she had a headache and took an aspirin. It seemed an adult thing to do. "I have a headache, too," I said. "I need one."

Mother shrugged and gave me a pill. Mike made no comment. Then we went across the street to see a picture at the Egyptian theater. As we sat down, Mike whispered to me, "If someone take aspirin without headache, the right hand must be hold higher than the heart, or you die."

I was terrified. I could not admit I had no need of the aspirin and I had no wish to conclude my life. As the feature came on, I found it necessary to run the fingers of my right hand through my hair, as though it were in disarray. Then I put my elbow on the back of the seat and leaned my head in my hand as though bored by the picture.

"Are you all right?" Mother asked. I assured her I was fine but by a series of stratagems made sure my hand never dropped below the critical heart line. By the time the film was over, my right arm was cramped and in agony but I was still alive. Walking up the aisle, I pretended to be searching in the left upper pocket of my jacket when Mike whispered, "I think so is enough time, is safe now you put down the hand." There was a curious twinkle in his eyes. I shrugged as though this information was of no concern to me. It did occur that I had been tricked but I refused to give him satisfaction in any way. I kept my hand elevated for a while longer, gingerly lowering it, inch by inch on the walk back to the hotel.

I rushed to my room where I could vigorously massage the cramped and aching limb.

That summer, since I was out of school and had nothing but mischief to employ me, Mother decided on a course of elocution lessons. It is possible that I mumbled. It is also possible that she simply thought I should be out of the hotel for some period each day, out of mischief. At any rate, speech lessons were decreed.

Josephine Dillon lived in a tiny house only a block from the hotel. She had been a New York actress when she met young Clark Gable and became his first wife. She had coached him, made him an actor until he got his first big break on Broadway, which brought him to Hollywood, to success and, in due time, led to their divorce. He was on his way to becoming an MGM superstar and she lived on what she made teaching others.

I do not recall how long I went on walking the short distance from the hotel to her house but her instruction failed to lead to the next logical step: I did not become a movie star. The family moved to Beverly Hills and I continued at a new military school.

The Pacific Military Academy was founded by Col. Harry Culver, eponymous father of Culver City where Metro-Goldwyn-Mayer was located and where my mother worked. I was surprised, during my first school graduation exercise, to hear an announcement awarding me a scholarship medal. Stunned would more accurately describe my reaction. The ceremony was attended by parents. When the award was announced, I heard a wild peal of laughter and an attempt to suppress same. As I crossed the stage to get my unexpected and undeserved medal, I could see my mother in the first row, trying to turn her laughter into a coughing fit. I cannot imagine why I was so honored except that this was during the time of the Great Depression and the school was concerned to have tuition renewed for the following year. I was pleased to have gotten any award but shared Mother's opinion that, considering my grades, it was an exceptionally silly one. I later pinned this medal to the chest of a Piglet doll someone gave me.

Then, as happens so often in life, tragedy followed on the heels of comedy. After the commencement ceremony came the annual school dance. We were in our dress uniforms, which, for some reason, known only to Col. Culver, resembled Cossack costumes—dark blue pants with a wide gray stripe topped by a gray blouse with brass buttons up the side of the neck. The blouse had epaulets and was cinched by a wide white belt with a brass buckle. I was perhaps ten years old and had never danced. I did, however, like music. The school band was playing an almost recognizable version of "Willow Weep for Me." The floor was jammed with my classmates shuffling to that rhythm with the students of a nearby girls' school.

A senior classman approached me as I sat watching the action. "See that?" he asked, pointing out two girls of perhaps 12 or 13 who were dancing together. I followed his accusing finger and saw them. "Let's break it up," he said.

Obviously the girls were doing something quite wrong and, though I was never one to volunteer, I obediently followed the lead of the elder cadet, determined to stop their illicit action. We reached the girls and he tapped the shoulder of the prettier one. She turned, smiled at him and stopped dancing. My elder classmate took her in his arms and danced off with her. I stared, stunned. Were they to receive no punishment, not even a reprimand for their action? The remaining girl was looking at me strangely. She smiled tentatively, exposing her braces where a morsel of cake was lodged. The music went on. "Aren't we going to dance?" she asked.

I watched the elder classman whirl his girl around the floor and finish the dance with a graceful dip. When the band raggedly struck up "Evergreen," they danced off again. My girl was still waiting. Slowly, the horrible realization dawned on me. When he had said "break it up" he didn't mean to throw them off the dance floor. He meant that we should—I swallowed, almost gagging. "I don't know how," I said miserably. Leaving her in the middle of the crowded floor, I ran to my room. I have never learned to dance.

Hollywood in those days was a small community, everybody knew everybody else and there was a great deal of home entertaining. I, being decidedly minor, did not attend these parties. The one that had introduced me to Eve was a later trial, which was not thereafter repeated for some years.

During most of Mother's parties, I was sent to Uncle Bill and Aunt Vi's house. They would, some weekends, take me on camping trips or on various tours in their "motor," as Uncle Bill called it. He was a very responsible driver and, in his open touring Buick, was well aware of any sign of improper action by other drivers on the road. He would shout suggestions to them intended to make them mend their ways. "Woman driver!" was frequently on his lips as more of the fair sex ventured to go automobiling. But Uncle Bill's most caustic comment, reserved for really serious breaches of roadside etiquette was "Why, you fried egg!"

Our excursions could run from day trips in the mountains to overnight camping, often on the beach at Oceanside in their tent. Uncle Bill, before marrying my aunt, had been a Royal Canadian Mounted Policeman and knew the great outdoors. His name was William A. Reynolds and someone (probably Mother) had given him a monogrammed pipe stand, which occupied an honored place on his mantle. On the stand were his initials in silver. They spelled WAR. I thought that was really keen.

Auntie Vi had been unable to have children. Whether the problem was with her physiology or his was neither known nor important. She thought of me as hers, and I was always preferred over my cousin, Sandy, her other nephew who, when my multi-millionaire Uncle Will was cleaned out in the crash of the late '20s, came to live with them. Sandy and Aunt Florence, the formerly wealthy Detroit society lady, shared a small back room of their modest Glendale home, an incredible comedown, which must have embittered Sandy as much as it did his mother. On her, however, it showed.

Back in the days following my encounters with Eve, I was usually sent, on party weekends, to Auntie Vi's. But there was one alternate destination—Collins' house. He lived far downtown on 130th Street, in the colored district, with three children and his alcoholic wife, Irene, who worked for Mother on and off as a maid. The children were Joe, Bootsy and Margurite—two girls, one boy. The same number and gender combination I was later to have.

At Collins', his son Joe and I slept on the day bed on the porch and would talk long into the night. Together we would roam the neighborhood. I do not know what 130th Street thought of my white face but there was never any deference shown to me by Collins' family as Massa's child nor was there any evident hostility from the neighbors in those gentler days. But there was a certain caution, a recognition of my difference. Collins' brother-in-law, George, sharing his sister Irene's love of the bottle, was expanding one night about some friend who had a bar fight. "Them niggers like to kill theirselves," he said.

"Atchway ethey ofay," Collins snapped in pig Latin. I realized it was a warning not to use what later to be termed the N word in front of me.

Once or twice I went with his family to the colored beach. It didn't seem odd to me that there should be a special place for colored people to enjoy the beauty of California in that pre-smog era but a rope, stretching out to a float, separated their beach from that of the Jonathan Club, a very exclusive White Establishment to which my Uncle Will belonged. The two separate peoples shared the same ocean, indeed the same waves only a few feet apart but that thin rope was an impregnable barrier, not to be crossed.

Toward the end of the '20s had come the agonizing transition from silent pictures to talkies, a period that saw the sudden demise of many stellar careers—handsome leading men with high squeaky voices, idolized vamps with grating foreign or regional accents. Few people had any clear idea how to handle the new technology. Actors from the stage were hired because they knew how to speak. Playwrights were sought to write speeches for them to say. The change was chaotic—for many, catastrophic.

Directors, used to storytelling with imaginative camerawork, now had to let the actor's lines explain the action because, on top of everything else, the new technique was clumsy and immobile. Actors were forced to stay within range of microphones concealed in flowerpots or lamps, or strung overhead. With no freedom of movement, scenes became static talkfests. Movies no longer moved. In this time the sound man, the mixer, was king. No one dared dispute him because no one knew exactly what he did.

Mike fought a running battle with mixers, insisting on movement in his scenes. If the camera couldn't move, the actors must. He would no longer stage static scenes with actors chained to a microphone. Mike demanded that the mixer find solutions. "Lazy bum, why you don't listen harder?" Mixers were not fond of Mike. Vitaphone, which started the sound revolution, was a Warner Brothers patent. Sound was recorded on a large disk and synched up, with great difficulty, to the action, causing occasional unwanted comic results when the actor's lips moved some beats ahead or behind his speech. Audiences put up with this because sound was such a miracle.

As a child, long before I myself was employed in the industry, I would visit Mike's set and watch the creation of this new wonder, a talking scene. On what was to be called the sound stage were two small soundproof booths, called "iceboxes" by the crew. They were stifling. In one was the camera, enclosed to keep its noise from ruining the sound. This restriction was the reason why early talkies were so static. At the end of each take, I went with Mike and whoever else could squeeze into the other small booth to hear the recording of the scene played back. If the recording quality was acceptable, the take was okayed. If not, Mike would stomp out, mumbling curses which might have been in English and reshoot the scene, glaring constantly at the mixer.

It was Auntie Vi who came up with a summer vacation for me. In 1928, Pacific Military Academy was having its camp at Lake Elsinore, some 60 miles south of Los Angeles. There I spent part of one forgettable summer. We slept in tents and had swimming, boating, baseball and football. Both of the latter I managed to avoid. Swimming there was not a great deal better as the bottom of Lake Elsinore was a mass of mud, slimy grass and God knows what else, frightening to the feet.

It was to this camp that Uncle Bill and Auntie Vi came and found me sitting in front of a tent marked Company D. I was the sole occupant of Company D. Uncle Bill was clearly uncomfortable and, after several attempts at speech, Auntie Vi took over and calmly explained that Mother had been in an accident. She was all right but was in the hospital. They had come to take me to her.

In the hospital I remember Mother's face swathed in bandages and the unintelligible words that issued from the bandages. She had been in the back of the Lincoln, on her way to pick up Mike when their car was broadsided by a speeding hit-and-run driver, who then took off. Mother was thrown forward into the glass that separated the rear compartment from the chauffeur. Her lower lip was split wide open and, for the rest of her life, she carried a visible scar despite plastic surgery.

I did not realize at the time how close to death she had been. Jagged glass fragments penetrated her chest, narrowly missing her heart. All I remember are the bandages and the muffled voice.

Some 15 years later, Joan, who was to be my first wife, while driving to Warner Brothers, was hit by a drunken driver and, like my mother, carried a lifelong scar from the impact that almost killed her. While on a gurney, waiting to be treated in the emergency room, she was in and out of consciousness but heard the E.R. personnel saying, "Isn't it a shame, she had such a pretty face." She had just been signed as a Warner contract actress and was convinced that she would never be able to work. The face was repaired but Joan had been a concert violinist and the fracture of the frontal sinus made the vibrations agony. She was forced to give up the instrument.

Within weeks of her injury, Mother was back home and I saw more of her. We talked and I played cards with her but after just a few weeks, Mother was back at the studio and life resumed its normal course.

I was often taken to previews. I remember vividly one occasion, at the Alexander Theater in Glendale. I cannot recall the picture but Darryl Zanuck was the producer and Mike directed it. As was the custom, viewers were asked to fill out cards, rating the film. Studio officials crowded about the tables set up in the lobby, scanning the cards for signs of a hit. The cards that night were very good but both Darryl and Mike had a feeling that something else was needed before the film was ready for release. They disagreed, however, on what that something should be. In front of the theater I stood before the line of limousines with Mother and Aunt Virginia while Mike and Darryl, standing apart from the main body of studio personnel, argued about the benefit of cutting out one scene. Darryl, a small man with a big cigar and an even bigger ego, advanced his viewpoint with extreme vigor, getting so fervently into the matter that he flicked the ash of his cigar in Mike's face. There was a hush. I could feel Mother's tension as she stood beside me. Aunt Virginia grasped Mother's arm. There was an audible gasp from the lower-ranking studio officials. Mike's only reaction was to calmly reach out, lift Darryl by the coat front and set him down in the gutter. Then he walked away. Studio employees rushed protectively to Darryl's side as he sputtered in rage.

Mother got us all into the car and Collins drove us home. The next day, Darryl came down to the set and discussed the preview results rationally with Mike. The night's confrontation was never mentioned. They were friends.

It was about this time that I decided to take my life into my own hands and change my name. When I was still unborn but kicking and causing discomfort, Mother referred to me as Jake the Monster. When I emerged, I was officially called by my father's first name and my mother's last, Wilfred Meredyth Lucas. But the name Jake stuck. When I squalled, I was again Jake the Monster.

Julia, my grandmother, thought this too harsh a name for one so young. "Not for a little boy, Bessie," she insisted and, instead, called me Jadie. So the family was divided as to who I was. After a period of this confusion, Mother started to call me Jack—I have no idea why but it momentarily satisfied both family factions. Then, at the age of eight or so, I read a book whose hero was a famous World War I ace. His aerial feats, dogfights, kills and acts of gallantry raised me to the peak of ecstasy. His name was Ronald Raven. I thought Ronald Raven was the greatest name I had ever heard. I campaigned to be so called. Mother was not as thrilled with the idea as I had hoped. I remained Jack to her. To Mike I would always be Jick.

Undaunted, as my hero would surely have been, I read and reread the book, then began a more subtle approach. I left notes for Mother signed Ronald Raven. On her birthday (which was also Lincoln's), I sent her a telegram at the studio wishing her many happy returns and signed, "Your loving son, Ronald Raven."

This supplied conversation at the dinner table and laughter, the last thing I expected or wanted. My campaign was clearly off on the wrong foot. I did not like the name Wilfred and Jack was little better. I had presented them a perfectly good name and met amused stonewalling. I remained Jack for many years. Finally, when my importuning became too much to bear, Mother struck a compromise and legally changed my name to John. This partial victory I did not find an occasion for unqualified celebration because, in my mind's ear, I could still hear the chatter of the machine gun, see my hero gallantly salute as the enemy plane, with its sinister black cross, spiraled down in flames. I could hear the cheers of Ronald Raven's fellow officers as he landed on the tarmac, the wings of his plane shredded with bullet holes, the mechanic saying, "Lord, Capt. Ronald Raven, it's a miracle you got this old crate back at all."

After that, who could be satisfied with John?

5

Resisting Education and Other Pursuits

Before her birthday in 1967, Mother mentioned that she had had a lifelong desire for a Mynah bird. Since Mother had always instantly bought everything that even momentarily interested her, I found this exceptional. I also found it a difficult present to obtain. After searching everywhere, I finally found a pet shop that contained such a bird, young enough to be taught speech but already able to utter a few phrases. I presented it to Mother on her birthday, dramatically drawing off the concealing cloth from the cage. The bird's name, I explained, was Ronald Raven. It looked at her solemnly and said, "Hello, Dolly." Mother was absolutely fascinated by the bird and did not allow it to leave her side. She diligently taught it to swear.

At this time Elizabeth, my elder daughter, was thrown from her horse, her leg badly fractured; the head of the tibia resembled shrapnel in the X-ray. After two surgeries she was confined for months in a body cast to the orthopedic bed we had set up in the children's playroom. Ronald Raven was sent down to her, the novelty of Mother's feathered friend having worn off.

Since Elizabeth was unable to attend school, the nuns from Louisville brought her lessons to the house and brought her up on all the latest news of the school. On one of their visits the phone rang. Angelino, our houseman, must have been in the garden because it rang many times. "Somebody," Ronald Raven screeched, "get the fucking phone."

From then on, whenever the nuns came, Ronald Raven was relegated to the rear of the house.

My very earliest memories are filled with all the nastiness of asthma, which lasted into my late teens. It is a horrid affliction. The constant battle to cough up the semi-solid mucus coating the bronchial tubes. The panic, the fight to get air into my lungs. It is really the difficulty of getting air *out* of the lungs past the heavy mucus and the bronchospasms. I was allergic to almost everything. Nighttime, for some reason—perhaps just the act of lying flat—was the worst. I came to loathe the dark, waiting eagerly, like one of *les malades* at Lourdes, praying for the miracle of dawn. In the morning, I knew, things would be better; and, for some unexplained reason, they would be. A good part of my missing the usual school curriculum was the fact that I got such sympathy for my illness that I was allowed to remain in bed when I felt ill. This would usually entail a house call from the doctor but, since doctors had little idea of the cause of asthma, my need for bed and rest was almost never questioned.

Although it is a disease, and a bad one, there is a good deal of psychic input in asthma and in Mother I had an excellent role model for psychic input.

The most memorable demonstration of this was back in the 1930s, when I was still a child and Mother was still at MGM. She had begun to develop a series of mysterious illnesses. For weeks at a time the house would be filled with the bustle of nurses and the visit of doctors. Then, suddenly, Mother would return to work as though nothing had happened.

As an adult, trying to reason what had been happening, I would guess that she was going through what today are called anxiety attacks.

At the time, the anxiety was all mine. There would be long nights when she would run hysterically through the house, then faint. At such times I would cower outside her bedroom door praying she wouldn't die. Doctors would come, sometimes bringing nurses. It didn't strike me as strange that the next morning she would get into the limousine and Collins would take her to the studio. I was merely relieved.

I had no way of knowing the frequency of these attacks. I saw them only on weekends. The rest of the time I was resisting education in my current military academy.

In this period Mike did a few pictures that harked back to his UFA days in Berlin. *Doctor X*, the first Technicolor horror film, is still a classic. It starred Lionel Atwill, who had also played in *Captain Blood* and many of Mike's other pictures. Atwill had been a stage actor and director who finally gravitated to Hollywood. He was a character actor rather than a star, as the term was used in that day. Among his other credits he took, as his second wife, Louise Cromwell Brooks MacArthur. He was her third husband. Her first had left her a very rich Washington socialite.

She had then married a promising middle-aged general, Douglas MacArthur. MacArthur was annoying the entrenched military powers by suggesting many changes in the peacetime army. In 1932, at the height of the Depression, he became a very unpopular figure because he was unlucky enough to be chief of staff of the army troops ordered to drive the "Bonus Army" from the hovels they had built in Washington. These veterans had marched on Washington to force Congress to grant early payment of their bonuses for service in World War I. These were men MacArthur had commanded in that conflict but orders were orders.

Tired of Army routine and missing the glamour of her former social life, Louise divorced MacArthur. He remarried and it was his second wife, Jean, who went with him when, before the Japanese attack, he was "exiled" to Manila and into history.

In 1937, Louise married Lionel Atwill. Hollywood, she thought, would bring her the glamour and excitement that a stodgy military husband and the Washington social scene couldn't provide. Soon, however, she found that life with an actor wasn't all that exciting either. They were divorced.

Then came World War II and MacArthur became the stuff of legends. A war hero, never out of the news, mentioned in the class of Alexander and Napoleon, and, finally, with the occupation of Japan, uncrowned Emperor of the East. All that glory might have been hers but for the divorce. Few people can correctly read life's road maps.

When I was home from school on weekends, many of my Sundays were spent at the Uplifters Club in Santa Monica where Mike's team played polo. He, Darryl and some of the Warner people had started a polo team. The third player changed from time to time but the fourth was always Aiden Roark, a society player from the East Coast, a three-goal man who made up for any deficiencies in the others players. The team played mostly at the Uplifters but had matches at various Southland clubs. I have a trophy from Midwick Country Club.

May 4th 1937
The J. M. Spalding Tournament
Won By
Mike Curtiz, Darryl Zanuck, Aiden Roark and Peter Perkins 11–10

My father had been a founder of the Uplifters and now, having returned from New York, officiated as timekeeper at the polo matches, a voluntary honor. Mike and Mother's box was right in back of the timekeeper's platform and I would split my allegiance between their box and my father, sitting beside him, waiting for him to ring the bell that would indicate the end of chukkers. I'm not sure if I felt a sense of divided loyalties but it was always a little uncomfortable. As an adult I realize it must have been uncomfortable for my father, too—uncomfortable for everybody. I may also have felt that being a timekeeper was slightly demeaning; too much like an employee. Hollywood breeds a status mentality.

After my military academy years came Beverly High School. This posed a cultural shock to me, having for so many years been required to put a bright shine on my shoes, have my tie correctly knotted—in short, been used to the constant formality of militant scholarship. I was surrounded here by kids in sweatshirts and corduroys. I did not deem such dress proper and, one cold California morning, I became the center of attention when I elected to wear a black velvet-collared tweed overcoat borrowed from my stepfather's closet. I failed to achieve the hoped-for effect—man of the world, bon vivant. The Dean of Boys suggested it might be well to follow current school dress custom. Later that night, Mother said, "He also called me at the studio with questions about your home life and suggestions that you get counseling."

After suffering the lack of appreciation and understanding of the Beverly Hills School System for a few years, I was sent to Cumnock. This was not exactly a school for problem children but it did have its share of unusual students. Here I fit in better than I ever had before. Here, also, I met Ariel, my first relationship with a girl who was my junior. Her father had been a musician who had walked out on the family. She lived with her mother and grandmother within a few blocks of the school. Ariel had one pronounced peculiarity. This was the golden era of the drive-in. Wherever else we went, our evenings always ended at a drive-in. Ariel never, in all our relationship, ever ordered anything other than a hot fudge sundae and french fries. How she maintained a stunning figure on such fare I can only attribute to youth and a very rapid metabolism.

Many of the students at Cumnock were children of movie or business celebrities. A group of us would spend many a lunchtime listening to William Hammerstein, son of the famous lyricist, play the piano. I could appreciate the music despite my unfortunate inability to get all the way through "Ramona" after two years' instruction. William's mother, Oscar Hammerstein's second wife, Dorothy, was born in Australia and had lived in a house directly across the street from the childhood home of my wife-to-be, Joan. Houses in Australia were frequently named. Joan's was St. Roche. The future Mrs. Hammerstein lived in Halloween.

At Cumnock I did well in a few subjects that interested me—French, physiology, drama and ancient history. Mathematics remained a constant mystery to me and does to this day.

My rejection of the world of Pythagoras, Euclid and Einstein had been made permanent some years earlier by a Lt. Taylor, a mathematics instructor at Southwestern Military Academy in San Marino. He was large, gruff and wore a brush mustache. We developed an instant mutual antipathy. I was singled out for much adverse comment in class.

Study Hall was meant to give us time to work out our lessons. I, however, had been taken to see a submarine movie—I think it was an MGM film. I was fascinated. My periods in Study Hall were spent rewriting this story and adding crudely drawn pictures of submarines with doors carefully labeled Sally Ports, lest there be any confusion as to their purpose. That is what they were called in the movie. I once felt an ominous presence. Lt. Taylor, standing over my shoulder, cuffed me on the back of my head, thus physically suggesting that I use my time on more useful pursuits. I could not help myself. For months I lived aboard that sub in my mind and was unable to resist transferring the experience to my copybooks. I did, however keep an anxious eye out for Lt. Taylor, covering my work when he appeared. I fear that he was not entirely deceived.

Weekends at military schools are a time of anxious interest. Cadets, unless they have accumulated too many demerits, were allowed to go home after Friday afternoon Dress Parade until Sunday evening. Those burdened with infractions, those unlucky ones, were campused.

One weekend I was lucky in the demerit area but hadn't finished a test in algebra. Lt. Taylor made it very plain that I could not leave until I had done it to his satisfaction. I was still sweating over it when Collins arrived. Explaining my problem, I got into the back of the limousine to complete my work, trying not to hear Collins' grumbling and the constant checking of his watch. I had finally come to terms with an especially tricky problem when Lt. Taylor, his face red with wrath, materialized out of nowhere and dragged me from the car. "So," he thundered, "you were going to sit in the back of the car and never notice when the chauffeur drove away. Well, that game won't work."

I was sent back to the classroom to rework my assigned problems, angry, hurt and annoyed—annoyed mostly because that excellent idea hadn't occurred to me. It took another hour to get the paper done to Lt. Taylor's reluctant satisfaction. I then had to listen to a bitter litany from Collins as we drove at maddeningly reckless speed all the way to Culver City to pick up my mother at the studio. "I'm supposed to tell your mother she had to wait 'cause that peckerwood don't like you?"

I wasn't sure of the definition of peckerwood but it did seem to fit Lt. Taylor.

At the opposite end of the pedagogical spectrum, when I was a Beverly

High student, was Mr. Druart. A Scot, he had been a professor somewhere or other in the United Kingdom. He was retired. I have no idea how Mother found him but during one of the frequent calls my mother received from the principal of Beverly High it was decided to hire a tutor for me to improve my dismal math. Mr. Druart was chosen for the job, I shall never know by what process but I loved him. He was short, old, frail-looking and, in all weathers, wore a black overcoat and carried rubbers. Having been raised in an unpredictable climate, he was not, at his age, about to make concessions to the sunny skies of Southern California. "Druart, " he would introduce himself. "My name is Druart. D-r-u-a-r-t."

He had been employed to remedy what today's polite euphemism would term my numerical impairment. We would repair to my room each afternoon to get out the math books. Soon, however, I discovered that he was a Classicist and loved poetry and Greek. I found I could easily distract him from the dreaded numbers and into the realm of the Muses. He would recite poetry to me and later bring me his personal volumes, which I devoured. He could also be encouraged, with a minimum of prompting, to recite passages of *The Iliad* in Greek. I never learned Greek but I can still recall the sonorous sound as it poured from his lips. Through his watery eyes I saw the topless towers of Ilium fall and Priam dead. I cannot count beyond my fingers but I have loved poetry all my life.

At Beverly High School I had an English teacher who made a definite attempt to interest us in that subject beyond parsing, etc. She read and assigned reading, most of which I found interesting. In her class I wrote my first poem. There was, in the '20s and early '30s, an organization called World Peaceways. I knew it from the magazines Mother subscribed to, expensive magazines. Every ad for World Peaceways quoted the loss in lives and property in the First World War, describing the terrible suffering it had caused. I do not recall what exactly they proposed to do about it but it fired my imagination. I wrote:

THIS IS THE GLORY OF WAR.

He lay in the van of the legions
Of the legions that marched ahead,
He lay in the van of the legions
Among the rotting dead.
It's us that our kings always sell
To the devils of war in this man made hell,
In this lice filled trench with the stench of death
Where our lungs rebel at every breath

And our screams drown out the cannon's roar.
This is the glory of war.

My teacher praised my effort and said it showed real promise. I had to read it to the class. Then she explained that van was a short form of vanguard, the units that went ahead of the troops. I had assumed van meant the rear and was so embarrassed and humiliated that I tore the poem to shreds. I did not take criticism well and have ever since lived with a dictionary at my side.

Mother had a masseuse, Bertha, who came to the house regularly over a long period of time. Her daughter, Isabel, was five years my senior. Once, at the Crescent Heights house, for a reason I do not remember, she babysat me. I would have been perhaps 8 and she 13. I recall that she was not pleased with the assignment. Later, when we moved to Beverly Hills, Mother's massages continued and Bertha would occasionally bring her daughter, now 19, to wait for her. I had a brief romance with this girl, despite the disparity of age. As I was a mere 14, I do not think Isabel cared much for the idea or particularly liked me but her mother promoted the relationship. They lived in an apartment owned by the family of Amos Johnstone, who was later to become my friend. Isabel was a thin, angular girl not given much to smiling and not very pretty but she was a girl. My earlier experience with Eve had aroused, if not fully awakened, my interest in the opposite sex.

As I was too young to drive, Mother got me a chauffeur and a car, a Ford sedan. The chauffeur, Alex, was a young black student at UCLA who made some spare money when he drove me on dates, to movies, dinner. Isabel was somewhat more worldly than was common for girls in that era, more worldly than I was prepared for. One night, dispensing with Alex, we went out with a group of her friends, driving to the beach in a convoy of cars. Two by two, like animals going into the Ark, the couples vanished into the night carrying blankets. We followed to the sand, spread the blanket and Isabel lay down. I was unsure of what, exactly, I was supposed to do. With an annoyed sigh, Isabel showed me, adding. "If you come in there, I'll kill you."

In 1933, the new President, Franklin Roosevelt, took office and fulfilled his campaign promise to end Prohibition. Repeal started gently so as not to overly alarm what "Drys" were left in the country. Beer with an alcoholic content of 3.2 was to be allowed.

On the first night of its permitted sale, there were beer stands erected on the Santa Monica and Venice piers. Amos Johnstone, scion of the family that owned Isabel's apartment, drove me down to the pier. Amos was considerably older, perhaps 20 or 21. Why he struck up a friendship with me I cannot imagine. He lived with his sister and her husband. His brother-in-law was a builder and Amos worked for him as a carpenter. But, off the job, Amos was a sharp dresser. He actually owned a pair of spats, which, even then, seemed something out of the last century. But with his pencil-thin mustache he did look dapper. On that night at the Santa Monica pier I consumed 12 bottles of beer. At 3.2 percent I doubt that I got drunk. Perhaps I simply vomited the vast volume before it could take effect but I remember thinking of it as a very adult and exciting experience.

Through Amos, I later learned of the wonders of Alturas. Las Alturas had been, in the early days of movies, a hotel. It was up in the Santa Monica Mountains above Brentwood, remote, secluded. Silent film star Wallace Reid had spent his last days there, deep in the drugs and alcohol in which his promising career had drowned. It was now, in the last days of Prohibition, a speakeasy. It had a bar, a huge kitchen and a head-waiter-manager called Joe. Alturas' main attraction was illegal booze but Joe could be persuaded to whip up food for the hungry. The dining room was unused and the bedrooms where employed for far shorter stays than originally planned.

Amos and I were currently going with two sisters, Mabel and Blondie, who lived in Atwater, near Glendale. Amos' girl, Blondie, was everything the name implied. Mabel was 16 and protected by her older sister from the wildness Blondie, herself, enjoyed. While Amos and Blondie went through the rooms at Alturas like a cyclone, I could never get Mabel beyond the barstool and she remained, as far as I was concerned, a virgin. I had only Joe's booze to comfort me.

Then came a true, memorable and (in many ways) traditional Hollywood experience—Maggie's wedding. Maggie Ettinger, who had shared our beach house in Venice with Mother and Louella Parsons, had chosen as her bridegroom an advertising man from New York—Ross Shattuck.

The wedding was at Louella's house and, of course, an elaborate affair. Set up on the rear lawn were many tables and umbrellas. Most of Hollywood was there. Louella's husband, Doc Martin, a well-known Hollywood urologist, had gotten a slight start on the drinking and was already slurring his greetings. Mother told me that she had been at a party at Louella's earlier in the year. The festivities were at their peak when someone discovered Doc passed out under the piano, and tried to wake him. "Let him get some rest," Louella pleaded. "Poor Dockie has to operate early in the morning."

At Maggie's wedding there was a great deal of table-hopping, gossip exchanged, deals made. Agents grabbed at Mike, trying to sell him this or that client—star or starlet. Mother joked with old friends. I usually felt out of place at such functions but, having managed to sneak a glass of champagne, I was delighted with the whole party.

At the table next to ours, Orry Kelly, head designer of Wardrobe at Warners, held court, commenting about every dress in sight and having stars come up to receive his approval of their clothing choices. Orry was massively overweight but immaculate. He wore his gray hair long and flowing at a time when short military cuts were the male fashion. He dressed in extravagant elegance. He flaunted his "alternate lifestyle" at a time when the closet was the only safe place for what was called a "pansy."

One of the celebrities to stop by was Cary Grant with Virginia Cherrill on his arm. Cary, when fresh from England and still named Archie Leach, had shared an apartment in New York with Orry and another friend. Virginia, gorgeous and halfway between starlet and star, was his new bride and was gushing to everybody about how happy she was, how wonderful Cary was. "Don't tell me, honey," Orry said, "I had him long before you did." It was a short visit.

The wedding itself went off smoothly and I managed to sneak another glass of champagne when my table partner was turned away, watching the ceremony. This was the second glass she'd lost and she must have questioned her memory.

The wedding bouquet was thrown and, as I stumbled to my feet to watch, the bouquet missed the assembled young ladies leaping excitedly for it, hit the top of our umbrella and slid down into my arms, making me, according to popular folklore, the next bride. I never heard Orry Kelly's comment on that.

By 1935, Mike had begun to assert himself and fight for more challenging scripts. "If I don't follow my head, I'm a shoeshiner" was how he put it.

Finally he got a picture with action and romance. *Captain Blood*. Various casting was discussed. It had been planned for Robert Donat but he was ill—extremely bad asthma—and had to drop out. Cary Grant was a favorite but Jack Warner thought he was too polished and effete. Finally the part went to a young actor under contract to the studio—Errol Flynn. Flynn had been brought there by Lily Damita, a glamorous foreign star getting on in years but rich and clearly capable of getting what she wanted. She persuaded Warner to hire Flynn as an actor. Warner agreed but did little with his acquisition. He had played a corpse for Mike in *The Case of the Curious Bride*, which starred Warren William. Now as a last resort in a tough-to-cast picture, he was given to Mike.

Michael Curtiz and Errol Flynn on the set of *Captain Blood*. Mike sits in the "Major Curtiz" director's chair presented to him by the crew so that he would "outrank" Flynn (1935).

Part of *Captain Blood* was shot on location in the coves of Laguna Beach, which easily translated into the Spanish Main. Laguna Beach, as a matter of fact, had been the site of the first movie made in California. In 1907, the Selig Studio in Chicago suspended filming of *The Count of Monte Cristo* because of heavy winter storms. They sent the star, Francis Boggs, to California to find more suitable weather. He found it in Laguna Beach, south of Los Angeles, and the shooting of their film was concluded there.

We had a Laguna summer cottage my parents had built in 1930. The *Captain Blood* filming took place in summer. Since I was out of school, I got to be an extra, watching the climactic sword fight between Errol Flynn (whose name Mike translated into Earl Flint) and Basil Rathbone. Mike, given an actor of very limited experience, designed every scene like a painting, with Flynn at the focal point to give him stature. The rest is history. Despite having made him a star and done many subsequent pictures with him, Mike's opinion of Flynn never improved. "Earl is a terrific anti-talent," he said.

As an extra on *Captain Blood*, I remember a day spent in a costume too large for me with a mixed bag of Laguna residents, all dressed by the Wardrobe Department in equally riotous gear, and cheering Captain Blood's swordfight at appropriate moments. I received extra's pay and a very severe sunburn.

Our house at Laguna was small, with two bedrooms and one bath, a large living room and solarium, a tiny dining room and a small kitchen. But it occupied a whole block, was covered with bougainvillea and surrounded by riotous gardens. Outside, by the garage, was the chauffeur's room and bath.

Maggie Ettinger, perhaps remembering the shared rental of the Venice house, had bought one in Laguna and had talked Mother into building one of her own. Maggie's was across the street from ours and I played with her son, Gordon, who was several years my junior. Sundays both houses were always filled with artists, friends and parties, ocean swimming optional.

The local architect who had designed and built it had been driven nearly to the point of suicide by Mike's constant changes. He seemed to regard the project as he would one of his studio sets. When he said he wanted a room wider, he expected the walls to be moved back as they were at the studio. He was not interested in protests about building codes or the necessity of changing rooflines.

Collins would drive me to Mother's studio on Saturday night, pick her up, then go wherever Mike was shooting to get him, drive some 60 miles to Laguna to spend Sunday at the beach. In those pre-union days, film was shot six days a week and generally late Saturday night, since the company had all Sunday to rest. If we did not take the maid, Collins' wife, I would sit in front. If she went I rode in the back, often falling asleep on the floor of the limousine rather than using the jump seat.

In Laguna I would sleep on the large day bed in an oriel window in the living room. In the morning I would walk to the corner grocery to buy the Sunday papers so I could read the comics. After breakfast, we would generally go to the bottom of the street, with Collins carrying rugs umbrellas and pillows for a day on the sand. The house was all of knotty pine and, with a fire going in the grate, it was a wonderful place.

We lost it some years later when Mother found that Mike had taken one of his actresses there when he was supposed to be shooting all night. Mother ordered the house sold the next day.

Mike had a European attitude about marriage. It formed a stable home, provided comfort but was not expected to confine one's pleasures. Such adventures, Mike claimed, had no effect on men. With women, of course, it was quite a different matter. One of Mike's friends and countrymen, producer Alexander Korda, once gave a well-reasoned Hungarian defense of the double standard in sex. "If you step with your boot in shit," he said, "you can wipe it off. But—" He paused for emphasis. "If you shit in the boot—" He shrugged expansively.

Mike's extramarital ventures may have contributed to Mother's "illnesses." I have never been able to determine what happened to all that drive that made her a working writer while still in school, that took her to the upper reaches of the infant film industry as writer, actress and director and had her writing some of the biggest films of her day.

It is a drive I have never had, probably because I never needed it. I had only to ask and things were given. Hunger is a great instructor and my stomach was always full. In a strange way I have always envied those who fought their way up from poverty—as Mike and, to a slightly lesser degree, Mother had. Whatever her drive had been, it was gone by this time or, perhaps, transmuted into self-destruction. She had always made the rules—she divorced Burton, she got rid of my father. Now that she had someone she couldn't control, it made her "sick." Today her illness would probably be diagnosed as depression. Whatever the value of my amateur psychiatric speculations, she spent a lot of time in bed.

Instead of writing, jigsaw puzzles occupied her for long periods. They were expensive ones made of wood and came from some place in New York. Each would take days to solve. A folding board on the far side of Mother's huge bed held them. Her nurses—they came and went—would help. After endless searching, I might occasionally find the right piece. Vivian Tennant had an antique store on Highland Avenue and a husband who seemed contented to remain home with his bottle. Vivian would come alone to dinner with Mother—always served in the bedroom—and would join in solving the puzzles or play cards with her. In the course of these activities, we acquired a lot of antiques.

Mother was also addicted to mystery stories and could go through a book in a night. She belonged to the Crime Club, which sent books almost weekly. Several booksellers would send her new titles as they came in. Reading was a hedge against insomnia, along with the sleeping pills she had taken for years.

For me, mystery stories had a different appeal. They were a ticket to pleasure. We had no swimming pool. They were not common in the early '30s. Monte Blue, an early film star who lived next door, had one. Mother had worked with him on Westerns and he told her I was welcome to use his pool at any time. On location shoots, Monte Blue had one inflexible working rule. Whenever he went into a town, he would examine his hotel room, go to the nearest hardware store, buy an appropriate length of rope, tie it securely to the leg of his bed and leave it, neatly coiled, near the window so he could escape in the event of fire.

To the best of Mother's knowledge, he had never had to use this precaution but it did show resolute forethought. The use of his pool was a generous offer and I only had to climb over the wall but, alas, he had older daughters who had older friends. It was not just that I did not like to have others watch me swim. Conversation might be required and I did not feel adequate to manage that.

And, anyway, I was then in love with Virginia Zanuck. Love is never a pure emotion and mine was mixed with the fact that the Zanucks had a pool and had not yet begun their family. The pool was thus vacant during the week and I could have it all to myself. Although it was a trip of several miles, I could ride my bike down and swim all day unwatched and unmolested.

To express my gratitude, I took Mother's Crime Club books to the Zanuck house. Mother welcomed the idea of sharing her mysteries with her friend but finally drew the line when I took books, unopened, to Virginia as soon as they were delivered by the mailman.

"If I'm not allowed to read them, at least let me unwrap the damned package," Mother complained. In those pre–TV days, reading was one of the few uncensorable things one could do in bed.

Mother's health problem, physical or emotional, continued and she was treated for several months by a Dr. Tandowski, a man with a dark beard and heavy accent. He prescribed many different medications including morphine. After some time in a semi-stupor, Mother came to the conclusion that morphine wasn't a good solution to whatever ailed her and little by little had the nurse cut back on it until she was completely off. She was very proud of herself and told us all of her accomplishment.

When next the doctor came, she proudly announced that she had been able to get herself free of the drug, expecting his delighted reaction. Dr. Tandowski, unused to having his orders changed or challenged, puffed up. "I have, myself," he told her brusquely, "given secret orders to the nurse to decrease the doses." The nurse's startled expression made it clear that this was untrue but Mother broke into tears. Mike having overheard the last of this speech strode into the room like an angry God and, pointing his arm melodramatically toward the hallway, thundered, "Dr. Tandowski, go out!" That ended the physician's dealing in our home but "Dr. Tandowski, go out!" became a standard family response to any unwanted occurrence.

Mike was convinced that America was the greatest country in the world and wanted citizenship. He hired a teacher who would come to the house at night, sometimes go with him to the studio, working with Mike on the set between takes. He learned American history, the theory of government, the list of presidents and would ask us to test him at the dinner table. He knew far more than any of us did about the history and running of the country.

When the citizenship test came, it was done before a judge. Mike, who had been up most of the night going over the questions that might be asked, nervously entered the judge's chamber. The Judge turned out to be a great fan of motion pictures and was very familiar with Mike's work. The questions he asked were mostly about the stars Mike had worked with. The citizenship test was somewhat less than cursory. Mike was very disappointed. "Goddamn," he said. "Why hell, all this time I break my head to be American and he ask me only goddamn actors?"

6

Coming Up for Air

In 1934, the Zanucks were going to Europe and begged Mother and Mike to join them. Mother's illness, real or imagined, had left no permanent damage. She eagerly prepared to travel.

This required passports. The required photographs were taken and sent to the passport offices. When the documents came back in the mail, Mother examined them and let out a scream for Mike. "You were born in 1888," she told him. "You're two years older than me." Mike nodded. "Then what the hell is this date?" she demanded, waving his passport. "This makes you ten years younger. How do you think that makes me feel?" Mike shrugged. "Why you don't lie like I am?" he asked simply.

It was from their extended European trip that I got my raspberry silk pants. Such pants were all the rage on the French Riviera. Douglas Fairbanks, father of my rival for the affections of Joan Crawford, and many of Mother's friends in the Zanuck entourage had bought them. Mine were mailed home. I considered myself very daring and sophisticated but after Collins collapsed with laughter, I never had the courage to wear them outside the house.

Their European trip, however, came close to ending before it started. Mike was finishing a picture, which ran over schedule because of the illness of one of the stars. Mother went to New York the civilized way—on the Chief. The train took three days with a brief stopover in Chicago, allowing time for lunch at the fashionable Pump Room of the Ambassador East before changing to the Twentieth Century Limited, which carried passengers in luxury into New York's Grand Central Station.

As soon as Mike called the final "Cut," a studio driver rushed him to Burbank airport. The plane, slow as they were in those days, would cut two days off the trip and get him to New York with plenty of time to meet Mother at the boat. Unfortunately, however, Mike got himself on the wrong plane. It was going to New York but with innumerable stops along the way and would arrive after the ship had sailed.

The studio driver realized what had happened and reported it, setting off a series of telegrams to Mother's train en route to the rendezvous. Studio personnel made telephone calls to the airline and the mayor of New York. With all that pressure exerted, the plane was speeded up, a stop or two omitted. A studio employee from the New York office and a police escort waited at the airport to rush Mike, with sirens wailing, to the dock where the boat had been held an hour past its scheduled departure. All that effort was still not enough. The dock was empty. The ship had waited until the last possible moment, then sailed. However, the city of New York was up to the challenge and Mike went by Harbor Patrol boat to the ship where Mother watched his precarious transfer from the patrol boat to the ship's improvised gangway. They then watched as sailors bundled his luggage aboard. "Is not bad trip," Mike told her, "but I think so I like better the train."

From Paris, Mike took Mother to Budapest, wanting to show her his roots. At the station he received a welcome worthy of the most extravagant Hollywood premiere. Everyone turned out to meet the local boy who made it big in the golden land. Mike had begun his career as an actor, then was credited with directing the first Hungarian feature film before moving to Denmark to work for Nordisk Studios. Then came World War I; after serving in the Cavalry, he went to Austria to work for Sacha Films, then to Germany before being brought to the United States. But, to the Hungarians he was their own native son who could help all of them, either through loans or influence, to go to America and suck at the bountiful breast of Hollywood. Budapest is a beautiful city and Mother saw a good deal of it. She met Mike's innumerable relatives, including his mother and the two brothers he was later able to get out before the Nazis took over.

After all the sightseeing, the endless banquets and receptions, Mother's most vivid recollection was her departure from the railway station. There had been many farewells and handshakes from Hungarians who saw Mike as a ticket to fame and wealth. The speeches were so protracted that Mother had to go to the bathroom. She whispered this to Mike. He told it to an official who smiled reassuringly at Mother and went quickly away. He returned with an imposingly uniformed guard who carried a large key resembling the ceremonial mace that is carried into the opening of the English Parliament. The guard bowed formally to Mother then,

Bess and Mike in Budapest (1934).

while she cringed with embarrassment, preceded her down the length of the station under the eyes of all the interested onlookers. He unlocked the toilet door, bowed her in, stood watch and, when she emerged, escorted her back with the same solemnity.

They went on to Vienna. Mike, of course, was very familiar with the city and took Mother on tours. They went through antique stores and picked up furniture for the house they were redoing in Beverly Hills. One dealer sold them a portrait of Katherine Schratt that had been commissioned by the emperor. He also gave them Schratt's address. Kati Schratt had been an actress at the Burg Theater and, for years, the mistress of Emperor Franz Joseph. He built a house for her, his beloved Kati, and had an underground passage from the palace to that house. Now, in 1934, she was a very old woman who lived by selling off her jewelry, her furniture, all the possessions amassed in the imperial glory of her pre-war years. Mother and Mike bought Biedermeier furniture from her, including a massive dining room suite, an exquisite Meissen clock and candelabra and many individual Meissen pieces, all to be shipped home along with her portrait.

They then went on to Berlin. Mike had worked there and the reception was again exuberant. Although one saw evidence of the Nazis everywhere, famous Jews who traveled in such state as Mike were not molested—not yet. From Berlin, they went south to the French Riviera to meet up with Virginia and Darryl Zanuck and their party that included Joseph Schenck with Merle Oberon and Mike's boyhood friend from Budapest, Alexander Korda. As a kid in the streets of Budapest, Mike had two special friends, Korda Sandor and Lehol Gabor. Their names ultimately were translated into Alexander Korda and Gabriel Pascal. All were poor. All, after much wandering, did extremely well. Korda became possibly the top producer in England and, eventually, was knighted. Pascal also ended in England where he secured the film rights to the George Bernard Shaw plays.

During World War I, Mike was in the Austrian artillery. He returned to a defeated country as divided by ethnic and racial factions as the former Yugoslavia. With the collapse of the Habsburg Empire, civil war erupted. The strongest force to emerge was Bela Kun and his Communist "Soviet Republic." Amid Red Terror, returning officers were stoned or shot as representatives of the old order. In the interest of safety, uniforms were quickly stripped off and hidden. Mike went home and remained quiet until, one night, came the dreaded pounding on the door. Red Army Guards were there for him. He said a quick good-bye to his mother and family, expecting it to be his last.

He was taken down to a former palace of the old regime, ushered through long corridors to massive doors, which were pushed open and Mike thrust inside. In the far corner of the enormous room, a man sat working at a desk, his back to the door. Mike waited uncertainly, not knowing whether to speak or simply wait. After what seemed an eternity, the man turned toward the light and jumped up, throwing his arms wide. "Mishka!" After a stunned silence, Mike drew his first easy breath. It was Korda.

"Mishka," his friend repeated, "Come over here. We've got it made." He explained that he was now Minister of Propaganda in the new Communist government. He led Mike to a large safe and stuffed his pockets with money. "Buy yourself some clothes. You're going to work."

"What work?"

"We've got a wonderful thing going." Korda said. "I'm appointing you Managing Director of Phoenix Studios. You begin directing your first picture tomorrow—*Red Banner*."

"Tomorrow?" Mike was stunned. "Where is the script?"

Korda shrugged. There was no script.

Mike was assigned a detachment of Alpine troops and for weeks shot

6—Coming Up for Air

Mike directing *The Red Banner*.

them charging through the snow, Red banners flying. No scenes, just footage of the valiant Red troops charging, dropping and firing. On the mountaintop, he was remote from all the fighting and political turmoil going on in Budapest. The Communist regime was overthrown and Bela Kun fled the country. Romanian troops moved in. No one was certain what would happen. Communists now found themselves in jail and Mike had worked for the wrong regime. Korda had gone into hiding. Pascal, who had dexterously managed to straddle both sides, found Mike and was able to sneak him aboard a train and out of the country.

Mike went back to Denmark to work, then to Sweden where he made a few films. With things looking better, he moved to Germany, to UFA, the company on the cutting edge of the new film technology. There he did many films, including *Sodom und Gomorra* and *Moon of Israel*.

One day the guard from the main gate came to the set. There was a man outside who claimed to be a friend of Mike's. The guard's manner said clearly that he thought this impossible but did not want to turn the man away until he checked.

Mike went to the gate. Thin, ragged, dirty, the man threw wide his arms. "Mishka!" It was Korda. Mike got him a job as his assistant.

As for Pascal, no one had heard of him until years later. He had finally been forced to leave Hungary and ended in England. He was looking for work—any kind of work but he was particularly fascinated by the plays of George Bernard Shaw. He wrote several long, laudatory letters to the old man, asking for an interview. Receiving no answer, he finally borrowed money, took the train as far as the money would carry him, then walked the rest of the way to Shaw's country home, Ayot St. Lawrence in Hertfordshire.

He waited until Shaw came outside to get some sun, approached him, explaining that he was a film producer and rapidly outlined his plans for filming Shaw's plays, most particularly *Caesar and Cleopatra* and *The Devil's Disciple*. Pascal was at his most charming. His speed and enthusiasm attracted Shaw's interest.

Shaw had been asked before, many times, and had turned down deals with some of the world's largest motion picture companies. Shaw was said to have negotiated once with Sam Goldwyn for one of his properties and the two had failed to agree on the exorbitant fee Shaw demanded. Goldwyn brushed aside this aspect of the discussion and elaborated at great length about casting, the magnificent production he would be able to provide and the showcasing of Shaw's artistry, his wonderful words.

"The problem, Mr. Goldwyn," Shaw is reported to have said, "is that you are only interested in Art and I am interested in money."

"Your plan sounds interesting, Mr. Pascal," Shaw said at last. "Where do you propose to produce these works?"

Pascal assured him production would be no problem once he had the rights to the plays.

Shaw nodded. "How much money do you have?" he asked.

Pascal showing his impish, gypsy smile, turned out his pockets—empty.

Shaw laughed heartily. Pascal got his permission.

On the Riviera, Korda and Mike discussed Pascal and the vicissitudes that had brought the three of them to their present positions.

They also discussed the obvious infatuation of Darryl's partner, Joe Schenck, with Merle Oberon. "She has him by the grip of death," Korda said ominously. "He buys her very expensive jewelry. I worry that he plans to marry her." Korda found this idea shocking. "She merely works for what she can get from him." He told everybody, in the strictest confidence, of her past, hinting at very unsavory events.

He hammered his fears home to Darryl who, as Schenck's partner, should be most concerned. Finally there was a confrontation and Korda's viewpoint won. Darryl had a long talk with Schenck. Schenck reluctantly broke off his relationship with Merle. She returned to London. A short time later, Korda, having scored a triumph for Virtue, also left the Riviera.

After Mike and Mother got home, they were stunned to learn that Korda had been seeing Merle regularly and later married her. When he was knighted, she became Lady Korda.

Mike shook his head. "Hungarians!" he said.

The aunts, Mattie, Ella and Agnes Woodward, with whom Mother had lived and studied piano, had moved to California where, in the fullness of time, Mattie, the Virgin Aunt, died.

Mother and I went to her funeral. She lay on view in an open coffin. We joined the solemn line to pay our last respects. As we came to the coffin, Mother giggled. I looked and tried hard to stifle my own reaction.

Hurrying quickly back to our seats, Mother brought out her handkerchief, making little gasping sounds. I fought down the laughter building in my own throat as we tried hard not to look at each other. The rest of the mourners must have thought we were deeply touched.

Aunt Mattie, that stern Calvinist woman who had turned her loved one's picture to the wall when she undressed had, helpless in the hands of the mortuary cosmeticians, been made up with bright scarlet lipstick, heavily rouged cheeks and layered mascara. She lay on her pink satin pillow, looking like a superannuated hooker.

Later that year I was so involved in the problems my school provided that I did not really pay attention to the dinner table conversations, did not realize we were in for a move far away from the safe, familiar streets of Beverly Hills into a wild and alien land.

Virginia and Darryl Zanuck had bought some property in Encino, in the San Fernando Valley. That part of the Valley then consisted of agricultural land with a few buildings along Ventura Boulevard. Zanuck's building plans called for the erection of the stable before the house was constructed. The stable was a kind of horse palace with 20 stalls and a saddle room as elegant as any mansion in Beverly Hills. It was, however, as much of their spectacular new home as they would ever build. I have no idea what prevented its completion but on Sundays we, and other invited guests, would visit the polo field in front of the stables. There, on the rolling lawn, polo games would be played amid elaborate picnics.

Despite the fact that Zanuck went no farther with his estate, Mother had become excited with the idea of country living. A realtor showed her a hilltop house farther out in the Valley.

In a flash of *déjà vu*, it was the house she'd seen once in the Scottish Highlands when she was in the British Isles writing *The Iron Duke* (Wellington, the victor of Waterloo) for George Arliss.

She had gone to see Blair Athol, the castle of the Duke of Athol, head of the Stuart Clan. Stuarts had once been kings of England as well as Scotland. Her brother, Will, had found the family crest and, when in any new city, would look up MacGlashans in the phone book. MacGlashan is a sept of the Clan Stuart, a sort of poorer relation but there were seven townships owned by the MacGlashan line that he wanted to repossess. The properties were hopelessly entailed and the legal work would never have been worth the trouble but it was his hobby.

The exterior of the Duke of Athol's castle was a squarish white stone structure, not very interesting although the interior was quite grand. But, farther up in the Highlands, Mother had spotted a manor from the road. It fascinated her and stuck in her mind. The house the realtor showed Mother in the San Fernando Valley reminded her of that Highland manor. It was constructed of gray brown stone supporting a monstrous slate roof and seemed to be growing out of the hilltop on which it stood.

It had been built by a very rich and, up to a year before, very clever investment broker. Fortunately for us, unfortunately for him, his cleverness was not in line with the law. He was now living in prison. He had spared no expense on the house, which was surrounded by 110 acres, 90 of it in citrus. Huge pine trees lined the curving entrance drive down to the stone gate at the bottom of the hill. Mother fell instantly in love with the place. Mike was dragged to see it and, coming from a poor family where land was the dream of everyone, his consent did not require much urging.

Before they sold the place in 1946, it had grown to 265 acres, with stables for 12 horses—riding and polo ponies, cow barns, numerous outbuildings, including my photographic studio. An exquisite formal hilltop garden separated the main house from the swimming pool and a small complete house, designed by Mike's favorite art director, which was Mother's office and included a secretary's room, bar, fireplace and library as well as pool changing rooms and showers.

On the main road, just before the huge cobbled motor court, stood the Tower. This started as a one-room gardener's cottage to which Mike added a Hungarian style bar-kitchen and a round tower room that was lined with bookcases and had a curved stairway leading up to the bedroom and bath. Having completed it, Mike decided he preferred to live in a lovely second story room in the main house. I inherited the Tower.

Weekends were a time for entertaining, though not with the huge parties that had been the fashion in Beverly Hills. Mike had friends out for skeet shooting, on the field built up the canyon beyond the practice polo field. Mother and I would also join in this sport. She used a 20-gauge

Hal Wallis and Michael Curtiz on their favorite polo ponies, at the Canoga Ranch (1941).

shotgun, which lessened the recoil. Our 12 gauge ones had a hell of a wallop and invariably produced sore shoulders.

On our practice polo field, Mike would sometimes play stick and ball with guests or members of his polo team. These, of course were weekends when there were no actual matches. For competition polo, Mac, our stableman, would load up the horse trailer and all the needed equipment and drive to the designated field. Mac had been a cowboy in Wyoming, and the Levis belted below his protruding belly seemed to have been cut to display his bowlegs. During the war, Mac slaughtered the animals we raised. There was never a wartime shortage of meat at the ranch.

Sometimes Mike simply rode in the hills with Hal Wallis, who kept his horse at our stable.

Mother and I had horses, too. Occasionally Mother would ride with me in the hills. She had put on some weight but was still an excellent horsewoman. She had to be. Her horse was named Shadow because, like the fabled horse Alexander the Great tamed, it spooked at the sight of its

Mike on the lawn of the Canoga Ranch.

own shadow. She would also ride with Mike. But these bouts of exercise never lasted long. Inevitably she would retire to bed.

The living room at the ranch—in England it would have been called the Great Hall—had a peaked ceiling some 25 feet high, with huge crossbeams. There were two bay windows with bookshelves on either side of the fireplace. Both windows had desks and Mike sat in one or the other when he was working on his scripts. In my memory he is always there, making notes in his nearly indecipherable handwriting and unique spelling. Through the window, beyond him, stretches a long sloping expanse of lawn down to the fishpond which reflects the Image and, beyond that, across the valley, the far mountains, crystal clear in the pre-smog air.

Less than a year from the time we moved to the ranch, there was one of the catastrophic brush fires for which Southern California is infamous. Every few years they happen. Today we have helicopters for chemical drops and the Super Scoopers that load at sea and pour tons of water on the flames. Neither of these was available in the '30s. Men manned the fire lines and did what they could with the equipment available but many homes and lives were lost with each outbreak.

First, the sun over our southern hills was obscured by billowing smoke. Then we spotted the monster flames at the crest of the mountain. With a sudden burst they were across the firebreaks and racing down toward the ranch.

Firemen arrived but only to order us to evacuate the house immediately. They were going to set up their fire lines at Ventura Boulevard, some distance below us.

Mother called Mike on the set to tell him that we could get the horses out but the whole place was being abandoned. Warner Brothers had its own fire department to safeguard the sound stages and the sprawl of tindery wooden sets on the back lot. Mike called Jack Warner and told him he was going to have to close down the picture and go home to fight the fire. After a stunned moment, Warner told him to continue shooting. He would send help. Within half an hour, we had the Warner fire hose trucks and equipment rolling down toward the polo field and the oncoming flames. Although ranches near us suffered damage, we lost not a single building.

Either Jack Warner was a kinder man that many of his employees would admit or the thought of losing all the money it would cost to shut down production for a day gentled him. We were saved.

The ranch was sold in 1946 and we moved to Encino, considerably closer to town. The entire estate, 265 acres, citrus groves, main house, pool office, Tower house stables and barns, was sold for the then incredibly high price of $300,000—the price of a small middle-class house today.

It was sold to a man from Oregon who owned nurseries. At the last moment Mike had seller's remorse and tried his best to stop the sale, taking away objects that had been agreed would be left. He almost broke that camel's back when he removed two iron horse-hitching posts in front of the stable. They were old though not particularly valuable items but the buyer had had enough and walked away.

Mike was very cheerful. But, after two days of fuming, the buyer gave in. Mike got the hitching posts but lost the ranch. I still have the posts at my home.

After the sale, the property went through God knows how many hands until it was broken up and sold by a developer as 35 "estates" called Forest Hills. Our main house, with only the formal garden, the pool and Mother's office and bathhouse left, was owned for a while by Gene Hackman. I peeped in the pool house and Mother's MacGlashan coat of arms in stained glass was still there in the window over 50 years later.

For six years Jodie Foster lived in my Tower house. Some owner down the line had added a carport with a loft room above it, enlarged the kitchen and the bathroom. It sits now on a minuscule lot. In 1996 she had the Tower for sale. The asking price was $1,100,000—almost four times what the entire 265-acre estate had sold for in 1946. It does call attention to inflation.

It was at this ranch that Ethel came to us. Ethel Stern (whom Mike called Miss Sterlie) was a hairdresser at a beauty shop at Sunset and Highland, across from Hollywood High School, where Lana Turner was discovered. It was only two blocks from the Hollywood Roosevelt Hotel where we lived at the time Mother and Mike were married, before we moved to a succession of ever larger homes in Beverly Hills and then to the Valley. A few times Mother took me with her to the shop for a haircut or a manicure. I imagine I was something of a puzzlement to some customers as there was, at this time, a sharp division between male barber shops and female beauty shops. This distinction did not bother Mother and did not concern me. It was there that I met Marti, who was my age and Ethel's customer. Her father was a cameraman at Fox. Ethel acted as the go-between and soon Marti and I were "going steady." We acquired friends who were heavy drinkers and we kept up with them. It made my early arrivals at the studio painful.

Ethel had a husband, a farmer from the Midwest, who fell somewhere between American Gothic and Grand Guignol. He used to beat her regularly and, at one point, actually chased her into the yard with a knife and tried to kill her. Ethel was going to get a divorce and Mother offered her asylum to insure her safety until the divorce went through. Ethel moved in. The divorce went through and Ethel stayed on. She continued to do Mother's hair and looked for odd jobs around the estate, finally settling on accounting. She kept track of all bills and ultimately became a sort of unofficial housekeeper as well as member of the family. She remained with Mother from 1937 until her death in 1965.

Before moving into the ranch, we had gone through an interim period of some months when, the house on Roxbury having been sold and some major changes having been ordered for the new estate, which, despite the lack of cattle was called "the ranch" because this was California, we needed a place to live.

While waiting, we moved into the Colonial House, a deluxe apartment building on Hayworth, at the Hollywood end of the Sunset Strip. Many movie stars have lived there, including Cary Grant. It was next to the fabled Garden of Allah where there were never-ending cocktail parties with Robert Benchley and Scott Fitzgerald. Around the corner to the west was the Chateau Marmont, home away from home for many theatrical people come to dig the gold of Hollywood. On Sunset, a block in the other direction, was Schwab's Drug Store, where many young aspiring stars came to be seen and where some were actually discovered.

The Colonial House was one block west of Crescent Heights, almost opposite the home we had occupied before moving to the Roosevelt Hotel. That house, long since demolished, was now a high-rise apartment building. It could be seen from our balcony at the Colonial House. I was now back in the neighborhood where I had spent much of my early life. Life is a whole series of circles.

Just across the street from the Colonial House was the simple, staid mansion where Lee Francis, Madam to the Stars, plied her trade. Many of her beautiful girls had been drawn by the Hollywood dream of fame and fortune. Most settled for fortune although a few went on to more vertical careers. At any time of the day or night the rear of her house was crowded with the expensive cars of some of the biggest names in town. The Madam went on to write a best selling book, *A House Is Not a Home*.

Our apartment had a large living room, two bedrooms, a dining room, kitchen, maid's room and a huge balcony overlooking Hollywood and the distant buildings of Los Angeles. As it was only a temporary arrangement, I was to use the second bedroom, which was also a library. Now in my teens, I found that arrangement somewhat confining, coming-and-going-wise. I discovered, in the entrance to the apartment's large garage, a small room and bath, used as a chauffeur's room or resting place for the garage attendants. I pleaded and it became mine.

Three doors south of the Colonial House was Polly Moran's home. Polly had been under contract to Metro when she was teamed with Marie Dressler for a series of successful comedies. Dressler had been a stage star before coming to MGM for several memorable pictures including *Anna Christie* and *Min and Bill*. She was teamed with Polly in a small comedy film—as close as Metro would come to a B picture. But, like the *Andy Hardy* series with Mickey Rooney that made such a fortune for Metro, the Dressler-Moran team was used in a series of very popular films.

On a street bearing an ever-increasing load of elegant apartments, Polly had an old, ramshackle house where she lived with her elderly mother, a young alcoholic husband who occasionally showed up and her son, Jack. Polly was a funny, vulgar and wise woman. Jack and I had been together at Pacific Military Academy. Jack was small, dark with black curly hair. Officially, he was Polly's adopted son although gossip suggested he was her son by a black or Hispanic lover. Jack had a quick mind and a viciously funny tongue and at school had risen to the exalted position of Cadet Adjutant.

It had been some years since I'd seen him but here, three doors from each other, we almost daily rode the double-decked Sunset busses to Hollywood to visit movies and bars. I spent a lot of time at his house. Polly was generally slightly drunk and anyone was welcome.

One memorable day the doorbell rang and it was a salesman from Forest Lawn Mortuary. Forest Lawn is the sprawling Glendale cemetery where many of the movie—as well as other greats—find final rest.

Polly was feeling no pain and invited the man in to make his pitch. He obviously thought he had a sure thing here and would impress his employers and maybe earn a bonus. Handing around brochures of Forest Lawn's lovely setting, its works of art, he proceeded to tell us how he'd admired the wonderful pictures Polly had made, what happiness she and Marie Dressler had brought to millions. "And, since you and Miss Dressler were united so long in life, I thought how wonderful it would be if you could be together in the afterstate." He went on to explain, "When I found that the Mausoleum where Miss Dressler is interred had an empty niche directly above hers, I could hardly wait to get over and offer it to you." He waited for her pleased acceptance.

Instead she broke into raucous laughter. "I'll be goddamned," Polly guffawed. "I have to die to get top billing."

The sale was not made but Polly later let us tag along as she went off to a cocktail party in the neighborhood. Such parties were almost nonstop and we frequently accompanied her. After one, where she had vigorously over-drunk, we thought we were going to have to carry her home. She rejected help and went weaving wildly down the street. We got her into the house and upstairs with the promise of a drink waiting there. We got her almost onto her bed when she suddenly screamed and squirmed out of our hands. I thought she was having a heart attack. She resisted all restraint. Finally she managed to rip open the front of her dress, reach in and recover her false teeth, which had slipped and taken a tenacious bite of her over-ample bosom.

When the reconstruction work was done on the "ranch," we said farewell to the Colonial House and moved to the San Fernando Valley.

I saw much less of Jack and Polly because, after this move, I was sent to Cumnock and into the arms of Ariel. It was not a stated requirement but Mother always expected to see me at dinner. So I spent a few after school hours with Ariel then went home. The drive to the ranch and then back to Ariel's was a long one but most nights I managed it. She lived with her mother and grandmother in an apartment near the school. Our relationship continued until I went to UCLA. I had decided or, at least, agreed to decide on Journalism.

6—Coming Up for Air

Life at home went on in the same old way. The Hungarian community in Hollywood was a very tight-knit group. Paul Lukas, Bela Lugosi, actors, writers, directors and many who wanted to be any of the former. It was being constantly augmented as people managed to escape from what was clearly going to be Hitler's Europe. One evening Mike came home and announced that his cousin Ince Sandor had just arrived and would come and make dinner the following evening. Ince had owned and run the largest theatrical magazine in Hungary and through whatever twists of fate had come here to try to repeat his triumph in this new land.

"Ince is terrific gourmet cook," Mike assured Mother when she voiced some concern. But the invitation had been issued. Mother had met Ince in Budapest and been entertained by him. She could hardly be rude to him now.

Before noon, Ince arrived with multiple sacks of viands. The servants were told to give him whatever help he needed. He announced that he needed nothing and no one. The servants were banished from the kitchen and he was in there all afternoon, clanging pots, singing in Hungarian and probably sampling the cooking wine. When Mike came home from the studio, all was in readiness. The butler and cook were called in and Ince told them how the dishes were to be kept warm and how they were to be served.

We sat at the table and watched an incredible array of food brought in. Ince gave Mike spirited explanations of the courses in Hungarian with brief translations for us. Bell peppers stuffed with meat, Chicken Paprikas, all manner of side dishes, an elaborate salad and two desserts, one I had never heard of, the other red cabbage strudel—all excellent.

Mike, who was not a heavy eater, was urged, bite by bite, by his cousin who, himself, consumed monstrous portions.

Fortunately Ince's concern that Mike get enough nourishment allowed the rest of us to take small portions without his notice.

When the meal was finally over, Mike called the butler. "Would be kind, bring the soda."

The bicarbonate of soda was served in its cardboard box on a silver tray with tall glasses of water.

"Was terrific good, Ince," Mike said, "but I spoil my stomach." The cousins concluded their reunion with double helpings of the medicinal powder.

Mike complained he did not sleep that night. "Why you let me eat so much?" he demanded of Mother.

"How the hell could I have stopped you? You invited Ince."

"A good wife would tell, 'Don't goddamn be a pig.'"

There followed what had seemed to me a period of increasing domestic tranquility. Mother would come downstairs more often to dinner, a few times had even gone out to parties. This happy period was followed by scenes muted by closed doors. Perhaps abandoning her bed and getting involved in the world outside had made Mother more aware. She discovered another of Mike's extra-marital adventures. After much discussion, to which I was not privy, Mother moved with me, Ethel, Collins, a maid and a cook to a house that she had rented in Bel Air.

This was convenient for me as the house looked down, across the golf course of the Bel Air Country Club, at UCLA, where I was presumably absorbing Higher Education.

7

Hungarian Goulash

Mike was shooting *The Charge of the Light Brigade* with dashing "Earl Flint" and David Niven among the "gallant six hundred" who rode into the Valley of Death and performed the most spectacular cavalry charge ever photographed up to that time. Mike's technique has been copied so often that it is now clichéd. Miles of roads for the camera cars were laid and, in one continuous shot, the gallant attacking troop of Lancers began at a walk, then a trot and at the command "Charge!" broke into a full gallop toward the main Russian cannons. The Lancers dropped like flies as they were hit by fire from the hills in front and on either side. In the Valley of Death "the six hundred" was decimated. When the shot was concluded, Mike called for closer, detail shots. Wanting to show the continuing charge of the horses whose riders had fallen under the deadly hail, he ordered, "Bring on the empty horses." Niven later used this command as a title of his book.

At our rented Bel-Air home, deciding on a divorce was a challenge that seemed to revive Mother's spirits. She went to work again at a studio—Fox. Once again she was working with Darryl. I was vaguely aware of calls from Mike, visits from lawyers, but I had other things on my mind. The main other thing was Camille. Some friends had taken me to a club in Beverly Hills called Theroff's. Camille worked as a singer in the bar. I was fascinated and went there every night, usually with friends, drank enough to keep the proprietor happy and, when she had finished singing, took her home. Camille had been around a bit and was probably somewhere in her mid–20s. During the course of our relationship, she introduced me to a friend of hers, Martha, a diminutive blond who was also a bar singer. We went to watch Martha work one night. The room was

Mike with Olivia de Havilland and Errol Flynn on the set of *The Charge of the Light Brigade* (1936).

especially noisy, full of shouting drunks, not the most rewarding crowd to work. Camille would sing a song of the period, which ended several lines with the words "For you, for you." Over the tumult of the room that night, in her sweet, lilting voice, Camille's friend sang the song to the crowd finishing, "Fuck you, fuck you."

Under the drunken roar of the crowd, no one noticed the alteration of lyrics. Martha told us she did this whenever the place got too loud to stomach. I found the world of bar entertainment fascinating and instructive. Camille was also a good teacher in more intimate subjects. All my education seems to have been non-academic.

Meanwhile Mother, having decided to restructure her life, took a call from the distant past. A man she had met during the filming of *Ben Hur* had tracked her down at the studio. He was in town on business. She had known him in Paris. He was a French war ace and, when they met in the early '20s, was still in uniform. He was charming, dashing and had obviously made an impression on Mother. She invited him to dinner at the

Bel Air house and dressed very carefully that night. I was off to Theroff's for dinner, drinking and Camille but I sat for a few moments in the living room while Mother and her ardent guest had cocktails. The ex-ace was now middle-aged, somewhat balding, and had a belly that was beginning to distend. While still displaying a charming accent, he had not managed the intervening years well. Mother later laughed at her attempt at time travel, did not invite him back and spoke no more of the matter. My own affair with Camille ended just as suddenly when she discovered to her horror that I was only 17. Soon the divorce lawyers ceased to come to the Bel Air house with their documents and one evening Mike appeared at the dinner table. We moved back to the ranch.

When college worked no better than all other educational schemes, discussions were held to determine what was to become of me. Mike solved the problem by securing me employment as an apprentice script clerk at Warner Brothers. I was apprenticed to Fred Applegate, a plump, friendly but unusual man who had worked on many of Mike's pictures. Fred was always fully but conservatively dressed—suit, tie, well-shined shoes. He worked from an apparatus the likes of which I have never seen before or after. It was called, by everyone except Fred Applegate, Apple's Horse. It was, in effect, a school desk on wheels with a sort of saddle attached behind it. Fred could wheel this mobile workplace between the tangles of cables and lights and do his job in equestrian comfort. Under his tutelage I learned to use a stopwatch to time the length of each take, to write in the script a description of the wardrobe of each actor, to note each actor's position at each line of dialogue so that subsequent shots would match the action of the master scene. I learned to record the camera positions, size of lenses, whether we were photographing a group shot, a two-shot or close-up. I also learned some bizarre things, which were Fred's alone. Lifting the top of his mobile desk revealed Fred's working equipment— Script, Production Reports, Cutter's Reports and a rainbow assortment of pencils. He had developed his own system of Cutter's notations, efficient but incredibly complex. A Master Shot had a blue pencil line running as far through the script as the shot went. A Two Shot had a red line. A Close-Up was green. Pick-ups (a break in the scene caused by an actor's flub or a camera problem, which was continued in another take) were in black. There were colors for every eventuality. Apple's dream was to write a textbook for script clerks. Even at my age and lack of experience in the publishing game, I wondered at the range of the market for such a book, how vast an audience was waiting and willing to pay for the chance to learn a job that probably hired—industry wide—less than 100 persons.

The first picture I worked on was not one of Mike's but was under the direction of Joe May, an aging German director who had done well in the country of his birth but here, for whatever reason, had lost confidence in his ability. The film was called *Confession*. The star was Kay Francis, who was nearing the end of her career. Joe had made this film in German (as *Mazurka*) some years before and now had a Moviola on the set to view his old picture. A Moviola is a small, one-person projector that cutters used in selecting, cutting and splicing scenes together. Joe would run and rerun scenes from his German *Mazurka* on this machine and set up the new scene in exactly the same way, trying to recreate his prior success frame by frame, sometimes running back and forth during rehearsals to be sure he had it right. This earned him the ill-concealed laughter of the crew. It was, in retrospect, a depressing way to begin my career, watching the pitiful end of his.

At the conclusion of that picture, I was moved to a musical short starring Dennis Morgan and a young bouncy girl called Candy Kane. Movies, in those days, ran short subjects, newsreels and perhaps a cartoon before the feature.

Dennis had come to the studio as Stanley Mourner. Warner considered this a melancholy name for a star and promptly changed it to Dennis Morgan. He was to be groomed as Warners' singing star. The bouncy female lead in *The Border Cantina*, Candy Kane, was rumored to be the lesbian lover of Ann Alvarado, who was married to an actor, Don Alvarado, and would ultimately marry Jack Warner. Don had come to Warners as Don Page but, in the era of Valentino's seductive success, Warner ordered him to take his mother's maiden name, Alvarado. He took it. Then Jack Warner took his wife. Don Alvarado became an assistant director and had a lifetime job at Warners. I think he probably got the better bargain.

Mother was not fond of Ann. She was a longtime friend of Irma Warner, Jack's first wife and the mother of Jack Jr., who was some years older than I was but always came to my birthdays. At my age, all the gossip I heard in my early teens passed over my head. Warner and Ann lived under the same roof until she got an instant Mexican divorce. Then Jack divorced Irma and Ann and Jack were married in 1936. Ann had an air that Warner considered ladylike. She became a treasured hostess for him and anathema for Warner's family. They liked her even less than they had Irma who, despite her being from a good Jewish family, they called "the shiksa" because of what they considered her "haughty," non–Jewish ways. The dislike was mutual as Irma was embarrassed by the elder Warners' old country ways.

Mother had a decent relationship with Jack and wrote many pictures for him but it was never a very warm friendship. Her favorite was Sam. He was "the one nice Warner." Sam came up with Vitaphone—the first successful method of making pictures talk. He had to almost force it on his brothers. Jack thought sound was a passing fad and Harry was horrified by the expense it would involve.

But Sam insisted and a musical score was used in Mother's *Don Juan*. That, the Warners agreed, made some sense because it would eliminate the cost to the distributors of hiring live orchestras to accompany Warner Brothers films. Sam would not let go of the idea that pictures could actually talk. Al Jolson sang a song in *The Jazz Singer* and then ad-libbed, "Folks, you ain't heard nothing yet." The audience was stunned and delighted and history was made. Unfortunately Sam, always in delicate health, died the day before the premiere of *The Jazz Singer*, which rang the death knell of silent pictures.

This history came casually from Mother and Mike over the dinner table along with all the current gossip. The revelations of Mary Astor's diary during her divorce was a continuing sexual saga in a time long before today's soap operas. All this was of real interest. Life, for me, was a far better teacher than school. When the original director was dismissed at the beginning of filming of *Robin Hood*, Mike assumed the reins with the ever-more-popular "Earl Flint."

When the musical short to which I had been assigned finished, Mike had me move over to *Robin Hood*. My script mentor changed from Apple to Pam, whose last name I have regrettably forgotten. She was excellent at her job and *Robin Hood*, with its multitude of costumes, presented a far greater challenge than *Confession* had. Flynn was united with Olivia de Havilland as he had been in *Captain Blood*. He also took his role of romantic hero seriously off-screen. The crew used to bet on how often the girls were changed in his dressing room during the day. Each star had a small portable dressing room, which was hauled on the stage, following its owner from set to set. These were tiny wooden bungalows with dressing table, chairs and a daybed for actors to rest on between takes. The rumor was that Flynn never rested. "In like Flynn" would later become a term of praise among the high testosterone set. Certain crew members would sneak up and listen beneath the dressing room's windows and report the sounds emanating from Flynn's couch. Despite the contempt in which Mike held Flynn's thespian talents, he got a good performance from him and Flynn was confirmed as a top star.

Mike had accumulated a crew he tried to use on every picture. Chief among them were Jack Sullivan and Sherry Shourds, assistant directors, and Limey Plews, the prop man. Mike loved jokes and every time Limey

Left to right: Hal Wallis, Errol Flynn, Olivia de Havilland and Mike on the set of *The Adventures of Robin Hood* (1938).

came up with a joke that could be used in the picture, Mike would give him $10.

Then there was Irving Rapper, the dialogue director, who went through many films with Mike and eventually became a director in his own right. It was on *Robin Hood* that I first met Irving. He had come from the New York stage and was small, elegantly dressed and fussily busy. His job was to run lines with the actors, make sure they knew them and recited them properly in the scene. At the close of one take where Basil Rathbone, the corrupt Sir Guy of Gisbourne, had completed a long speech, Mike called "Cut." He turned to Rapper. "Is right."

Before Rapper could answer, Pam, the script clerk, said. "The dialogue isn't correct."

Mike looked back at Rapper. "What he said made perfect sense," Rapper assured Mike.

But Pam was insistent. "It wasn't the script. It wasn't accurate."

"Accuracy," Rapper told her, "as Napoleon once said, is the virtue of clerks." It brought down the set.

On my next picture, another dialogue director taught me the words

Mike on the castle set of *The Adventures of Robin Hood* (1938).

of the Gershwin song "It Ain't Necessarily So" in Yiddish. Such lessons were my real interest. My actual assignment was as apprentice to the script clerk, Frank Fox. Frank was born Francisco Kowalski, son of a Polish Jew married to a Mexican woman, a man with a sense of humor and incredible vitality. His children have done very well in the business. Again I was an apprentice with no real duties except to make a clean cutter's script each evening. This was often done at Marti's, with whom I was then involved. The reason for this work is so that the cutter would know exactly how much film was available to him in every set-up, where it started and stopped and a short description of each shot. It was not very demanding work. I much preferred talking to the actors, exploring the props on the set and, when possible, taking long walks on the back lot. I had brought my school habits of learning rejection to the workplace.

At home, we had another Hungarian visitor from Mike's past—Gabriel Pascal. With the right to do Shaw's plays in his pocket, he was constantly trying to get Mike to go into business with him. Pascal was a small man, slightly overweight, with a gypsy's eyes and complexion. He had great charm and a beautiful new wife. After dinner, we retired to the solarium where the studio projectionist had already set up for a picture in the projection booth Mike had built. The picture was projected through a small window behind the bar. The screen came down in front of the billiard table. On weekends the studio projectionist would arrive on Friday or Saturday night carrying one of the new, often unreleased films that made the rounds of executive projection rooms. Studios contributed prints of their pictures and were, in turn, shown the product of their competitors. It was a wonderful arrangement—for the executives. In the solarium, guests would dispose themselves on couches and chairs and we would go to the movies. Our greatest movie fan was our Boxer, Cappie (short for Capital Gain). Boxers are a wonderful breed, faithful, gentle (except with other dogs), brave but are notoriously flatulent. Cappie was always the first one seated. He would leap on the couch of his choice and, as soon as the film would start, fall asleep, contentedly emitting great quantities of gas. When it became too offensive, we would throw him out. The night Pascal came to dinner was a banner night for Cappie. No sooner were the main titles over and the picture begun than an odor so penetrating occurred that Mother and I were moving simultaneously to evict the dog. As I started to rise, I noticed Gabriel's wife glaring and angrily slamming her elbow into her husband's side. Mother saw it at the same time and it was such a wonderful spectacle that we were tempted not to reveal Cappie as the culprit.

While Mike was shooting *Kid Galahad*, Mother took a trip she had

7—Hungarian Goulash

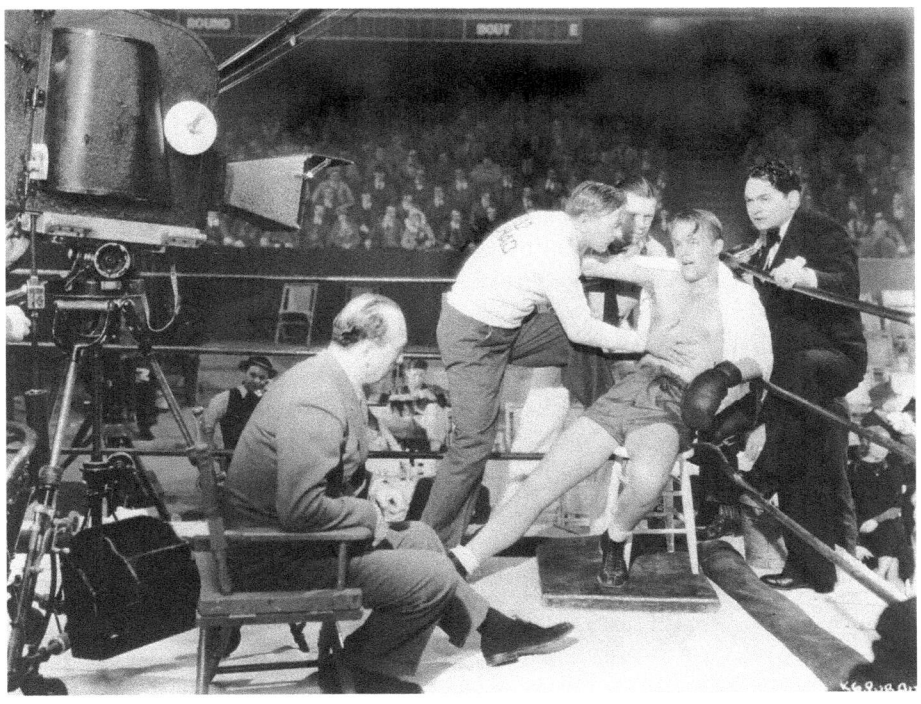

Mike directs a boxing sequence in *Kid Galahad* (1937).

always wanted to make. She and Ethel sailed through the Panama Canal, from New York, then up the West Coast, stopping in Mexico. She had phoned from Mexico City and said they were taking a car and guide next morning to drive to Taxco, an ancient silver mining town. She would call from the hotel there. Dinnertime came and there was no call. Mike was concerned. I had arranged to go to the movies with Frank Fox that night and drove to his house in Hollywood. Mike called to say there was still no word. Frank took over and called the hotel in Taxco. No, Mother wasn't there. It is only a few hours' drive from Cuernavaca, where they had spent the previous night. I became worried. Frank arranged the whole matter. He called the Federales, the government Federal police who patrol the roads. There were constant translations. I was asked for a description of Mother and Ethel and all sorts of seemingly insignificant information. I responded in English and Frank translated into Spanish for the police. After a good half-hour of bureaucratic back and forth, they announced that they had already dispatched two motorcycles to locate the women. "Now," the Captain asked, "when we find them, on what charge do you wish them held?"

We had to start all over again.

It turned out that Mother's guide had convinced her that the hotel she had picked was not the best one, taken her to the alternate place and, there, she had been unable to get a call through. The whole matter was straightened out in the morning. All turned out well and Mother returned home with a vast supply of presents.

Around the house, we had become familiar with Mike's speech and it seemed quite ordinary. On the set, however, I was first acquainted with its humorous currency among the cast and crew. Irving Rapper kept a list of the best samples. One scene, where Robin's men ambush the superior and heavily armed troops of the evil Sheriff of Nottingham, had Robin's Merry Men swinging down on lianas or dropping onto the Sheriff's troopers from the concealing limbs of the giant oaks. What he wanted, Mike explained to the actors, was that "when the Sheriff guys ride on the horses in, boys should fall from the trees like fruits." In this same period, involved in a philosophical discussion with Basil Rathbone, Mike explained, "Christ, Buddha, Confusion, is all the same."

Some time earlier he had done a picture—*Cabin in the Cotton* with Richard Barthelmess and Bette Davis in her first significant role. She had

Mike jokes on location during a break filming *Cabin in the Cotton* (1932).

third billing after Barthelmess and Dorothy Jordan. Barthelmess played the son of a poor sharecropper who insists his boy not work in the fields but go to school and "make something of himself." The father, worked to death by the cruel plantation owner, dies in Barthelmess' arms. The owner, feigning an act of generosity, puts the boy through school then, having obligated him, employs him as a clerk to keep the plantation books and bleed money out of his own starving people. Davis is the planter's daughter who almost lures him away from his true love, a simple tenant girl. Davis begins her seduction of the innocent Barthelmess with what she later described as her favorite line, "I'd love to kiss you but I've just washed my hair." Set dressers and prop men had been working for weeks on the Warner back lot, planting bushes and wiring cotton balls to make a cotton field. Central Avenue, in the colored district, had been denuded for extras as pickers along with the poor white tenants. Mike had several cameras on the cotton-picking scenes. He, himself, on a 30-foot tall camera platform, spoke through a bullhorn to the hundred or so black extras, explaining how they should behave "like Southern peasants." There were dazed expressions on the extras, due, perhaps, to the distortion of the bullhorn. "You should be steeped on the tradition from the terrible time when the South was fighting the East." Barthelmess, torn between his people's needs and his obligation to his employer, at last breaks away from the spell of the seductive Davis and plantation luxury. He defends his people in court, forcing the planters to sign a contract guaranteeing the tenants a fair share of the profits of their work. The tenants and pickers are overjoyed and, Mike instructed them over the bullhorn, "When the hero come out from the courthouse, all the niggers should throw up the hand and shout happy from—" He broke off, startled as the assistant director apologetically snatched the bullhorn from his hands.

"Jesus, Mike, you can't say that!"

"What I say wrong?"

"You can't call them that," the assistant explained. "They're colored. You have to say colored."

"Oh," Mike took the bullhorn again. "I am terrible sorry what I say," he apologized to the extras. "I speak so lousy my English." Then, more firmly he began again. "When the hero come out, all the *colored* niggers should throw up the hand and—"

The assistant had already collapsed.

Mike made an effort to instill some of his own enthusiasm for film in me. Indeed, he was a teacher to anyone who would listen. His passion was pictures. He could neither understand nor abide anyone who did not share this enthusiasm. He never ate lunch, claiming that it destroyed all the momentum built up during the morning. When hungry actors looked at their watches as the afternoon rolled forward and the assistant director explained for the twentieth time that there was a contract mandating lunch breaks, Mike would mutter, "Why hell they not take a aspirin?" He would finally give in. Then, when work resumed, he would mutter loudly about the slowness of the "after lunch bums."

Although I enjoyed the ambiance of the studio, I was more of a spectator. Mike's attempts at teaching his own enthusiasm had small effect. By osmosis, I must have absorbed many of his precepts that I would use later. He loved his work, lived his work.

"When you know right the lines," he would tell actors, "the scene will flow like butter." He regarded all who would listen as his pupils and admonished then, "You should be like a tiger on the camera, fighting for the success from the picture." This may not have been instantly intelligible to his listeners but it perfectly expressed his philosophy.

It was sometime in this era that Pek came to us. Mike was always trying to help Hungarians, to help anyone who was sincere. Though he could be brutal on the set, he had a warm fuzzy heart.

Desider Pek, in his native country, had been, at one time or another, a professional mourner, attending funerals and weeping copiously. He was ideal for the role as he vaguely resembled Boris Karloff in the *Frankenstein* makeup. He had also worked at a sanitarium for people with eating disorders—from anorexia to simple lack of appetite. His job was to sit at the head of the table and eat gigantic amounts of whatever was served, thus demonstrating the joy of food. How successful this was among Hungarians I do not know but, when Pek would accompany us to lunch or, on a few occasions, dinner, he would wolf down his own food, then go around and clean whatever remained on anyone else's plate.

Mike always dressed for the studio.

Mike kneels at Bette Davis' feet on the set of *The Private Lives of Elizabeth and Essex* (1939).

This performance never stimulated my appetite but perhaps things were different in the old country.

Pek became Mike's secretary. I am never sure exactly what he did but he was always there in the outer office, typing, most often in Hungarian, and chewing pods of the garlic he kept in his pocket.

Michael Curtiz in a lighthearted moment on the set.

On one occasion, Mike found him doubled up over the desk with a terrible stomach ache. When the pain did not let up, Mike called Mother, who told him to take Pek to the Branch Clinic. Dr. Branch was our family physician. She would call and prepare him.

The doctor did a thorough examination, temperature, blood pressure, pulse, palpated his stomach. Pek bore it all stoically. Dr. Branch finally came out and said he had sent some blood work down to the lab and would wait for the results. "But I can't find anything wrong with him."

"Then," Mike protested, "why hell he hold his stomach and sweat from the pain."

The doctor had no explanation to offer.

I told him Pek ate raw garlic all the time. "Could *that* do it?"

The doctor said he had been painfully aware of the garlic but doubted that would have caused the symptoms.

At that moment, the lab assistant came in and reported that Pek had a tremendously high white count, indicating acute infection.

Mike and the doctor went into the examining room where Pek lay in a fetal position. The doctor rolled him flat on his back and again palpated his stomach, pressing on McBurney's point.

This finally elicited a howl from Pek.

"Appendicitis," the doctor said. "Acute. He's got to have surgery at once."

"Goddamn," Mike demanded of the supine man, "why you don't tell him where it hurt?"

Pek managed a baleful look. "If he is a good doctor," he explained, "he would *know!*"

Pek was taken to the hospital, the appendix was removed. Soon he was back at his desk. So was his garlic.

While Mike was thus engaged at Warners, Mother, at MGM, had done *Red Headed Woman* for Jean Harlow and *Strange Interlude*, from the Eugene O'Neill play, for Clark Gable and Norma Shearer. Then she went with Darryl's Twentieth Century Company, which was renting space at the Samuel Goldwyn Studio. Later, when Darryl was able to buy William Fox's failing studio on the outskirts of Beverly Hills, it would become Twentieth Century–Fox.

Mother wrote several of Darryl's first productions—*The Affairs of Cellini* with Fredric March, *Folies Bergere* with Maurice Chevalier and Merle Oberon. Then she undertook a collaboration with Gene Fowler, a best-selling novelist and former newspaperman who learned the technique of film from Mother as they wrote *The Mighty Barnum*, with Wallace Beery in the title role. The screenplay was later published as a book.

Gene and Mother got on beautifully. They shared a bizarre sense of humor. On *Timberline*, one of his first hit books, he wrote a dedication to Mother:

> For Bess Meredyth—my pal. A man's man. With deep appreciation for one of the finest associations I have had in this or any other profession (including my pimp days at Bryn Mawr).
> Gene Fowler
> 1934

In many ways their relationship was like the one she had with John Barrymore.

Gene, too, had a reputation as a considerable lover and had managed to cut a wide swath through the bedrooms of Hollywood. But he was Mother's friend. As I grew up, he became my friend, too.

Gene wrote my favorite Barrymore biography—*Goodnight, Sweet Prince*. He also became the godfather of my daughter, Victoria.

Elizabeth's godparents had been her great-uncle, Max von Bernuth, and Joan's sister, Maurecette. Michael's godmother was Louella Parsons, a large lady. Those resenting the incredible power of her newspaper column, when it wasn't used to their advantage, called her fat. She was, indeed, most heavily endowed above the waist. When she held Michael at the baptismal font and he looked up at those mountains of potential nourishment, he was mouth-wateringly delighted and cried not at all.

Years before, in 1938, Mike shot *Gold Is*

Bess Meredyth, publicity photograph circa 1930.

Michael's christening (1957). *Left to right:* Joan (holding Michael), Louella Parsons, Father Murphy, Bess, Nell MacGillicuddy.

Where You Find It, starring George Brent and Olivia de Havilland, on location near Weaverville in Northern California. The location was an old hydraulic mining site where, during the gold rush, huge pumps forced river water at tremendous pressure into the gravel deposits and through sluice runs to wash out the ore. I was along as apprentice script clerk.

The set decorators had carefully researched the technique and great wooden sluice runs were built by Warner carpenters to carry the water and slurried ore down the mountain to the settling vats where the gold was extracted. The whole atmosphere of the '49 Gold Rush was recreated. It was a gigantic project and the construction workers fiddled constantly with the sets, even in the long shots. Their unnecessary delays caused Mike, always impatient with anything that held up filming, to shout over the bullhorn, "Hey, carpenter, don't do a genius job out from it, Mr. Warner won't see it."

The project had the feel of a military operation. A huge tent city was built in the wilderness, housing the crew, actors and hundreds of extras. There were streams of limousines to carry them all up the steep mountains.

The picture was in Technicolor, the old three-strip process, and all that monstrous equipment had to be gotten into very difficult country. The Technicolor cameras of those days were huge blue boxes, many times the size of modern cameras. They carried three strips of film, the three primary colors, which were exposed simultaneously. Despite their vast size, the cameras were delicate and this was the first time they had been required to function in such a hostile environment.

The military atmosphere of the camp was intensified by the constant warfare between Mike and the Technicolor technicians. It was like the early days of sound again and Mike's battles with mixers. Under the guidance of Natalie Kalmus, wife of the founder, the Technicolor people claimed to be the only ones who understood the use and limitations of their equipment. Mike had little patience for the long delays taken to set up cameras and adjust them. "Hey, Technicolor bums, when you write your memoirs for the next generation, tell them how goddamn slow you work on your things." Beside the large camera crews and engineers, there was a Technicolor Associate, a grand title matching the grand manner in which he ruled his fiefdom.

One late afternoon, Mike had lined up a love scene played against a gorgeous mountain sunset. The Technicolor cameraman looked questioningly at the Associate. There was hasty discussion among the technicians and Mike was told the Technicolor cameras could not possibly shoot into backlight. Mike said, "On my responsibility, you goddamn do it."

"But, Mr. Curtiz," the Associate sputtered, "Mrs. Kalmus gave explicit instructions that—"

"Mrs. Kalmus," Mike told him, "don't shoot my goddamn picture."

The Associate, his ashen face resembling a French aristocrat awaiting his turn at the guillotine, watched as Mike continued to rehearse the scene.

"Please," he begged, "at least let me phone Mrs. Kalmus and tell her." The assistant director reminded him the nearest phone was many miles away over terrible roads.

"The sun don't wait for Mrs. Kalmus," Mike said. "We make the shot, then you call." It turned out to be a sensational scene and changed Technicolor's thinking about that particular rule. In his lifetime, Mike was to break many rules.

I formed a sort of friendship with George Brent despite the difference in our ages. He was often referred to as a "wooden" actor. Some directors claimed he always went to sleep in the close-ups. It is strange what a calm and easygoing guy he was, considering he had been in a very rough section of the IRA as a teenager and was said to have escaped from Ireland with a price on his head. George talked very little about this part of his life. Coming to America, he studied acting on Broadway, then, moving to the movies, had married, in succession, Ruth Chatterton, Constance Worth and Ann Sheridan. He was also a licensed pilot, at a time when such were rare. I, remembering Ronald Raven, was worshipfully impressed.

As an apprentice script clerk, I was essentially a sightseer, unnecessary baggage on a very tough location. The resentment of nepotism was generally concealed among the crew but could be felt. At the conclusion of an especially long day, we were crammed into a limousine for the trip back to camp. I sat on a jump seat. Uninterested in the flow of conversation among the crew, I closed my eyes and, helped by the jolting of the car over the mountain roads, began to nod. Someone, I think it was a makeup girl, noticed and said, "He's asleep."

Behind me rode the unit manager, a stocky man, balding and with a cigar constantly clenched in his teeth. Our first meeting was like that with my math teacher, Lt. Taylor. We formed an instant mutual antipathy. "Don't wake him up," the unit manager said. "He's finally found something he's good at."

Amid the ripple of laughter I had three choices. I could come up with a clever remark that would turn the laughter on him; I could angrily confront him or I could pretend not to have heard. Noël Coward would have been able to destroy my antagonist with one cutting comment. I do not confront well. I was not Noël but I chose the coward's way and feigned sleep.

When *Gold Is Where You Find It* was finished and we were back at the studio, I was finally given a picture in which I was the sole script clerk. Who decided I had successfully passed my apprenticeship, I will never know.

It was a low-budget picture directed by Ray McCarey, brother of Leo McCarey who did *Going My Way* with Bing Crosby and a lot of very successful pictures. As I remember, this was one of the *Torchy Blane* series that Warners made with various actresses in the title role. Ray was a very nice, laid-back guy and things went well for a week or so and I thought I was doing my job perfectly, timing the scenes, marking the position of the actors, what they were doing when they said a certain line so that subsequent angles would match and the cutter would not be confronted by an actor with his hands in his pocket at the end of one shot and his hands above his head at the beginning of the next. Part of the script clerk's job is to make sure the wardrobe conforms from one scene to another, down to the distance from the pocket an actor's handkerchief protrudes. All things must match. They did until one fatal night.

While preparing the cutter's script after dinner, I was suddenly horror-struck to realize that an actor about to rob a bank had left the getaway car and entered the bank wearing a blue pinstripe suit. On the interior of the bank, shot on a soundstage weeks later, he had come in through the door wearing a plain gray suit. We had, of course, shot him coming out of the bank with the loot in the blue pinstripe because all scenes at a particular location are shot together. Movies are almost never shot in sequence. They are broken up to take advantage of sets, locations and availability of actors. That is the reason for script clerks. The interior scene in the bank and the exterior scenes on the street, being weeks apart, had allowed my notes to fail me. Retakes would have been impossible since the set had been struck. So, I thought, was my career as a script clerk.

I stayed up most of the night, pondering the problem, hoping for a solution.

I rewrote a scene which had not yet been shot, in which the robber confronts his "moll," adding a couple of lines of dialogue in which he tells her the bank was so crowded and the guards so heavily armed that he had decided the robbery would have to be postponed. If this were done, the story would be only slightly modified and the film we had would work. He brings off the robbery on his *second* attempt, using the scene we had just shot of the robber in the gray suit getting the money from the teller and exiting. We need never show his coming out in the ill-starred pinstripe suit. The audience would take for granted that the getaway car was there.

I was the first one on the set. When Ray came in, I explained what I had done, let him get out his angry expletives and over his shock. Then I showed him my solution. It took a few moments but he slowly nodded. "Yeah," he acknowledged, "that would work." He added a couple of lines of his own in which the "moll" berates the robber for his cowardice. We shot it. I think it was actually a better scene. Ray did not, however, allow me to forget what I had done. He kidded me a lot but it could have been very serious.

At dinner, I related the story, expecting Mike to be upset, having gone to all the trouble getting me the job but he burst out laughing. "Jesus, Maria! Jick should be writer. He have the talent like you, Besky."

So, at the end of Ray's picture, Mike having talked to the proper authorities, I became a junior writer with a salary of $50 a week. That was not what Earl Flint made but it was decent money for those days. Men supported a family on less.

For my first assignment, I was teamed with another writer who had never written but whose brother was an associate of Walter Winchell,

Winchell's leg man. We talked a lot, even tried an adaptation of a book called *Horse and Buggy Doctor* We had infinite discussions, many notes but not much writing. The project came to nothing.

I was then assigned to the Short Subjects Department, it being the practice for theaters in those days to run a short subject, comedic or informative, along with the feature picture and the cartoon or newsreel. Instead of the 15 minutes of promos we sit through now, those audiences got entertainment.

I was ordered to write a short on Clara Barton, founder of the American Red Cross. This period, shortly before Pearl Harbor, was a time for building patriotism. War had been raging in Europe for two years. Hitler had swallowed up many countries. The draft had been decreed and despite America First's attempt to keep us out of foreign entanglements, a feeling of war was in the air. America First was a movement with which Col. Lindbergh (formerly Lucky Lindy) was associated. Lindbergh had gone over to examine the German Air Force and had high praise for it. It was an evaluation that made him a hero to some, a traitor to others. My friend Bill Rogers, once my roommate in military school and the son of writer Adela Rogers St. John (they had a house next door to the one we rented for Malibu summers), had gone to Canada to enlist in the Royal Canadian Air Force. He was later killed staying at the controls of his bomber while his crew bailed out over the French coast.

Even Mike, a top director, was asked by Jack Warner to direct a short on Chaim Solomon, a Jewish banker who helped finance the American Revolution. It was called *Sons of Liberty*. Shorts were normally assigned to minor talents but this was a favor for a cause. It won several awards.

My Clara Barton story limped along until the producer of the Shorts Department gave me a deadline. Following my natural instincts, I had done a lot of research but put nothing on paper, waiting until the last moment. Then I called the stenographic pool for a secretary and dictated the entire script in order to meet the deadline. I chose to dictate for two reasons. First, I couldn't spell beyond cat or, rather, I couldn't spell simple words—complex ones, words from history or science that I had chosen to learn, came out right, the others I had never paid attention to. The second reason was that it was faster—my typing skills matched my spelling skills. We worked late the night before the deadline and the secretary promised to finish typing, send the script to mimeo and have it on the producer's desk before eight o'clock the following morning. I went home, tired and pleased that my first real writing had gone off so well.

Arriving at my desk at nine the next morning, I found a copy of the script. On its cover was the title and my name. I gazed at it in wonder and pride. Then I began to read it. If I had typed and spelled it on my worst day, it could not have been more horrible. I finally came to the spot where Clara Barton sees a newspaper on the stand with a banner headline reading PRESIDENT MCKINLEY EXECUTED. I threw the offending papers down, rushed to the producer's office and begged his secretary to give me back the script before he saw it. He was in. It was on his desk but she was reasonably sure he would not read it before lunch. As soon as he left, she promised, she would sneak it from the stack and call me.

I ran back to my office and, with dictionary in hand, made hasty corrections. Then I went to the stenographic department and got the secretary who had taken my dictation and told her of my distress. "Sometimes you mumbled," she said defensively.

"Maybe," I agreed. "But when was the last time we executed a president? We've been mean to some, assassinated others but never have we executed one. McKinley was assassinated."

The head of the steno department, overhearing this and listening to my anguish, gave the corrections to a more experienced typist who also corrected what spelling I had missed.

The producer's secretary had sneaked my first script to me and the producer had the new copy on his desk before he left for home. I drew my first easy breath of the day.

The Clara Barton Story was never made.

8
Off Camera

Hollywood, for those working in it in the Golden Years, was a silken cocoon, isolating its inhabitants from the ugliness going on in the real world, the grinding poverty and humiliation of the Depression—millions out of work, hungry, their only meals those from the volunteer soup kitchens. Formerly rich men sold apples for a nickel on street corners. Mother was not insensitive to trouble. She was an easy touch, gladly raining asked-for money on the just and the unjust. But she never quite believed how terrible those times were. She claimed she had never seen a soup kitchen. I am sure that was true. Soup kitchens did not line the streets of Beverly Hills. While the rest of the country suffered, Hollywood prospered. The movies were a relatively inexpensive way for people to forget the tragedy of their daily lives.

Sneak previews were generally held out of town so as to avoid the supposed "sophistication" of the audience in the movie capital. Often sneaks were held at the Alexander Theater in Glendale. Glendale was then a rural community and was thought to have an audience representative of the average American. Such previews were held unannounced—they were truly sneak. Today the term has become ludicrous with sneak previews being advertised in the newspapers. It was customary for the director and most of the top echelon of the studios to attend, judge the reaction of the audience during the running of the picture and then read the cards that the viewers were asked to fill out as they left the theater. The lobby would be filled with clots of studio personnel, studying the cards, trying to decide if they had a hit or a miss. The cutter was there to take instructions if there was any rearrangement to be made or any scenes excised before the film went into its final form for release. The cards for that preview

Mike talks with the stars of *Daughters Courageous*, the sequel to *Four Daughters*: Priscilla, Rosemary and Lola Lane, Fay Bainter and Gale Page. James Wong Howe is the cinematographer on the set (1939).

were excellent; the audience had obviously loved it. Jack Warner, customary large cigar in hand, congratulated Mike and invited him to go with his party to the Cotton Club, an illegal but widely known gambling club. At the time, Mike was shooting *Four Daughters* with the Lane Sisters and a young actor in his first film role, John Garfield. "Thanks you, J.L.," Mike said, "but I am terrible tired. I take only a sandwich and go on bed." Warner promised him wonderful sandwiches at the Cotton Club and said there were a few things he had to talk over. "We talk on the morning," Mike countered. "I am terrible tired. I take a sandwich and go home." Warner was flattering and persistent. Mike finally agreed to go but added, "Only I take one sandwich." At the Cotton Club, Warner headed for the roulette table. "Get Mike a drink," he ordered one of his underlings.

"Is very kind, J.L.," Mike said, " but I want only take a sandwich."

Warner would not hear of such a thing. He shoved some chips in Mike's hands and told him, "If you're as lucky with roulette as you are with your picture, you'll clean the pants off them." He flicked his cigar in the manner of Groucho Marx. "And, with these women dealers, that's not a bad idea." Warner had the reputation of a man who would rather make a bad joke than a good picture. Mike reluctantly went to the table. Within ten minutes he had lost the chips and went back to Warner, who was now deep in blackjack. "Thanks you, J.L.," Mike said. "I am terrible tired. I take a—" But Warner had already pushed more chips on him. "Play. Let me finish here and we'll get something to eat." Once again Mike returned to the table and played out his stack of chips. When they were gone, he started back to Warner, changed his mind and sneaked out the back way. On the drive home, everything was closed. No restaurants, no all-night diners. Even the drive-ins, so popular in that period, were all closed. Nothing. He went to bed late and hungry, having to rise at five again the next morning. "Goddamn," he told us at dinner next night. "On the set I get from J.L. a letter." He showed it.

> Dear Mike,
> Congratulations again on a wonderful picture. You certainly have the magic touch.
> Jack
> P.S. Please send your check for three thousand for the chips.

"Sonabitch," Mike said. "Next time I am hungry, I want a sandwich, I get on a stand-in."

As our nation came out of the dark cloud of the Depression, the critical nature of the European situation had become evident to anyone who would look—the massive German rearmament, the takeover by the Nazis of country after country. Clearly they planned to redress the Versailles Treaty as Hitler had promised. Mike knew the horrors of war and its effects on civilians. He was working to get his family out of Hungary and to California with him. The Hungarian counsel and lawyers were working on the problem but the quotas were filled. Too many others had come to the same realization. Mike continued his own battle to make good pictures. Among the other results of the sound revolution had been the creation of a new breed of man—the dialogue director. Irving Rapper was an example. A dialogue director generally had stage experience but the term "director" was a misnomer. His job was merely to rehearse the actors, making sure the lines were correctly learned and correctly pronounced without any unwanted accent. He did not direct but, like the mixer, his word was unchallenged because he also protected Sound. As technology progressed, the mixers became more flexible, the director more used to sound as a major part of the picture. A soundproof "blimp" was added to the camera, allowing it to come out of the "icebox" and restoring some of its mobility. The dialogue director gradually became a sort of coach who would rehearse and prompt the actors. By my time, the job had lost much of its meaning but it did afford some assistance to the director, relieving him of the tedium of hearing line rehearsals. Having, as an apprentice on Mike's sets, seen dialogue directors at work, that became my next job. I was, of course, to work on a B picture. On the first day of my first picture as dialogue director, I met my first wife, Joan. She played a corpse. Errol Flynn's first part had also been as a corpse in Mike's *The Case of the Curious Bride*, starring Warren William. Errol had gone on to stardom. Joan played supporting parts in A pictures and leads in Bs. We were married in 1951.

Joan MacGillicuddy, an Australian, had gone to the Royal Academy of Dramatic Arts in London, and then was signed to a contract at Warners. Our union produced two girls, Elizabeth and Victoria, and a boy, Michael. Then, in 1959, a year after the birth of our son Michael, I took Joan back to her people for a year while I was shooting a Down Under Western series in Australia. The series was called *Whiplash* and was a production of Viacom, an English company. I was associate producer and alternate director. By British law, every other episode had to be directed by a British subject to maintain what was called British Content. Only the producer, Ben Fox, the star, Peter Graves, and I were American. Our alternating director was named Peter Maxwell, a Hungarian but one who had been raised and schooled in England in what he described as "a rather good public school." His English was flawless. He thus qualified as British Content. I was associate producer and alternated with Maxwell directing every other episode. In the transition from Australia to England, the Royal Academy and then America, Joan had lost her Australian accent and was amused when the tradesmen of Wahroonga, the village where we lived while I was doing the television series, called her the American Lady. But that was far in the future.

In 1939, settled into my job as dialogue director, I was beginning to enjoy work for the first time. There were many perks. The service man would bring chairs and I would sit with the actors and rehearse the scene. Even B pictures had service men — Negroes in resplendent uniforms, looking like doormen at exclusive hotels. They worked under the Prop Department. It was their job to make coffee, bring it to the stars and upper echelon crew (which, happily, included the dialogue director), run errands, keep chairs in proper locations for those who were entitled to chairs. The whole system was highly hierarchical. It was a comfortable institution that went out with the demise of the big studios.

From this distance, I now realize how humiliating it must have been for those men. As far as I can remember, theirs, with the exception of shoeshine "boys," were the only black faces to be seen in the studio. They had to listen to such things as the gaffer calling, "Put a nigger on that arc." These were the black cloth squares the grips used to keep a lamp's light from hitting an unwanted area. They are now called "gobos."

This was also the time when black dogs were often named Nigger.

The crew was highly unionized. Electricians handled the lights, grips handled gobos, pushed the camera dolly or handled on-set construction. The prop man handled props furniture and everything else that was wanted as dressing for a scene. There were union lines that were not to be stepped over. At times it became ridiculous. I have seen production held up for a considerable time by an argument over which union had the right to plug in an ornamental lamp used in the set. My work was all on B pictures. These were program fillers, meant, during the Depression, to offer the public two pictures for the price of one. Bs were cheap to make and rapidly done. They did not employ the top writers, directors or stars. But it was an opportunity for directors, some who had written or done stage work, to get a start. There was not as much at risk as with a costlier A feature. But many of the B directors were oldtimers who had been at it since early silent days. They knew how to keep to a schedule and bring the picture in under budget. A few knew little else. One referred to historical or costume pictures as "one of them filums where everybody writes with a feather." I once had a long argument with a director called "Breezy" Eason on the studio back lot one cold night. We were shooting a picture whose title I forget but whose lead character was called Capt. Craig Killian of the Commandos. That should give some clue to the quality of the production. The scene was wartime London, undergoing the Blitz. On a back lot street wall was a poster, which Breezy insisted was a mistake by the set dressing department. Underneath a picture of Winston Churchill were the words, "We Shall Not Flag Nor Fail." The line was from one of Churchill's speeches that continued, "We shall fight on the beaches, we shall fight in the streets. We shall never surrender."

"What the hell does that mean?" Breezy demanded.

"Does *what* mean?" I asked.

"We shall not flag. A flag's something you wave." he said. I explained that, in this context, it meant to be limp, it meant that the British would not lose energy or determination, they would not give up. I'm afraid I didn't make a very convincing case but he finally agreed to leave the thing in place. The poster was mere background and I doubt if even the most diligent viewer would be able to notice anything beyond the face of Churchill.

In this and in subsequent B pictures, while rehearsing the actors in their lines, I found some dialogue absurd, ungrammatical and otherwise troubling. I began to change words, then sentences. At the end, I was rewriting whole speeches, whole scenes. At first the directors did not notice. The actors were happy but, as my "improvements" got more extensive, the new scenes had to be learned. That caused some delays. B schedules were tight. If the picture was behind schedule, the producers—they were called supervisors at Warners—yelled at the assistant directors and, when necessary, at the directors. No one wanted to be known as a slow director. In B pictures, that was the highway to unemployment. My time of glory terminated with *The Gorilla Man*. We fell slightly behind schedule and my director, naturally, passed along the blame. "The dialogue director's rewriting confused the actors and caused the delay," our producer was told. This was true but there was no interest in a discussion as to whether or not the rewriting had improved the scenes. Quick, not good, was desired. I was allowed to finish the picture with a stern admonition not to meddle with any writing chores. After that, I was not fired but it was decided that I might best be employed as a second assistant director.

The first assistant runs the set. His loyalties are split between the director that he assists and the Production Department that hires him. The second assistant's job was more routine than that of a script clerk in terms of endless paperwork, filling out call sheets, orders and times for actors, crew, animals (if applicable), etc. It also required a lot of telephone work, giving actors their calls, requesting equipment, etc. This tedious work was broken by handling extras, helping the first assistant manage crowds, scouring the rear of the set and adjacent areas to find where extras might have gone for a nap or card game. Extras must be herded like sheep. A second assistant must be part dog.

For a time I was on the set of Mike's *Dive Bomber* starring Errol Flynn and Fred MacMurray. Errol sulked quite a bit of the time after he found that MacMurray, who had been borrowed from another studio, was getting a much larger salary than he was. But there was a good deal of fun working with units of the U.S. Navy, including the old U.S.S. *Enterprise* and her task force. I cannot say that Mike prepared the officers for war but he did test them under considerable stress. At one point, the *Enterprise* and the task force that provided its protection were steaming off Coronado for the cameras. Mike disliked the look of the formation as the wind was blowing from astern. "No," Mike shouted. "Cut! Tell them the smoke should go from right to left." It was explained how difficult it was to change the course of all the ships involved and that, when the wind

Mike and Fred MacMurray on the set of *Dive Bomber* (1941).

is astern, it is natural for the smoke to blow forward. Mike was unmoved. "When the smoke go in front, it looks lousy." The camera boats, the aircraft carrier and the entire task force had to come about to put the smoke in Mike's required position. At dinner, the admiral commanding told Mike that he was giving the fleet an excellent shakedown cruise. He could say this with a relieved smile because the carrier scenes were completed. The unpredictable picture people would be gone and he could return to more vital missions. The next day, however, he found his relief had been premature because the Navy switched from the old-fashioned biplanes to monoplanes for its air arm and so many scenes had to be reshot to reflect this technological update.

Back at the studio for the shooting of the interior sets, an historic event occurred. There was a visit to the studio by the Archduke Otto von Hapsburg, pretender to the throne of the Austro-Hungarian dual monarchy, the man who but for the fortunes of war would have been Mike's King-Emperor. There were tons of publicity photographs taken with the stars and the director. In one picture, Mike is instinctively bowing to his might-have-been sovereign. At dinner, Mother asked whether Mike had spoken to the Archduke in German or Hungarian. Mike shook his head. "Why hell I talk foreign? I speak English. I am American."

"I thought," Mother said with a straight face, "you might have forgotten your native tongue." Some of his friends had told her that he was no longer proficient in Hungarian. As a matter of fact, they claimed that Mike was intelligible in none of the languages he spoke.

Mike denied the slander. "Of all the Hungarians what are famous," he insisted, "I talk the best goddamn English."

A final decision of what turn my employment would next take was rendered unnecessary by the draft. The war was raging in Europe and, though we were at peace, our factories were gearing up for war production, for sale overseas, of course. America was not to be involved in a fighting war. We had the Lend-Lease Act, funneling munitions and ships to England, and Congress had enacted a precautionary buildup of our nearly non-existent military. Many of my co-workers were being drafted. On the day I got my 1A card, I saw a young man who had worked the guard desk until his number came up, sitting contentedly back at his post. I asked what happened. He grinned ear to ear. "I got lucky," he said. "I've got a bad heart."

Because of the war, Mike was able to get his mother and two of his brothers out of Hungary. His mother was allowed into the United States because of her age and health but the two brothers, Gabor and Desider, had to wait in Mexico until their papers could be pushed through the bureaucratic logjam. They waited two years. Mike's mother, a frail, stooped woman with a will of iron, was given a house and a housekeeper named Mrs. Alpert. Mama was strictly observant of her Jewish faith. All dietary laws had to be followed. Fish must come into the house alive. Mrs. Alpert then had to kill and prepare these unfortunate and terrified creatures in the sink. This job horrified her. But, what horrified her more was that Mama might find out her secret. She, too, was a refugee. She had been married to a Jew but was not herself Jewish and was terrified that Mama would learn this and discharge her. Then where would she go? There was, as might be expected, a great deal of friction between Mother and her mother-in-law.

We occasionally drove to Tijuana, across the Mexican border, to visit the "boys"—Mike's brothers—and deliver assurance that everything was being done to speed their entrance to the United States. They were not thrilled with the trashy border town but knew that their home had been taken by the Nazis and they would otherwise be dead or in concentration camps. One of Mike's sisters, Marget, who had lived with her husband in Romania, had been deported with her family in the cattle cars. Her husband and two male children died in Auschwitz. Marget and one daughter somehow lived through it. While I was waiting to be drafted, I suddenly, in quick succession, lost Collins and my father.

The maid came in after breakfast to say that Collins had just reported for work and seemed sick. He nightly made the long drive to his home on 130th Street and then back to the San Fernando Valley in the morning. I went down to the room that was kept for him next to the motor court and found him doubled up on the bed. I told Mother I thought it was serious and she called the Branch Clinic. When I drove Collins in, he refused a cigarette. "Now you know I'm really sick," he said.

I got a wheelchair and I took him upstairs to the clinic where he went through a series of tests. John MacDonald, my friend and internist, ran an EKG. It was a coronary thrombosis and there was considerable damage. I remember Dr. Branch, an excellent surgeon and a very kind man with a Texas accent, saying, "Collins, you're a very sick boy." I remember feeling the term "boy" was improper although Dr. Branch meant it kindly. Collins' wife and her brother arrived and Dr. Branch made arrangements to admit Collins to the Hollywood Presbyterian Hospital. It took considerable pressure because Collins was colored. His family was to take him in our station wagon. Dr. Branch suggested I not go. I think that, too, was meant kindly. Feeling that everything had been arranged and all would be well, I drove home. Within an hour and a half, we received a call. Collins was dead. It was stunning to me. He had been part of my life almost as long as I could remember. For the first time, I considered mortality.

Mother, of course, paid for the funeral. He was buried in a colored cemetery. The small chapel was overflowing. I had no idea he had that many friends. Mother and I were the only white faces there.

Many years later, when I was directing a scene that required large tombstones—modern cemeteries have only level grave markers—we shot there. I took my lunch hour digging through old cemetery records to find his unmarked grave. I wondered why his family had never put a stone up.

Well over a month after his death, a delivery van drove up into the motor court. A deliveryman came to the door with the papers for the new stove that was being delivered. The cook was delighted. The old stove had had problems and there had been much discussion in the kitchen. Collins' voice had been one of the loudest to condemn the stove. When it was brought to Mike's attention, he said, "Call up the plumber he should fix it."

But here was the new stove. The cook delightedly told Mother it had arrived. Mother had not ordered a new stove and came out to the kitchen to settle the matter. The deliveryman had all the papers. Mother insisted no stove had been ordered. The deliveryman insisted it had.

"When?"

"Last Friday, " he told her. "Your chauffeur said it was to be delivered this week."

Fred, the new chauffeur who had been hired to replace Collins, was called in. He denied any knowledge of the stove.

"Not him, " the deliveryman said. "Your regular chauffeur, Collins."

"When was this?" I asked.

"Last Friday."

"That's not possible."

"I was there," he said.

Mother and I stared at each other.

"Collins," she told him, "has been dead for a month and a half."

Now it was the deliveryman's turn to look stunned. "But I know Collins," he said. "He's been with you for years."

Mother told him he must have been mistaken about the time. Collins had a particular hatred for that stove since he had singed his hair lighting the oven when he thought the gas wasn't flowing.

"It was last Friday," the deliveryman insisted stubbornly.

Mother told him she was not superstitious and would not accept any supernatural explanation. She did, however, accept the new stove.

When Mike came home, Mother told him the story. He frowned. "You think so maybe really Colon have ordered it?" he asked. He was met with stares of varying incredulity from all concerned.

The cook looked particularly anxious. "You mean his ghost?" she asked with a shudder.

Mike shrugged. "Well," he said, "we have now a better stove. What we have for dinner?"

The shock of Collins' loss had not yet passed when we got a call from Sylvia, my stepmother, to say that my father had been taken to the hospital. I went there at once. It was an osteopathic hospital and they were treating him with enemas and adjustments. He proved to have a coronary. I arranged to take John MacDonald down to see him. This was a double problem for John. He was not only, as a medical doctor, venturing into enemy territory—an osteopathic hospital (the two disciplines were much farther apart then) but he had just come back from burying his own father, who died of a coronary. I wanted my father taken to Hollywood Presbyterian so John could treat him, but a quick examination made it clear that Luke could not be moved. There was nothing John could do. I continued to visit my father daily. He would be rational at times, then would describe little animals crawling up the wall to hiding places. After two weeks, the phone rang in the middle of the night. Mother called me in.

I was a half-orphan. Shortly after this, I began to exhibit what seemed to be heart problems. John ran an electrocardiogram and diagnosed it as NCA, Neuro Circulatory Asthenia—what we today call Anxiety Syndrome. My heart would race wildly and I would come close to fainting. I had probably absorbed some of my Mother's hysteria. I was told that there was nothing physically wrong with the heart but I kept going back for EKGs to reassure me during the frequent attacks. Simply knowing it was hypochondria did not change the symptoms, which were terrifying. I don't know which I feared more, that I was going to die or make an embarrassing spectacle in front of friends when I had an attack. When the symptoms continued long enough to bore my physicians, a psychologist was found and I went to him, off and on for years. We discussed many aspects of my life, including the obvious (even to me) cause of my trouble—the death of Collins and my father in rapid succession—but that did little to change things.

My therapist was a diabetic, drank coffee constantly and smoked even more than my mother. I had expected to lie on a couch in accepted Freudian fashion and reveal Significant Things in a stream of consciousness. My stream was dammed up when I found he was an Adlerian and not interested in such techniques. We had a direct, face-to-face confrontation to discuss the universal striving for Power. This was Adlerian psychology and this was the way it was ordained by the man who had worked with and then broken with Freud. Over time, distinctions in therapeutic techniques have blurred. Just as there are no Galenians or Pasteurians in medicine, there are no longer strict Freudians, Adlerians or Jungians. All those men were pioneers. All made contributions.

In search of my problem, my therapist kept coming back to my lack of a home life when very young—military schools, lack of contacts with parents. I could not accept any of that. As an only child, I had nothing to compare my relationship to Mother with. To me, it was wonderful. I was treated as an equal. She made no objection when I called her Bessky, as Mike did. Mere children would have had to say Mother. Grinning, she once told me that I am alive because of a misdiagnosis. Feeling ill, she had consulted a doctor who told her she had a bowel obstruction. I don't know what, if any, treatment was suggested but time passed and the obstruction turned out to be me. "When I found out," Mother told me, "it was too late. Otherwise, you'd have joined your little brothers and sisters down the toilet." I was an adult, or almost, at the time she told me, and I thought it was funny. Mother always had a wry twist on everything and I had always been proud of being treated like an adult, feeling that I could tell Mother anything—not that I did—not everything. I never told that story to my therapist.

If a patient has problems, it is almost a cliché for the therapist to blame the mother. He kept bringing up other things—military school, divorce—but I failed to understand his reasoning as most of the kids I knew went through the same upbringing. That's the way things worked. I later came to realize not all things worked that way but also to realize how difficult being a mother was for Mother. Her career came at a time when working in a male world required a lot of guts and full-time attention to the job. She couldn't have it both ways. I seriously doubt that it is really possible today. But even at the urging of the therapist, I was unable to see any blame to be affixed to her. No one sets out to be a bad parent. I am sure everyone would have benefited if I had been able to spend more time with my own children. You simply work with what knowledge is available at the time.

What I realized much later was that during their marriage, my father's considerable career went down as Mother's went up. With Mike it was just the opposite. Whether Mike's extra-marital actions caused her to withdraw from her work or whether it was just the way a very cruel and competitive business works, she hid her grief in illness. You keep yourself on top or you're on the slide to oblivion. But for whatever reason, Mother's career trailed off as Mike's ascended.

The one positive advantage of therapy was to give me a better insight into motivations, which helped in writing. In writing, everything helps. No knowledge, however obscure, is ever wasted. The proper shape for a writer is a funnel. All experience should go in the large end and come out, distilled, and ready to be written.

In one last effort, Mother was back with Darryl at Fox, writing the 1940 *The Mark of Zorro* for Tyrone Power. Finally, in late 1941, my draft number was called. My letter came:

> From the President of the United States, Greetings.

It was almost with relief that I prepared to leave the comfort of the ranch for military service. It would force my mind into new channels. For my Army career, Mother had bought me an elaborate suitcase. It contained a small short wave radio, a ditty bag with my electric shaver, pajamas, medications—many of the nicer things of life. The draft board to which I was to report was in Reseda, far out in the San Fernando Valley, then an agricultural community. I arrived at the Valley Selective Service Station carrying my very fashionable suitcase. The other draftees who reported at 6 A.M. that morning had a few possessions wrapped in newspapers or perhaps clutched in paper bags. They studied me as an interesting alien.

Because some official had discovered my military school background, I was handed a paper that appointed me Acting Sergeant with orders to get these men safely to the Induction Center in downtown Los Angeles. I studied some 20 farm workers, muscular from heavy lifting. Any one could have destroyed me with one hand. These were the men I was responsible for and must command. I was about to abdicate my honorary title but, as I studied the paper, I found that, as clearly as I could make out, should any try to escape, or otherwise disturb the peace of the journey, my commission entitled me to call the police. I was relieved. There need be no physical confrontations. So, I decided to handle them as I would herd movie extras—but more politely. I took my troop from the Reseda Draft Board to the downtown induction center on a streetcar. This was the first time in my life I had ridden on one. Despite that, we arrived without incident and, after the usual indignity of physicals, were shipped to Fort MacArthur, named for the father of the Douglas MacArthur who achieved much prominence in World War II. The fort was a holding area where inductees were kept until the Army processed and sent them to the desired locations or various boot camps. I had with me a letter from Col. Levison, head of the Warner Brothers Research Department, stating that I was a motion picture writer and requesting that I be sent to the Signal Corps Army Motion Picture Center at Monmouth, New Jersey, as a screenwriter. I presented this to the Induction Officer. Out of Monmouth were to come countless training and some propaganda films. Many top Hollywood talents spent the war in Fort Monmouth. There Frank Capra turned out his *Why We Fight* series. John Huston went overseas and made some superb combat films. The bureaucracy of the Army had Levinson's letter somewhere in its mills and was grinding on it very slowly. As days passed and many men from my barracks were sent off to various camps, I had begun to feel the letter had been lost and, with it, my hope of this relatively pleasant duty with my peers. I became resigned to the fact that I was in for a dull time. There was no war. Through Lend-Lease, we were providing arms to England and the forces of democracy in Europe so they could fight. We had no intention of becoming embroiled in the hostilities. The Army was being built up on a purely defensive basis. Citizen soldiers were being shipped to various camps to live in discomfort.

For me, this was military school all over again, in more primitive circumstances. There was some drilling—old stuff to me—and exciting assignments like taking a truck to round up all garbage cans in the upper fort where the big guns waited in their emplacements, unaware of their obsolescence, being designed to ward off a Spanish-American War attack. While waiting for orders, we were encouraged, while not otherwise occupied, to engage in sports. Encouraged, in Army terms, means "Get your ass out there and play." So I found myself on a volleyball court engaged in a game I neither liked nor understood. I have never liked or understood any competitive sport despite the tennis pro Mother hired once to teach me tennis and take me on hikes. Instead, I got him to take me to Catalina on a boat some of his friends had and where there was a lot to drink. I have never been athletic but I remember clearly this day on the dusty volleyball court. There were a group of us in the game, including a colored man of 19 or 20 who walked with a crutch, having sprained but not done any permanent damage to his leg which would cause the draft board doctors to dismiss him. He was a natural at the game, slamming the ball down in unreachable places while hopping on one foot. One of the players with what seemed a Texas accent called, "Hey, Sunshine, throw the ball to me." The crutch was hefted and the black man stood facing the other players, plus the spectators—all white. "Don't call me Sunshine." His voice shook with rage. "Don't any of you bastards call me Sunshine." His eyes blazed. There was a total and complete silence, which dragged on and on. One crippled man facing a dozen. The silence seemed endless. At last somebody called. "You can call *me* Sunshine. Let's play."

I regret that somebody wasn't me.

The monotony of waiting for assignment to Fort Monmouth was broken by our Staff Sergeant, a short wiry man with a leathered face who had been in the Army all his life. When he discovered that I had worked in the motion picture business, his interest was not primarily art. It meant that I had money. In what was probably a regular routine with him, he sneaked me off the base late one afternoon and we started a round of bars in the roughest part of San Pedro. I, of course, picked up the tab for all drinks for the sergeant and his friends. I waited in one seedy whorehouse while he got laid. I was offered the specialty of the house but made an embarrassed refusal and waited, not drinking, almost afraid to touch the soiled furniture. He had taken five dollars from me as the whore's fee but I am sure in that place it didn't cost more than two. Then we went back to the round of bars. God knows how many drinks we consumed. I remember only being in a taxi and coming to the upper M.P. post. I recall being shoved from the taxi and the sergeant telling the M.P.s to pass me. His speech was so slurred I could hardly understand but the M.P.s did. It was probably a stock routine. He shouted after me to tell the second checkpoint down the hill near the barracks that he had sent me. After stumbling a few times, falling once, I delivered the message to the M.P.s there. It must have worked because I remember swaying in the company street, trying to decide which of the dozens of identical wooden buildings was my barracks. Somehow I managed to find it because, still dressed, I woke at reveille several hours later with the world's worst headache and was forced into the lineup and the march to the mess hall. They were serving eggs, hash browns and bacon that morning. Bacon is cooked by being dumped into a garbage-can-sized pot full of boiling grease and then fished out, half-cooked and warm, to be slopped into one of the compartments of the metal mess tray, swimming in a pool of grease. I managed not to vomit, nibbled dry toast with coffee and somehow staggered through that awful day. Perhaps as punishment for my night on the town or perhaps just the luck of the draw assigned me to K.P. duty. I was set to work in the huge kitchen, scouring the monster vats where food is cooked for multitudes. Here, in the midst of a heavy winter rain, with open windows and steaming kitchens, I caught cold. In the barracks it worsened. I was sent on sick call, thence, to the base hospital. The chest cold got better there, amid more comfortable surroundings, but the asthma, which I had suffered since childhood, returned with a vengeance. It used to require a house call from the doctor and shots of adrenaline. At the base hospital, they took a full medical history.

Jani, with whom I was going at the time, got permission to visit me at the base hospital and was there when Mother arrived. There was a lot of sentiment about my being in the Army and the possibility that, if the U.S. got involved in the war, I might be sent to fight in Europe. Many people in our circumstances were getting married and this was discussed. Jani and Mother being more in favor of it than I was, the plan was put on hold. After several weeks in the hospital and numerous physical exams, the head doctor told me he was requesting a medical discharge for me. I was returned to limited duty and barracks life while my discharge was being processed.

Finally, on October 29, 1941, the paper came, an Honorable Discharge under CDD, Section II, signed by Lt. Frank Slaughter. Beside the obvious irony of such a name for a man in the fighting forces, I believe he was the same man who authored many historical novels. The paper announced: "Soldier is entitled to travel pay." I saved the Army the streetcar fare. The new chauffeur drove me home.

I took a little time during November and December to think about what I wanted to do. My father had been an actor. Mother had acted. Perhaps, I thought, that might be the solution for me. My previous career moves had not proven too fruitful. It was coming up on Christmas, always a big production at our house—at all the houses I knew. I went on shopping trips with Mother, usually to Bullock's Wilshire, probably the most elegant store of its time. The store is closed now but the building still stands, a wonderful example of '20s modern architecture. In contrast to today's expensive department stores, where it is impossible to find a human to even answer a question, Mother would sweep through Bullock's Wilshire followed by a large entourage of salesmen and women, buying scores of presents. On Christmas our living room would be stacked with an incredible array of gifts—not just our family-to-family gifts but from actor's agents, producers, people wanting something from Mike or, through Mother to Mike. It was the same way in every large home in Hollywood. Producer Hal Wallis' living room was almost impossible to navigate. Louella Parsons' entire house overflowed. She had the power of the press and everyone, high or low, curried favor with her. Secretaries opened her gifts and kept lists. It was the only efficient way her volume of presents could be handled. But it was not flawless. One year Mother got a gorgeous French embroidered purse from Louella. It had obviously cost a fortune. When she opened it, she saw the elaborate silk lining, the built-in mirror, comb and lipstick. She also saw a card that read,

> Merry Christmas and much love,
> Clark and Carole

The Gables, Clark and Carole Lombard, had given it to Louella the previous Christmas.

In our family, birthdays were easy to remember. Mother was born on February 12—Lincoln's birthday. I was born on May Day, and Mike on Christmas Eve. As it turned out, their wedding anniversary was equally unforgettable, December 7. Mike had Robert Stack and Henry Blanke (who had been Mike's assistant director and was now his producer) over to do some skeet shooting. I was reading when I heard a shout from Mother. I ran into her bedroom. She was not in a deep "illness" now but she still stayed in bed a good deal of the time. Over the radio we heard the ominous tones of H. V. Kaltenborn announcing the Japanese raid on Pearl Harbor. I grabbed the station wagon, raced down to the skeet field and relayed the news. The skeet match broke up quickly. I went back to the house because Ann Sheridan and George Brent had come to lunch. I brought a portable radio out to the pool and the three of us listened, drank and ate. The extent of the damage to the fleet was not yet released but clearly that damage was terrible. It was a very quiet lunch.

Even amid the excitement and horror we were hearing, I realized with mixed emotions that I was a civilian. I was not involved. Almost two months after my discharge from the Army, Mother had received a card from the authorities at Fort MacArthur. It was the third they had sent.

The first announced that I had arrived at the Reception Center, Fort MacArthur. The second said that I had been assigned to an army post on Luzon in the Philippines. It was not until over a month after my medical discharge that the third one came, finally assigning me to the Signal Corps Replacement Center in Fort Monmouth, New Jersey, which is what Col. Levinson's letter had requested and I had hoped for. That type of military foul-up was common, almost standard, in those times. SNAFU was the polite term for it. If I had not caught cold, been hospitalized while my contingent was shipped out, the second notice would have been the correct one. I would have been in the Philippines and probably have been in the Bataan Death March.

Germany, Japan and Italy formed the Axis Powers, bound by treaty to fight together. On the day Germany declared war on the United States, Mother went into her office at the pool house and smashed many of the expensive antique German mugs that lined the shelves above the bar. It was a senseless act that Mike protested but Mother, who had studied German and sent me to Berlitz to become fluent, which I never became, took Hitler's challenge out on the artifacts of a gentler German age. The next few days after Pearl Harbor we spent, like the rest of America, glued to the radio and H.V. Kaltenborn. Since I was out of the Army and doing nothing, I went back to my job.

The whole complexion of the country had changed overnight. Even at the studios, those ivory bastions, people felt suddenly martial. Ronald Reagan, though not on active duty, had somehow gotten assigned to the Cavalry—a branch of the service that was not to find much employment in the era of tanks. In his uniform he frequently used the Warner Green Room's tablecloths to demonstrate classic cavalry maneuvers to lunchers who would listen. Warners' eating facilities were divided into three parts. First came the large outer restaurant, which included counters for those in a hurry and checkered tablecloths for the meals of those members of the lower orders who had more leisure. The more exclusive Green Room was for actors with name value, writers and directors. There was a writers' table where writers could exchange ideas and complaints, mostly about those privileged to dine in the Executive Dining Room—the most exclusive one reserved for producers and the brothers Warner. Around the writers' table, Reagan was considered something of a joke in his gleaming cavalry boots and what was viewed as his limited acting abilities. But even the most analytical minds at the table could never have foreseen where his talents would take him. I witnessed, however, one shining moment on the set of *The Voice of the Turtle*. Reagan had previously had disagreements with the director, Irving Rapper, who had graduated from dialogue director status and done some quite successful "woman's pictures." Reagan regarded Rapper as non-macho and "overly fussy"—a euphemism for homosexual. One scene in *Turtle* called for Reagan to dance with his leading lady. After several calls of "cut" and repeated takes without explanation of the problem, Irving took Reagan aside and told him that he was holding his partner too close and it looked ugly. That did it for Reagan. He returned to his starting position muttering loudly enough for the entire set to hear, "What this picture needs is a technical director to tell this director how boys feel about girls." For that alone I would have awarded him the Presidency.

Feeling I had been around Warners too long under the aegis of Mike, I went to Twentieth Century as assistant director. Mike had, of course, spoken to Darryl Zanuck. I made a new start at a new studio. There my superior, the first assistant, was Eli Dunn. I did several pictures under him, working indifferently well. These were not difficult films—few extras to handle. My only real duties were to call actors and make out the call sheets for the next day. This was done in the late afternoon, when we could see how the schedule was going and whether we would be ready to shoot what was ordered, what time to call principals and their stand-ins. This gave me spare time to talk with actors and to make the acquaintance of Faye, a young contract player with whom I subsequently spent much off-work time.

We met on a picture starring Gracie Fields and Monty Woolley. Faye was under contract to Twentieth. She was the Gentile adopted daughter of a Jewish couple named Simon who had become Christian Scientists. Under the name of Fanchon and Marco, they had staged elaborate musicals to accompany the top films at the Paramount Theater in downtown Los Angeles. Faye was some years my junior and was very athletic. During our time together, she taught me how to swim and to ice skate. The ice skating I gave up but for many years I swam morning and night. Her education in music was flawless but in other areas that interested me— literature, history, etc.—she was extremely limited.

Sometimes we would watch movies at our house, sometimes at hers. On one of the latter occasions, we had run *The Scarlet Pimpernel*, which takes place at the time of the French Revolution. The Pimpernel is the alias of a titled Englishman, friend of the Prince of Wales, who, working undercover, saves French aristocrats from the guillotine. At the conclusion of the film, Faye's parents were discussing the plot. Her mother asked, "Now, that Prince of Wales—is he the one who resigned to marry that American woman?" I had to explain that the two events were some 150 years apart. My relationship with Faye was sweet but short.

At Twentieth I also, for some reason that I cannot now explain, studied Spanish. We had no great influx from below the border at that time and hardly anyone spoke it. Logic would have dictated my going on to improve the French I had learned at Cumnock. The big boss, Darryl Zanuck, had a French teacher who met him at his home, drove in the green Rolls-Royce limousine with him, speaking only French. The teacher waited all day in the office and, whenever Zanuck was not otherwise engaged, spoke French to him. He rode home with him late at night, after Darryl had screened all the studio's dailies. That came as close to total immersion in a foreign language as was possible while running a major studio in English.

Zanuck later received a colonel's commission and his French was put to use during the North African invasion. There was a good deal of publicity about his exploits—he went in with the Free French Navy by submarine. The praise and honor heaped upon a former employee, who had not only left him but, much worse, become very successful, so disturbed Jack Warner that he campaigned until he, too, had acquired a colonel's commission. As far as I know, the extent of his military involvement was to have the studio wardrobe department make up a vast array of uniforms to bear the weight of the eagles on his shoulders. He did, however, make many war pictures, all patriotic, all profitable.

During the war, our servants came and went, some to better paying war jobs, some to the draft. One of our many butlers was English, a thin, nervous man whose name escapes me but whose face is indelibly engraved in my memory. Mother was impressed with his credentials and with the way he took charge of the house, the maids and even our temperamental Filipino cook, Freddy. He was the perfect butler. For some reason, Mike took an instant dislike to the man and would watch him suspiciously as he served in his flawless manner. He could almost feel the weight of Mike's eyes from the moment he entered with his silver tray. Already made nervous by the expression on Mike's face, he would begin to gasp. With tightly closed lips he would make it most of the way around the table. As dish followed dish, he would fight heroically to stifle the convulsions occurring deep in his throat. Inevitably a faint cough would escape. By the time he finished his round of the table, his face would be cyanosed from the effort to restrain himself. As soon as the door of the butler's pantry swung shut behind him, a spasm of coughing could be heard from the kitchen. Mike's face would quiver slightly with repressed mirth. "Stop it!" Mother hissed. "He's the best butler we've ever had."

"Phony, " Mike muttered. "He talk phony."

Then it was time for the dreaded next course. The poor man, having recovered, served Mother, who smiled reassuringly at him. As he approached Mike's place and his scrutiny, the inevitable spasm in his throat became evident. With his mouth firmly shut, he began to make stifled coughing sounds. Mike's eyes never left him and as he reached the door, his cheeks blue and almost in a state of collapse. The coughing sounds could be heard as he rushed out through the kitchen to the servant's dining room in an effort to muffle the noise. It went on night after night. Mother would beg Mike to stop, to refrain from looking at the man, but he could not or would not change the game plan. After the butler nearly expired during one round, Mother threw a butter knife at her husband.

Mike looked up in innocent surprise. "What I do wrong?"

"You know damned well," she told him. "We've finally got a good butler. He knows how to serve. He gets on with the rest of the staff. Leave him alone." Mike looked repentant and did not stare during the rest of the meal although the butler acted like a horse about to shy every time he approached Mike. One night, as soup was served, Mike was still on his good behavior. Although the butler's hand trembled slightly as he went to serve Mike, he had not coughed once. I sensed a new era of good will. But as he lifted the soup bowl from the tray, Mike looked up, meeting his eyes. The man's hand slipped. "Why you put your finger on my soup?" Mike demanded. That did it. In a furious paroxysm of coughing, the butler staggered from the room.

This time Mother threw a lighted cigarette.

"Why you hurt me?" Mike's eyes were wide, innocent. "I doesn't do nothing wrong. He spoil my soup."

Mother fought hard to maintain her anger as a great commotion arose from the kitchen. A spoon flew toward Mike to follow the cigarette but missed by a mile. Mother was laughing too hard to aim. Soon we had a new butler.

We lived in the San Fernando Valley. Twentieth Century–Fox was a considerable distance over the mountain in Beverly Hills. Its vast back lot, where innumerable films were made on its standing sets, was later sold off to hold the high rises of what is now Century City. During the war, ration cards allowed civilians only the necessary gas to get to work and home. If I wanted to go anywhere, take a date out, I had to find some way to stretch my supply. To do this, I bought a motorcycle which used very little of the gas that I siphoned from my tank. The plan worked well until I left the studio one rainy day, gunned the bike to get out of the way of an oncoming car, skidded and crashed. I had some road burns but the main damage was to my left ankle. The shift lever had dug in and almost surgically cut a groove up along the Achilles tendon. A fraction of an inch one way or the other and I would have lived the rest of my life with a dropped foot. A kind woman picked me up and drove me to the emergency room next to the Beverly Hills police station. All I can remember of the ride was holding my shoe under my foot so that the dripping blood would not stain her car's carpet. I was stitched and released. The chauffeur picked me up. That night I called Eli Dunn, the first assistant, to tell him what had happened. Then I spent the next week in bed.

At the end of that time, I received a call from the Fox Production Department, under which assistant directors work, and was told not to bother to come in. I was fired. Shocked and indignant, I had simply assumed that Eli would tell them of the accident and everyone would feel sorry. The production department took the view that it was my responsibility to have informed the department myself. I had to admit the correctness of this view although responsibility had not been part of my upbringing.

9
In the Wings

With my leg healed and having been fired by Fox, I decided that, with an active war on, I should, even though I had been declared unsuitable soldier material, have some part in the conflict. Early in the war there had been a huge fright when a Japanese sub shelled some oil wells north of Malibu, doing no appreciable damage. Japanese, mostly American citizens, were rounded up and moved to detention camps. It seemed reasonable at the time, terrible in retrospect. But there was a good deal of panic then. For the first time, American soil had been attacked. Nobody seemed to have any clear idea of what to do about it. A large wooden platform was built in the hills a mile or so from our ranch. I became an aircraft spotter, taking night shifts. I had flash cards of Japanese aircraft, which were useless in the dark, but it was possible to tell a single from a multi-engined plane, guess at its height and direction and report it through the phone to a combat center. I heard very few planes sitting there, bundled up against the January nights. Mostly I read by flashlight. It was dull and did not seem very heroic, sitting in the dark, awaiting a Japanese air attack that never came closer to our shores than Pearl Harbor, some 2,500 miles west of California.

Timm Aircraft was located at Van Nuys Airport, headquarters of the California Air National Guard. There I took on some real war work and found myself in a strange situation. Factory work is stunningly different from working in a studio. Timm made training planes for the Army Air Corps. I was doing war work as a Special Expediter, which grand title required me to go and fetch any parts that were in short supply. War Production put a strain on all businesses and the production lines had to be kept open. If one supplier did not have a part ready on time, another must be located and the item picked up. I did that pickup. A Special Expediter was a kind of gofer. But, as I had to go all over the world's widest city, I got special gas rations for my Packard convertible. To say the most, it was not very demanding work.

I had been at Timm for several months when I got a call from Marti, my ex-girlfriend. I was surprised at the call because of the somewhat traumatic manner of our breakup. I had met Jani, a young contract actress, at Warners. Her family was Christian Scientist. She did not drink. It was a different life from what Marti and I had together and, for various mixed-up reasons, among them several somewhat drunken fights Marti and I had, Jani seemed like a clean start. So I left Marti for Jani. For some reason I seemed to find girls whose names ended in i.

One night, about a month after our breakup, I opened my eyes to stare into the muzzle of the gun I always kept in my bedside table. It was weaving in the hands of Marti, who had been drinking more than usual. "You bastard," she kept muttering, "I ought to kill you."

I was instantly wide awake and talking fast, soothing and reasonable. It developed that Marti had persuaded her date that she needed to visit a friend in the Valley. He assumed it was a girlfriend. Once I talked the gun out of her hands, I put on a robe and went down the tower steps to meet him. He was a tall, thin guy who, realizing what had happened, was very embarrassed and tried to reassure me he had no idea whatsoever that she meant to—

I shook his hand warmly, silencing his protest. "Come in and have a drink." I lead the way into the bar. Marti sat glaring as we talked cheerfully about his work and touched on various innocuous subjects, ignoring what had just happened. I finally walked them to his car, waved in relief as its taillights vanished down the drive.

I later heard that Marti had married a man who worked in radio. When I got the phone call from her, she explained that her husband had, at the start of the war, been appointed program head of the San Francisco Office of War Information. All her hostility seemed to have vanished. There was a place for me in the writing department. I was a naturally a little reluctant but her voice was warm and friendly. She seemed happy with her new life.

The Office of War Information was not quite the Signal Corps and I wouldn't get to wear a uniform but it seemed more useful than being a delivery boy. I left Timm Aircraft.

Then, before I could make arrangements and pack for San Francisco, I got a notice from the Selective Service Board stating that I had left war work and was therefore eligible for the draft. I was given a report date.

I thought about San Francisco and fresh starts. It did not seem right to be a civilian when most of the guys I knew were in uniform. That was a popular war. We had been attacked and American values were at stake. To a generation brought up on the divisiveness of the Vietnam War, that mindset may be difficult to understand. But everybody was for the war of 1941. In one way or another, everyone worked for victory. I called San Francisco and explained what I was doing, then told the draft board I would prefer not to wait. I volunteered to go at once.

When I arrived for the second time, I was looking forward to the service. Perhaps I would get another crack at the Signal Corps. If not, I would do whatever was required.

But when I came before the draft board, they had discovered the screw-up. Paperwork showing that I had been in the service and discharged had been found. I was given an apology, thanked for my patriotic motives and dismissed.

I drove the 500 miles to San Francisco to work for the Office of War Information. My boss, Mort Werner, Marti's husband, and I became best friends. He was later to work with me at our summer theater in Laguna Beach and then go on to become a top executive at NBC.

I loved San Francisco although it was very crowded with war workers and living space was hard to find. I got a room in a home out on the Avenues, a fair drive from 111 Sutter where the fourteenth floor formed our offices.

My bedroom was large and at the front of the house, overlooking a somewhat faceless street. It was near a school but I was never there on school days and therefore was not disturbed by the noise. Next to my room, with a private entrance, was a rather large bathroom with wash basin and shower but no toilet. That facility occupied a tiny room down the hall. It, and my bathroom, were shared by the other three occupants of the second floor. Such arrangements took some adjustment on my part but in wartime San Francisco, I was told I had found a real gold mine.

I was in a fascinating city and on my own. I found the Crocker Bank, a magnificent structure on Market Street with a marble entrance and imposing pillars and gold letters and screens before the tellers' windows. It breathed money and was near the office. I could hardly believe that I was allowed to open an account and deposit my meager pay from the O.W.I. here weekly. It must be admitted that I also received an allowance from home but I felt as though I was taking my first solo steps.

The Office of War Information, at least our part of it, was not as glamorous as it had sounded. I sat in a cubbyhole with a typewriter and stacks of United Press and Associated Press articles as well as whatever items the military services disseminated. From these, I (and others with slightly different targets) were supposed to create exciting and informative radio shows beamed across the Pacific to convince native peoples that we were coming to their rescue and beating back the bestial Japs. It sounded like good and useful work but I finally came to the realization that I was creating shows for a Pacific island native sitting under a palm tree without a radio. It was pointless work.

On the positive side, it brought research fully into my life. It was not just words I was hired for. This was the golden age of radio and music accompanied the programs, reinforcing the message. We had an incredible library of LP records, classical, blues and Broadway. I spent a good deal of time selecting the proper music and making up for the time I had lost when the piano lessons Mother had mandated for me at military school ended.

My inability to play did not affect my love of music, however. In my pre-teens, we had a player piano. Popular songs had the lyrics printed on the music rolls. I would sit by the hour with the mechanism exposed, watching the tiny square holes rush by and singing the songs, which were printed on the side of the unscrolling sheet. When we got the music roll for Gershwin's *Rhapsody in Blue*, I played it until Mother finally forbade me to run the piano when she was in the house.

At the Office of War Information I was able to hear music from all the new Broadway shows on the recently released LP albums and integrate the music into the programs we broadcast.

Mort played piano by ear and was very good. He could instantly play any song he heard. I later realized that this was not amazing among musicians but, at the time, I was suitably impressed.

I loved the time in San Francisco. Mort's wife was doing a radio show he had created for her: *G.I. Jill.* Jill was a sort of girl-next-door answer to Tokyo Rose, who so enraged the military brass because, broadcasting from Japan, she injected enemy propaganda along with the music. Most of all, they hated her surprisingly accurate information of our troop movements and strengths. Despite the enemy source, the G.I.s loved the music Tokyo Rose played. G.I. Jill was the answer. The show got a lot of fan mail from troops posted all over the Pacific. Some of Marti's broadcasts were done from military camps. When she was away, Mort and I would go to three different movies on a Sunday and drink rum with a constantly changing array of mixers.

I also managed to form a relationship with Mort's secretary, who lived on Telegraph Hill. Her name was Fran. I had broken the ending-in-i pattern. Fran was a wonderful girl. We saw a lot of San Francisco.

We went out often with Marti and Mort. Marti seemed to bear me no grudge and Mort had no undemocratic objection to mixing socially with his secretary.

There was an Italian restaurant on Kerney Street where we ate often. It served a four-course dinner, salad, pasta, main course and dessert, along with a carafe of wine, for $1.25. Wonderful food. A year into the war, they had to post a notice.

> The management regrets that, due to wartime shortages and the rising cost of available food, we are forced to raise the price of our dinner to $1.45.

San Francisco was fun. But, increasingly, the work I was doing seemed to me useless—perhaps even more so than Timm Aircraft. At least Timm was making something that could fly. Where my radio programs went, no one would ever know.

The really bad case of flu I caught gave me the excuse to resign for health reasons. I was sorry to leave Fran and I knew I would also miss Mort and Marti but I had a feeling for the first time in my life that I should take some personal initiative and decide what I was going to do with that life.

Back from the O.W.I., I got over the flu and then concentrated on what I really wanted to do. I knew I did not want Mike to get me work again. He had enough problems now trying to arrange jobs for his two brothers, whose visas were expected to come through any day. He also had some very important pictures coming up, *Captains of the Clouds*, with Jimmy Cagney and *Yankee Doodle Dandy*, also with Cagney, but he continued to behave in his customary unpredictable manner. At dinner one night he bit down on something and groaned. His tooth hurt, obviously a lot.

"You'd better see the dentist in the morning," Mother told him.

That thought shocked him. "I prepare my next picture. I have all day to talk on casting. Script is not right. I have terrible tough job. I wait until—"

Mother let him run through his list of reasons as to why it was impossible to go to the dentist. "On the forenoon, I sit with the writers. After, I have casting. On the afternoon, I have meeting with J.L. because the budget don't—"

Mother had heard enough. She called Dr. Gogerty, our family dentist, at home and got him to agree to stay late at the office to take care of Mike the next afternoon.

9—In the Wings

James Cagney and Mike chat between takes on the set of *Yankee Doodle Dandy* (1942).

"You go after your meeting with Warner," Mother said. "Gogerty can see you as late as six. If you can get away earlier, he'll fit you in somehow."

"Thanks him his kindness," Mike said gratefully. "Last night I doesn't sleep."

At five o'clock next afternoon, Mother called Mike's office to remind him of the appointment. The assistant director told her he was in Warner's office.

Mother got Warner's secretary and asked if she had any idea how long the meeting would last. She was told they were discussing casting and had been at it for over two hours. "It can't be much longer. I'll be happy to interrupt."

"No," Mother told her. "But, if it goes beyond another half-hour, remind him he has a dentist appointment."

Three-quarters of an hour later, Mike walked in the house. It was a half-hour drive from the studio.

James Cagney and Michael Curtiz rehearse a song for *Captains of the Clouds* (1942).

"Where have you been?" Mother asked. "I called the studio to—"
Mike stiffened. "Why you spy on me?"
"I'm not spying. You had a dental appointment at six and—"
Mike grabbed his jaw. "Yeah," he groaned. "That goddamn Gogerty, he hurt like hell. Next time I go on other dentist."
"You never went near Gogerty," Mother told him. "You were in J.L.'s office until well after five and Gogerty is probably still waiting at his office. You don't have to put on an act for me."
Mike drew himself up indignantly. "A good wife, " he said, "would told to me right away. I know you wasn't on Gogerty." He stalked off to his room. Mother patiently called the dentist and apologized. Mike bore the pain two more days, then Gogerty drilled and filled the tooth.

I had, in the past, thought about an acting career but now I gave it serious consideration. I talked it over with Mike and Mother, then enrolled in the Pasadena Playhouse School of the Theater.

The Playhouse had an excellent drama school and had turned out a good number of successful actors and directors. I found myself very excited by the project.

But, once enrolled, my usual study habits came to the fore. The course involved much classroom work, Theatrical History, Costume Design, Set Design, Set Building, Makeup, etc. I was interested in the history of the theater and we studied it from its Greek roots to the present. There were speech classes and poetry. The actual acting I liked, though not as much as I'd thought. I even enjoyed the fencing lessons although any type of exercise was foreign to me and it was a very long drive from Canoga Park in the San Fernando Valley to Pasadena. Those were the days before freeways. Fencing class started at eight and was followed by showers, then off to the classrooms. Later in the year there were scenes we had to prepare and perform. There were two smaller theaters but we all dreamed of playing on Main Stage. At midterm, with the entire academic staff assembled, we were each required to do one scene on Main Stage. My effort was a scene from Marlow's *Tragical History of Doctor Faustus*. I did Faust's final speech before Mephistopheles drags him down to Hell. I got words of approval from my instructors on my handling of Kit Marlow's speeches and, more important, a good review when I performed it at home for Mother.

But homework was required and that suffered. Mostly because of my natural dislike of homework but also because I met Marjori Hunt (another -i.) She was from Arkansas. She had graduated from law school but had never practiced. She decided instead that she wanted to act. I am ashamed of the Shakespearean banality but I called her Portia from our first meeting. Portia went on, during our long relationship, to join a large advertising agency, McCann and Erickson—the agencies controlled radio in those pre–TV days. The networks bowed to them because they controlled the advertisers. Portia started as a secretary, progressed to assistant producer on *The Eddie Cantor Hour*, then, solo, as producer of *The Dinah Shore Show*.

Portia was older and in her second year at the Playhouse. She also, having passed Law, was obviously an excellent student, graduating at the top of her class. At the conclusion of my first year, I was stopped by my favorite teacher, in whose class I did well. She was a Southern lady with the unforgettable name of Fairfax Proudfit Walkup. We used her book as our class text in costume design but she taught far more of theater than mere costume design. Reluctantly she told me that because of my other grades, I would not be asked back for the second year.

I was shocked. In military school I had gotten by and passed from grade to grade. I realize that was chiefly due to the Depression and the need for student income. But even at Beverly High I had squeaked through. This was my first positive rebuff. It bothered me.

On my last day in acting class, my teacher, Tom Brown, who was also a professional working actor, said, "Lucas, why don't you shit or get off the pot?"

It was not a matter of choice. I had been pushed off. Some years later, when I was directing *Ben Casey*, I used Tom as an actor. I reminded him of that incident and thanked him for the shock he gave me.

In 1942 Mike was shooting *Captains of the Clouds* with Jimmy Cagney, much of it on location in Canada with the Royal Canadian Air Force and, of course, *Casablanca* with Bergman and Bogart. Mother, as always, worked with him on his scripts from her bed. Her participation was unofficial but it was fairly common knowledge. *Casablanca* had a lot of rewriting done while the picture was actually shooting and at one conference with the writers, the Epstein brothers, Mike announced that he was dissatisfied with a particular scene. When Julius Epstein pressed for the reason for his displeasure, he frowned. "Goddamn," he said. "I don't remember what hell Bess tell me." I regret that I was not in town for the shooting nor for the award ceremony when he got the *Casablanca* Oscar from Jack Benny, who was hosting.

Although *Casablanca* is probably his most memorable legacy—it plays all the time and has lost none of its original punch—*Yankee Doodle Dandy* plays on television every Fourth of July and *White Christmas* every Yuletide.

Mike's problem was that he was too good at his trade. He would direct any script the studio forced on him. Among actors there are real professionals whom you might not recognize from picture to picture, so well do they throw themselves into their roles. Then there are *stars*—not necessarily good actors but with a special personality that holds an audience. Examples of star directors are Hitchcock, Capra and Ford. They were also excellent directors but they put their individual stamp on every picture. Stars, instead of being given roles, had roles contrived for them. Mike could do—and did—too many things too well. A great director can make a bad story better but never make it great.

I was home again after my time at the Playhouse and as aimless as ever except that I was writing volumes of unpublished poetry. Gene Fowler told me he also wrote a good deal of poetry. "Nobody makes a living as a poet," he said, "but it's satisfying, like a good bowel movement."

The war had gotten Mother out of bed. She was very involved in a group called Bundles for Britain. Virginia Zanuck, most of the English stars and many of their friends, most of the movie wives, got together and

Humphrey Bogart, Ingrid Bergman and Mike on the set of *Casablanca* (1942).

knit sweaters and did other such work to advance the cause of freedom in the world. This was indeed a popular war.

The government unleashed a massive campaign to promote victory gardens. People turned their suburban lawns into gardens. It did more to promote war unity than provide nutrition.

Mother had a plot of land on the ranch fenced off and she, herself, worked the soil, planted vegetables, watered, cultivated and would not allow the ranch hands to help. She was very proud of her work. But the enemy, it turned out, was not from abroad. The enemy within struck in the night, destroying her work. Rabbits found the vegetables a gift from Heaven, thanked the rabbit god and made vast inroads in the garden.

Mother had no idea what to do. Even fine-mesh wire fencing failed to keep them out. Finally, Mike took the matter into his own hands. "I will fix," he announced. Choosing one of the innumerable shotguns we used for skeet shooting, he went down one night and waited silently for half an hour. A rabbit came up to the fence and, with a few moments' digging, wiggled under and began the feast. Mike snapped the gun to his

Outside the Warner Bros. commissary, Mike is photographed after a lunch with Ingrid Bergman (1942).

shoulder and fired. It caught the rabbit in the rear leg, not killing it. Mike looked up, pleased with the shot at a considerable distance. The rabbit whimpered and dragged itself pathetically toward the hole it had made under the fence. Mike watched, horror-stricken. Then, calling for help, he carefully captured the wounded rabbit. We had a veterinarian we used for all our dogs. Mike had Mother get the vet out of bed and took the rabbit to the animal hospital. The rabbit made a slow but satisfactory recovery and was ultimately turned loose on the ranch again. "Why hell we need garden?" Mike asked Mother. "We doesn't eat so much vegetable." Henceforth we bought our greens at the market. Mike had always loved rabbit cooked the French provincial way but, as far as I know, he never again ordered this dish.

Then I got my big chance. Mike was to shoot *Mission to Moscow*, from a book by Joseph Davies, the ex-ambassador to Russia. At a time when the average American was used to thinking of Russians as dirty Communists, Davies' book granted Stalin something approaching sainthood. But since the Russians were now fighting Hitler, our common enemy, it was necessary to change the image of Communists as people who would gladly slit the throat of any decent American. The public and Congress had to be brought around to grant them war supplies to fight the Germans. Jack Warner allegedly had lunch at the White House where President Roosevelt requested that a picture be made of the book. It was needed as an aid to American acceptance of Russia as an ally in the war against Hitler.

When the picture went into production, Mike offered me the position of dialogue director, a giant step up from Bs to an A picture. I have no idea what strings he pulled. He had shot a few unimportant scenes, mostly action. I was thrilled and accepted despite my resolve to get no more work from Mike. I promised myself I would do no rewriting. At any rate, this was not a B picture and the quality of the script was infinitely better than I was used to dealing with. However, my tenure ran out after only one day. Having just been appointed, I had not read the script and, after looking at the previous day's rushes, I questioned an actor's pronunciation of Ambassador Davies' name. The actor was correct within the context of his part but I had posed the question in front of the producer. It was a stupid mistake on my part. I should have known the answer before I asked the question. Or I should have spoken to Mike in private. I cannot explain or excuse what I did and, to this day, cannot understand it. I can only conclude that I was trying to show off my brilliance in catching a mistake that no one else noticed. The producer had heard just what he wanted to hear. He was already annoyed that he had not gotten his own choice as dialogue director. The discussion escalated. Realizing my mistake, instead of admitting it, I continued to behave stupidly and was a little arrogant. The whole incident was unimportant and unnecessary but, as it took place before an audience, Mike could hardly protect me. I was off his picture and back on Bs, trying to forget the humiliation of my demotion. I had to constantly restrain myself from rewriting scenes as I once had but it was pleasant work. If I missed a great opportunity, I also missed the condemnation that followed from those who felt the picture was Communist propaganda. It was indeed, a whitewash of the Russian treason trials during the '30s. Ambassador Davies' book justified Stalin's ploy for getting rid of political enemies. There had been a Nazi-Russian pact, which was shattered by Hitler's invasion of Russia. It was now necessary for us to supply military arms and supplies to the Communists for our own sake. If the Russian forces had not held at Stalingrad, many German armies would have been released to the West and probably made the Allied invasion of Europe and the ultimate destruction of Germany impossible. But the movie received a great deal of flak after the war, climaxing in the McCarthy era. No arrows were hurled at Mike but Howard Koch, one of the picture's writers, was given a very bad time by the ambitious and probably insane senator. Jack Warner received death threats. Still I consider my stupidity at losing that job prime among the many dumb things I have done.

Mike had other relatives to help. By now the visas of the "boys" had finally been arranged and they came up from Mexico. Desider, now David, was put to work at Warners as an assistant cutter and Gabor, under the name of Gabriel, went to Fox as a second assistant. The boys and Mama came to the ranch every Sunday. Mother also had her family, Auntie Vi and Uncle Bill, Uncle Will, my cousin Sandy and Grandmother Julia. Aunt Florence had died by then.

These reunions usually took the form of a huge barbecue on a flagstone area below the house in the orange groves. There a great stone barbecue had been constructed beneath the shade of four 200-year-old oak trees. "Mama," Mike's mother, walked heavily with a cane. She was 78 and spoke no English. Julia, who was now 86, felt sorry for the "poor old woman" and always helped her down the walk.

A friend from military school, Rogers Brackett, had gotten a job as agency producer on a very popular radio show, *Vox Pop*. It did interviews of famous people and interviewed their friends, a sort of precursor of *This Is Your Life*, which Ralph Williams did for so many years on television. They did a show on Mike and had interviews with Mother and various people who had worked with Mike, including Joan Crawford, my first love, whose failed career Mike resurrected and got her an Oscar for *Mildred Pierce*.

Her career virtually over, Joan fought hard to get the part. She had become a caricature of herself—her clothes, a style designed for her by Adrian in the early '30s, were made with the wide shoulders suitable for a football player. They matched the wide, over-rouged lips. Mike had a long talk with her, letting her know that she would not play the "star" as she had when she was at the top of her fame at Metro. This was a different role, one that would require simplicity and a real performance. She was grateful and agreed to anything he wanted. On the first day of shooting, however, she appeared on the set with her makeup man and the mile-wide lips that had been her signature. Mike took one look, grabbed a box of Kleenex and wiped her face. Joan ran to her dressing room in tears. Mike ordered the makeup man to return her with the face of a woman who works for a living. It paid off. She was stunned and delighted when she was nominated for an Oscar but too frightened of not winning to attend the ceremonies. She sent word that she had a severe cold. Mike

Mike directs a scene with Joan Crawford and Jack Carson in *Mildred Pierce* (1945).

accepted the award for her and delivered the Oscar to her "sickbed" with the photographers snapping away.

As a present from *Vox Pop*, Mike was given a letter from George Washington to one of his generals. Nothing could have delighted Mike more. So great was his patriotism for his adopted country that he would have done an entire picture for that.

Although *Vox Pop* traveled a great deal, New York was its headquarters. Rogers invited me back. I had never been in New York and when I found that Mike was going there with Henry Blanke, to see some shows and look at actors, I leaped at his offer to go with him.

Heinz Blanke, born in Germany, was something of an enigma. A friend to Mike and Hal, a longtime employee of Warners, he had come to this country as assistant director to Ernst Lubitsch. When Lubitsch moved on to other studios, Blanke remained at Warners, working constantly with Jews. He expressed total loyalty to America during the war but snide remarks were often heard of his German sympathies—mainly because of his wife, Ursula. Her father was a Wehrmacht general. During

Following her Oscar win, Joan Crawford and Mike worked together again in *Flamingo Road* (1949).

the time when the Nazi armies were taking over all of Europe, Heinz did have a tendency to discuss the war news with us and, eyes glittering excitedly above a sad expression, would say, "Isn't it terrible what those Germans are doing?"

In those days, airlines were not the accepted manner of travel. Airplanes were not completely trusted. We went east in the luxurious, accepted way—by train. We took the Super Chief from L.A. to Chicago, then transferred to the Twentieth Century Limited. The trip took three days.

Aboard the same train and with the same destination was Alex Korda. Korda had been urging Mike to come to England with him, making him fabulous offers and expounding the wonders of English life. Each evening we three would have dinner served in Mike's drawing room. Korda would go on about the great opportunities and freedom for a director working in England, would denigrate the harsh commercialism of Hollywood and the uncouth American audience.

Mike would defend his adopted country. "I stay on my home," he declared. "I am American." He shook his head sadly. "How hell you stand on it?" he asked. "The English is terrible phony."

When I broke into uncontrollable laughter, both looked at me, amazed. It took me a while to explain the humor of two Hungarians patriotically refighting the American Revolution.

We had a large suite at the Sherry Netherlands with multiple bedrooms. Mike and Blanke were off at readings and casting offices during the day, theaters at night. I watched Rogers do a couple of *Vox Pop* shows and did some theater going of my own. I also called Marlon Brando's sister, Fran. I had known her briefly in Los Angeles during my photographic period and had many pictures of her. My favorite and, ego aside, I think an excellent picture, was Fran beneath a portrait of her mother, Dodie. I shot her in a pose identical to that of her mother in the painting. Fran had married and introduced me to her husband. I told them I was to meet Mike and Blanke at the hotel but they insisted in taking me to an early dinner at a small French restaurant on Tenth Avenue. The food was wonderful but drenched in garlic. I rushed back to the hotel, changed and hurried to the dining room to find that Blanke had provided escorts for us. Mine was gorgeous and obviously willing to be very friendly but I was walking in a cloud of garlic. I tried not to breathe as I made polite conversation. After the dinner I'd had, I could not eat but played with a salad, hoping the greens would combat the garlic. She wanted to dance. I told her I did not know how. "Everyone can dance," she insisted. So I was forced to rise, take her hand to the dance floor and demonstrate my inability. To lessen the impact of the garlic, I kept holding my head well back from my partner. Anyone seeing us would think I had something seriously wrong with my neck. When we got back to the table, I excused myself on some pretext. I imagine she was not sad to see me go.

In the morning I was awakened by a white-faced and obviously frightened Blanke. "Come quickly!" He gasped. "Mike. I think he's dead." I followed him into Mike's bathroom. Mike lay slumped on the floor, water pelting down on him.

I shook my head, walked to the shower enclosure, rapped sharply on the glass. Mike's eyes opened. He looked at me and at Blanke's white face. "What's happen?" he asked.

I explained that Blanke was concerned, thinking something was seriously wrong with him.

"You crazy," Mike said. "I come out."

We retired and I explained to Heinz that Mike did this all the time. He would finish his shower, then turn on the cold water and nap for a few minutes. At home, he would fall asleep sitting on the drain and cause the shower to overflow. The library ceiling had had to be refinished several times until Mother had a small wooden stool made for him with perforations so that the water could get past him.

"He sleeps in cold water?" Blanke shook his head. "They're right. He is crazy."

The newly created United Nations, dream of Roosevelt carried forward by his successor, Truman, was holding its first plenary session in San Francisco. Rogers Brackett was covering the event with *Vox Pop*, interviewing many of the foreign dignitaries. He offered to get me into the San Francisco Opera House where the session was held. I loved the town and was tremendously impressed by the proceedings.

I saw this new aggregate of nations as the start of a form of universal government. To me it was a giant step toward Utopia.

It was thought that the planners had corrected the faults of the old League of Nations, dream of the then-president, Woodrow Wilson. The League's main problem had been its rejection by the American Congress, many of whom were anti–Wilson and, after the strain of war, anti– any more foreign involvement. While still in its infancy, the League went down the tube when Mussolini invaded Ethiopia and no one lifted a hand.

The sight of the Opera House packed with hundreds of delegates from around the world was an impressive and unforgettable scene.

Vox Pop wanted to interview Jan Masaryk, the foreign minister of the Czechoslovak Republic, who, with Benes, had led the exiled Czech government in wartime London and had now reclaimed his country. Amid all the dignitaries, the pomp and speeches, my clearest memory of the entire proceeding was the breakfast we had with Masaryk in the Fairmont Hotel on Nob Hill. A chill wind blew off the bay through a window and onto the foreign minister's back. He was wearing only a thin shirt. I asked if he would like the window closed and he replied, "I am a farm boy. Cold does not bother me." He returned to his country and in 1948 was murdered by being thrown out a window in the Foreign Ministry.

But the inauguration of the United Nations was an exciting and hopeful time. The U.N. has not always lived up to those hopes but, well over half a century later, it is still here.

At any rate, those few days in San Francisco were exciting and wonderful—the beginning of a new world. Then I went back to my world of make-believe at Warner Brothers.

While working on the lot, I visited Mike's set a number of times when he was directing *This Is the Army*. Irving Berlin's fund-raising musical still had all its military cast, which had toured the world for Army Relief. Mike added to them the greatest array of stars ever assembled. Even Lt.

Ronald Reagan was ordered back from Fort Roach—the name its unsoldierly movie inmates called the old Hal Roach Studio in Culver City near Metro. Many army training films were made there.

Some of the soldiers who had toured the world with the stage version of *This Is the Army* were New York chorus boys, highly unlikely soldiers for this period, almost 50 years before the "Don't ask, don't tell" rule. Some were very special friends of the biggest names in the theater, certainly not your average G.I.s. They were under military command for the tour and remained so during the shooting of the picture. *This Is the Army* was, all considered, not bad war duty. Mike's picture made $11,000,000 for the Fund, probably more than the entire world tour of the stage version had made.

In 1945 I was visited by another old military school friend, Walter Rathbun. The war had just ended and Walter (who was always called Bunny) had been discharged as a lieutenant in the Special Service Corps. It had been his job in the Army to provide and coordinate entertainment for the troops. He would essentially see that performers were happy and received all the comfort that the Army could provide in their limited circumstances. He, too, was now looking for something to do. He had attended Yale with, I must presume, rather more attention to education than I had managed and had seen summer stock on the East Coast. He suggested that we open a summer stock season in Laguna Beach.

Beside the childhood time spent there, I had also, from time to time, visited another school friend who lived in Laguna, Dean Riesner. Riesner, D., as he was known at Urban Military Academy, had been my first roommate in first grade. I was Lucas, J. Such was the military formality observed by kids six years old.

Dean's father, Chuck Riesner, a director, and Mother had worked together at MGM. As a baby, Dean, under the name of Dinky Dean, had briefly been a child star with Charlie Chaplin. He later went on to a long and successful career as a writer, doing, among other things, many of the Clint Eastwood pictures, starting with *Play Misty for Me*.

I do not remember much about Urban, the military school where we attended first grade together, except that it was in Hollywood and many of the children of movie people—including a much older classmate, Jackie Coogan—were there. The school was jointly owned by Major Black and Earl Fox. Earl Fox was a movie star whose son attended the school. At football games, the Earl Fox auto was the talk of any playing field. It was a Stutz touring car completely covered in pigskin, inside and out.

Bunny Rathbun reminded me that there was a Community Playhouse in Laguna Beach. I had, over the years, seen several of the amateur plays there. Dean had acted in some. It seemed like a good idea. We negotiated with the board of the playhouse and they agreed to rent it to us.

Neither Walter nor I knew much about putting together a company of actors and the logistics of a theatrical season. At the Pasadena Playhouse, my concentration—the part that did not include Portia—had been on the interior aspects of acting, the techniques, the use of costume and sets—not the harsh financial part of theatrical production. We got the needed money together. Bunny's family was rich. I chose to use what I regarded as my own money, a life insurance policy taken out for me by Mother. I asked if she would mind if I cashed that in. The policy was for $10,000, a fair amount of money then.

She sent me to a friend of hers, a man on the boards of various important corporations, to discuss the project with me to see if it had any financial value. During her early acquaintances with Mike, before their marriage, she had been seeing this man. He was married, wanted to divorce his wife and marry Mother. She would not hear of it.

One night, when Mike finished shooting several hours earlier than anticipated and drove his Packard in second gear up to the house, Mother had to ask her friend to go over the second story balcony as Mike was admitted by the front door. Fortunately I did not know the story then as I faced this imposing man behind his desk at a large financial institution. He asked me innumerable technical questions about anticipated audience attendance, number of seats in the Playhouse, proposed price of tickets, etc., none of which I was prepared to answer. But I made it quite clear that I wanted to do it.

"And what about your life insurance?" he asked. "When you get to be 50, you're going to wish you had this all paid up and—"

"Fifty!" I shook my head at this ridiculous idea. "Who'll ever get to be 50?" My tone indicated he spoke of the age of Methuselah.

His face reddened. "I'm over 50," he said snappishly. The interview ended quickly but I got my money.

Bunny now brought in a third partner, Richard Irving, who had no money to add but had experience. He had been in *This Is the Army*. Dick was one of the Army cast who was not gay. I had probably seen him among the large number of soldiers on Mike's set but we had never met. He did seem able to answer many of the questions I had been unable to respond to when I was getting my life insurance money and we started to organize.

I went to Johnny Mascio, a talent agent who worked out of a house on Camden drive just below Santa Monica Boulevard. In 1946, Beverly Hills was not the sleek fashion center it is now. There was a garage in back of the remodeled house that was Johnny's office. He agreed to rent us for almost nothing. We got wallboard, tacked it up, painted it with Kem-tone, a water-based paint, took carpets and the necessary furniture from our family storehouse at the ranch. The whole procedure sounds like a Mickey Rooney–Judy Garland film. "We can use Grandpa's barn. Let's put on a play."

We had a sign made, Gryphon Productions, and were in business. I had fallen in love with the name and I wanted to use a gryphon on a heraldic shield as our logo but I needed a picture of a gryphon to copy. Dick Irving and I went to the public library and found a picture in a Heraldry book. I got out my pen to trace it but, before I could protest, Dick solved the matter in a faster way—I thought of it as a New York way. He simply tore out the page and stuffed it into his pocket.

We announced in the trades—*Hollywood Reporter* and *Variety*—that we were casting for a resident company and hundreds of eager actors came for the auditions. It was terrible for me to see how anxious they were for a job that would involve a good deal of hard work for nearly no money and less than ideal living conditions. All my life I have hated casting sessions because of that look, the pleading eyes of actors hungry for a part. We finally settled on our resident company and the plays we wanted to do. Maggie Ettinger, Mother's friend and co-beachhouse mate with Louella Parsons in my early childhood, agreed to handle the publicity.

I started calling stars. In the process, I antagonized many agents who were not eager to have their clients work in Laguna for Equity minimum, a wage that was almost nothing and from which the agents made no profit. The proper protocol was to call the agent and let him submit the proposal. I always told them that I didn't know the rules. Had I followed their rules, we would have had no stars.

Then I sat down and wrote a play. It was probably influenced by Tennessee Williams' work but with some original additions. I used a platform stage with many playing areas, no sets. In an adaptation of motion picture technique, actors moved from place to place by going to a different stage area and into other sets of lights. It had a fluid movement that I thought was revolutionary. Also, I understood motion picture technique better than stage.

Portia, who had gone through the birth pangs of the play, elected to leave her important job as producer of Dinah Shore's radio show to go to Laguna with me. This was wonderful for me, lousy for her career.

We rented three houses to contain our resident company and the apprentices. Following the practice of Eastern Summer Stock, we charged the apprentices a nominal sum for the experience. They watched, played occasional small parts, built sets and did a lot of the grunt work. It worked reasonably well except for occasional grumbling that they were not getting any decent parts.

Stars were always dicey. It was difficult for anyone to commit two weeks of time—one of rehearsal, one of playing—a commitment that might possibly block out a high-paying film job. Switches often had to be made.

Housing for the stars was even more difficult. The hotel accommodations were not attractive. We searched, asked around and finally found guest houses. The most elaborate one was in the home of Mary Miles Minter's mother. Mary Miles Minter had been a star in the early days of film and was involved in the shooting of William Desmond Taylor, her director. It provided the first and juiciest gossip of the infant industry. Some speculated that the mother did it to protect her daughter against the wiles of the older man, some that Mary, herself, had shot him out of jealousy. He was also said to be involved with Mabel Normand. It was a sensational murder case, one of Hollywood's first great scandals. At any rate, Mrs. Minter had a lovely house in the hills of Laguna and I housed the stars in that location which I named Mary Miles Minter's Mother's Magnificent Mountain Mansion.

10

Takeoffs and Landings

To design and supervise the sets, I got my former instructor from the Pasadena Playhouse, Rita Glover. Like everybody else, Rita received very little pay but she was used to working with students and handled the apprentices well. She came up, at minimal expense, with some very good sets. The one thing she asked was that I take her flying. She had never flown and wanted very much to see what the world looked like straight down.

I had learned to fly as soon as the war was over, when my small plane would not be mistaken for the vanguard of a Japanese attack. I had always been interested in flying—possibly inspired by my memories of Ronald Raven, the war ace. Also, the time spent as an Aircraft Ground Observer listening for planes in the cold Valley nights urged me to be up there, fighting off the sneaky Japs instead of shivering by the phone in my Arctic gear, waiting to report an enemy attack and heroically save our country.

At any rate, to thank Rita for the wonderful work that she was doing with the sets, I took her flying. She loved it, looking down on the mountains and coastline, the white lines of froth washing the beaches. She talked about it constantly and asked to repeat it, perhaps even take flying lessons.

The next week I was flying back from San Diego. I banked to look at something in the cliffs north of Del Mar and the rudder locked, locked solid. Nothing I could do would shake it free. I was at 4,000 feet when I banked and so was locked in a downward spiral, losing altitude rapidly. Any attempt to level the wings resulted in a stall. I fought down panic and debated about killing the engine to avoid fire when I hit but decided the engine was my only control. Fortunately I was over the coastline and could use my remaining altitude to ease out over the water, which looked softer than the rugged cliffs on shore. It occurred to me that this was it. I was going to be killed. They say your whole life passes before you at such a moment. Mine didn't. I remember thinking I was glad I didn't have Rita with me that day. Then I remember saying, "Oh, God, let me live through this and I promise I'll..."—I checked myself. I'd dealt with superstition years ago. I was enlightened. I didn't believe in anything supernatural and I wasn't going to let cowardice start me praying now. I forced myself to pull my seat belt nearly through my spine and opened both doors so they wouldn't jam shut when I hit. Then, at the last minute before impact, I gunned the engine, pulling the wings level and letting the plane stall in. The small aircraft I was flying had fixed landing gear and, as the wheels dug into the water, they flipped the plane violently on its nose. The cockpit was flooded up to my neck before I could get free of my seat belt and swim out through the door I had left open.

I made it in through the heavy surf to the shore. As I hit the beach, an advertising plane, hauling a banner, called through its loudspeaker to the trailer park on the top of the cliff, "Ship down to the south of you."

That seemed like a hell of an entrance cue so I climbed up the cliff. A woman in the trailer park had seen the crash and gave me an old pair of her husband's pants in place of my soaked clothes. She also let me use her phone. I called the theater and Portia drove down to pick me up. The plane was a total loss. Although it was recovered and winched ashore that same day, saltwater corrosion is very swift.

Mother and Mike had rented a house in Three Arch Bay, close to Laguna to attend the opening night. I thought I had better announce my survival before Mother heard of the crash. I spruced myself up and thought I looked fairly normal but when I walked through the door, Mother took one look at me and said, "What happened?" I assured her it was nothing.

"You've had an accident," she said. I admitted it and assured her I was fine and went back to the theater.

I must confess that I warmed myself in the fuss and concern of our stock company over my deliverance. I myself was not much concerned about it. Flying, I told them, involves a certain risk. Anyone not prepared to take that risk should not be flying. It had happened. It was over. We had a show that night.

It was a week before I took up a plane again. Just after liftoff, I began to shake. I looked in disbelief at my feet on the rudder pedals. They were vibrating out of control. I was dizzy and started to sweat. My vision blurred. "Oh, God," I thought, "if I can just get this thing on the ground,

I swear I'll never fly again." This time I did not check myself. That thought calmed me a little. Still shaking, I flew the pattern and prepared to land. As I turned on final approach, I realized I had meant exactly what I had said. If I stopped now, I would never have the guts to fly again. Fighting all my instincts, I made it a touch-and-go landing. Shoving the throttle home, I went around again. I made three more circuits. By then I was under control. I landed, shut off the engine and sat quietly in the plane, stunned to realize how much the crash had really affected me. Ronald Raven, my war ace, would never have had nerves like that. But, then, I never got his name so I never got the game.

The Federal Aviation Authority requires that a report be filed on all accidents. I prepared and sent off a brief description of the event and my guess as to the cause. That model of Aronca had a chain on the steerable tail wheel, which connects with the rudder for ground taxiing. It resembled an old-fashioned bathtub chain. It was that chain that had jammed. I have since talked to several people who had similar experiences and were able to finally kick it loose. My chain was sturdier.

Many years later when my first wife, Joan, and I were cleaning out some files, I found a copy of the report I had sent in to the FAA and was startled to discover that we had been married five years after the accident, to the exact day, the exact hour.

In 1946, before our first season at the playhouse, we held readings to form a permanent company of actors. I was surprised when Joan's agent brought her in. I hadn't seen her in the war years and my time at the O.W.I. She read very well but we didn't pick her as we weren't sure she had the range needed for all the different roles required in a stock company, with a different show each week. We had not had an intimate relationship at Warners because I was with Portia then. It was two years after the reading that I met Joan again. We started seeing each other and, after a long relationship, finally got married.

The first show for the 1946 Gryphon season was *Angel Street* with John Emery and Tamara Gave.

The opening night, thanks in great part to Maggie Ettinger, the audience was packed with Hollywood stars, some of whom did shows for us later. Keenan Wynn, Ruth Hussey, Constance Bennett, Claire Trevor, Lon Chaney, Jr., and Dane Clark.

All our stars were wonderful to the crew and interns but Connie Bennett insisted on something that worried me a good deal. I was not, however, about to lose her over the problem. She had a miniature white French poodle which, she assured me, would stay in her dressing room during performances. Ours was a very small theater and even the star dressing rooms were small. The door of the dressing room was left open while she was on stage. The miracle was that the dog never came out during the play. But, when the final curtain fell, she came out and waited in the wings while her mistress took curtain calls. She seemed to sense when the last bow was taken and the curtain was down to stay. Then she would streak across the stage and jump into Connie's arms. I could never figure out how the dog knew. But now, in the fullness of years, I have three miniature poodles, black, and they are fantastic. They are the only animals that do not bother my allergies. They manage to outsmart us in most things but I have never tried them out on stage.

We had the usual frantic and unexpected crises. On one show, which had a lot of music to cover scene changes. I came back from dinner a half-hour before curtain time to be met with the news that the sound system had gone out. The sound booth was upstairs, at the rear of the theater. No one knew what the matter was but it would need repair for which we had no time. The audience was just beginning to drift in. I told them to hold the curtain, rushed back to my house and got my portable phonograph with the 78 records that were popular at the time. The audience was getting restive. The curtain was already ten minutes late. I rushed backstage, hauled the player up the stairs to the upper dressing rooms. Aiming the speaker down at the audience, I ordered the curtain raised. With a good deal of sweat and anxiety, I worked with the records by the flashlight one of our interns held. Lacking the facilities of the sound booth with its properly cued records, I tried to get something resembling what we had rehearsed. Somehow we got through the performance and the audience didn't notice anything wrong—or were too polite to say so.

We used various directors at Laguna, including one of my instructors from the Pasadena Playhouse. We were getting a good deal of publicity. In mid-season I got a call from Mel Ferrer asking if we had any free week and would we be interesting in letting him do one show. He was working for the Selznick Company and wanted to do *Dear Ruth* with Ruth Roman, Guy Madison and a complete Selznick cast. Ruth and Guy were budding stars then and Selznick would pay the full cast and their expenses. It would cost us nothing and give us a free week. We could use a breather and agreed. Two days before their opening, Mel told me he wanted to replace Ruth Roman. It was completely his show and casting was none of my business as long as he could get the piece together in time. He brought down Natalie Schafer to play the lead. It meant frantic rehearsal for them but they made it. On their opening night, Maggie Ettinger was having a cocktail party and then taking clients to see the show. She was doing our publicity and was a dear friend so I went to her house for a quick drink. As I was about to leave for the theater, we heard the squeal of brakes and Bill Walsh ran in. He looked exhausted and badly in need of a shave. Bill worked in Maggie's office and had been in Chicago. He had driven all the way to the Coast with only a few hours' sleep to make it in time for Ruth Roman's opening. They had been going together and he promised to make it back in time for her show. I had to take him aside and tell him that Mel had replaced her. Understandably he took it very hard and we did not have many friendly conversations until years later when we both worked for Walt Disney. Bill was a producer there and, among other things, did the *Mickey Mouse Club* show.

For years afterwards I would meet Ruth Roman at various cocktail parties and, no matter how many time I explained that it was Mel's show and his decision, she would tell people, "This is the guy who thought I couldn't act."

The Gryphon season went on after *Dear Ruth* and we got Robert Milton, a stage director who had made many successful films. He was now a gentle old man who did several plays with us, one with Constance Bennett and one with Claire Trevor, both big stars of their day. Milton had a strange habit of vanishing during rehearsals and turning up later with the guarantee of elaborate furnishings for the sets he was to work with. In East Coast stock he had learned the habit of getting local stores to contribute for program credit. I got him to direct my play but he was a little confused with the technique required. I wrote it for multiple levels. Milton was used to a conventional stage, with real sets. As we rehearsed, Mike, who liked the play, sat in and gradually, almost imperceptibly, took over. He offered to take off a week from the studio to direct it. I was troubled and concerned for Milton. I kept thinking of Joe May, the German director on my first picture. I was tempted to thank Mike and refuse but my cold feet reasserted themselves at the prospect of losing what might have been my first big chance as a playwright. Although we gave credit in the program to Milton, Mike directed the play.

Signe Hasso did an excellent job in the part but, on opening night, a whole busload of her Swedish friends came down and insisted she have something to eat. The smorgasbord was accompanied by aquavit and followed by champagne. She arrived at the theater in a warm glow. She seemed a little unsteady in her dressing room but had regained control before she went on. The few lines she missed were covered well by the other actors and I was the only one who missed them.

At the party following the show, she came up to me in tears—her remorse heightened by more champagne. "John, darling, your beautiful play. I am so sorry I ruined your play. It was so lovely and I was so bad."

Then her expression changed and in a confident theatrical voice, she added, "Except in three or four important scenes."

That's why I love actors.

The audience liked the show. It aroused interest. Several agents talked about it but the only firm offer was from a Swedish company because one of the leads was played by Signe, a big star in Sweden, who went on make many American movies. The offer was to translate the play into Swedish with several suggested changes and seemed a lot more trouble than it was worth.

At Warner Brothers, Mike now had his own production company, which I would later join. Mother functioned as his story editor. With the challenge of work, she managed to be away from bed for considerable periods. She also hired Frances Marion, an old friend from MGM days, once the highest-paid writer in pictures and winner of two Academy Awards, to work with her.

Complementing her other talents, Fran, like Mother, had been an actress and was also an excellent painter and sculptor. She became a very close friend to Joan and me and was matron of honor at our wedding. She was also a sensational cook and would feed us at her apartment at least once a week. Fran was a real Renaissance woman. She was born in San Francisco and had been one of Hearst's favorite reporters before switching to motion pictures. She was beautiful enough to have been a star in her own right and, at the start of her career, had acting thrust upon her. She did not like life in front of the camera and had too many other talents, having worked as an artist and a newspaper writer like Mother. Also like Mother, she had been thrice married—once, briefly, at 17, to a young artist in San Francisco. Mother's first husband was named Leslie. Fran's was Wesley—Wesley de Lappe. After the excitement of the wedding, they lived in artistic poverty but discovered they had little else in common. They were divorced. Her second husband was Robert Dickson Pike, a businessman from a wealthy San Francisco family. He offered the luxury, which had been lacking, but was intent on his social position. Fran was intent on a career. It was not a happy union. Pike was stodgy and somewhat compulsive. Fran said that he expected fresh apples whenever he came home. He would chose one carefully, sit down and eat it before dinner. One night she had neglected to order her usual groceries and there was no apple. Pike complained bitterly. Fran apologized and said, "I'll take care of it." She got her hat and coat and left, never to return. They lived apart for some time while Fran moved from San Francisco to Hollywood to New York and back. Finally, they divorced and Fran went on to an extremely successful screen career.

Then, after two unsuccessful marriages, she met Fred Thompson, an Olympic athlete, twice winner of the triathlon who had studied for the ministry. He was a strong, handsome man. For Fran it was love at first glimpse. She married him and made him, along with Tom Mix, one of the greatest Western stars. She formed a company, wrote and produced his pictures and made a fortune. He was truly the love of her life. They built a huge estate above Beverly Hills with a lot of land and stables—both loved to ride. Fred, who did his own stunts in pictures, cut his foot while working with his favorite stallion, disregarded it, and, in a dramatic ending worthy of any of Fran's scripts, he died on Christmas Day of tetanus.

It took Fran a long time to recover. She started painting—which was her love before she entered movies. She did a portrait of me and some other pictures that hang in my house. She was also an excellent sculptor. She was a woman with a lot of guts. She now described herself as "an old woman with no control of wind and water." She was one of the most beautiful people I have ever known.

During the my Laguna Playhouse period, I used to fly up and use Mike's independent production office at Warners, close to Glendale airport, to call stars and arrange any other needed business of the theater. I presume, through Maggie Ettinger, my connection with Mike and my mother was known but I preferred not to use it. My name was Lucas, Mike's was Curtiz and he always introduced Mother as "my wife, Miss Meredyth." Using the connection with my parents would have opened many doors to me. Once inside, of course I would have had to prove myself, but it had become a stubborn matter of pride to try everything on my own. Somewhere along the way I had developed an interest in work, which all the years of attempted training had failed to provide. Maybe it was simply that I had been protesting against all authority, at school, in the studio. Now, with the theater season running, I felt, for the first time, I was my own boss. Mike was about to shoot *Life with Father* with William Powell, Irene Dunn and Elizabeth Taylor. He showed my play to Russell Crouse, the playwright who had done *Life with Father* on Broadway. Crouse said he liked it, wished he had written it but wouldn't have for commercial reasons. The play stayed in Laguna, I went home again.

Some Saturday nights, instead of running films at our house, we would go to the projection rooms of friends and watch movies there. Very often it would be the home of Hal Wallis, nearby in the Valley.

Hal had started in the Warner publicity department. He married Louise Fazenda, another of Mother's best friends, who had been a star in silents and moved on to comedy leads in talkies. She had a fantastic business sense and made millions in real estate in the San Fernando Valley.

Jack L. Warner, Mike and Hal Wallis at Warner Bros.

When Zanuck left Warners to set up his own production company, Hal took his place as head of production. He personally produced films he was particularly interested in—one was Mike's *Casablanca*, which won Mike an Academy Award. It also received the Best Picture award. When this was announced, Hal, as the producer, rose to accept the Oscar but Warner, running full tilt, beat him to the stage and accepted the Oscar for himself. That dramatic moment could not have been far from Hal's mind when he left Warners to set up his own production unit on the Paramount lot.

One night, after the picture we watched at his house, Hal asked what I was doing. I told him I was doing some writing. He asked me to play golf with him in the morning.

"But I don't play golf," I told him.

"I'll teach you."

I never have learned golf but, during our walk around the course, he offered me a job as a writer with his new company, which was shooting on the Paramount lot.

So I went to work for Hal. Since he was just getting his new company started, he did none of the high-budget, "important" pictures he had done at Warners and was to do so magnificently later. He wanted inexpensive films that would be instantly acceptable to exhibitors, ones with no risk that would build his cash position.

My first assignment was called *Dark City*, starring Lizabeth Scott, Hal's longtime mistress, and Charlton Heston, who had just been brought out from New York. Heston and I did our first picture together. Also starring was Viveca Lindfors and Don DeFore, who had also played for us at Laguna. The picture was directed by William Dieterle who, with Mike, had been one of the top directors at Warners. I don't know why Dieterle would do what was almost a B picture except that his career was winding down.

Next I wrote a picture for Alan Ladd. He was drinking heavily and his career was slipping but he was still a box office draw, still a star. Dieterle directed this also. I was pleased with the script and, on the day it started shooting, I received a telegram from Mother:

> HAVE YOU A SMALL PART FOR ME? I WAS A STAR OF THE SILENT FILMS. I ALSO DID SOME WRITING BEFORE THE PICTURES TALKED AND THE TRAINS RAN ON SCHEDULE. IF INTERESTED PLEASE CONTACT ME AND PERHAPS YOU ALSO HAVE SOMETHING FOR MY HUSBAND WHO DIRECTED PICTURES IN HUNGARY. SCHOLEM ALECHEM
>
> MRS. GENIUS MARTYR.

Mike simply wished me luck.

The background of the script I wrote was Civil War. Alan Ladd played a gallant young Confederate officer sent West to contact Quantrill, the outlaw Kansas raider, who had looted and burned border towns. Because the South was in such desperate straits, Quantrill, despite his evil reputation, had been commissioned a Confederate general by President Jefferson Davis. The plan was that his raids would draw Union soldiers away from the Southern front. It was up to Ladd to weld this bunch of outlaws into an army and use them strategically. Ladd was the brightest and best of the South, somewhat spit and polish. He quickly discovers what a foul mess he has gotten into with these men and their murderous boss.

In the introductory scene, Ladd rides into Quantrill's mountain camp. He is stopped and nearly shot by a half-dressed, ragged and bearded guard. Ladd chews him out for military sloppiness and failure to salute an officer.

When we saw the dailies, I could not repress a loud moan. Ladd appeared with his uniform jacket unbuttoned, wearing low-slung Western six-guns instead of the regulation Navy Colt. He looked as sloppy as the guard he was upbraiding.

He had refused the uniform as the wardrobe department had prepared it, fearing he looked too "sissified." His fans would expect him to look as he did in his Westerns and would not accept him any other way. From that point, the whole picture went down the toilet. It was released under the title *Red Mountain*. This is the first time I have publicly acknowledged it.

My only good memory is when the picture was shooting in New Mexico. Dieterle became sick and Hal got John Farrow to take over as director for a few days until Deterlie recovered. John was a writer-director who was married to Maureen O'Sullivan—Tarzan's Jane in many MGM pictures and mother of Mia Farrow. Later I was to direct Maureen in television.

We were all flown to the distant locations by Paul Mantz, a famous flyer who did a great deal of movie work, both in transportation and in

Bess, Mike and John Farrow (center) in Encino (circa 1947).

stunt flying. In the morning, while Farrow went out to take over the direction, Hal and I worked on a couple of new scenes for the script. When we drove out to the location, they were in the middle of a take. In the scene, Alan Ladd has been tracked down by the evil gang. "Throw down your guns," the leader ordered Ladd. "You're surrounded." Farrow called "cut" and said, "Print it."

Hal had the script in his hand and I saw him stiffen. The line, as I had written it, was "We've got you boxed in. Throw down your gun."

"Don't print that," Hal yelled. He showed the script page to Farrow. "We work to get some interesting dialogue and you change it to a cliché." That was a speech to lift a writer's heart but I avoided Farrow's eyes lest he think I had complained. The scene was reshot with the proper dialogue. I could have flown home without the need of a plane.

During the interval after this picture, Hal went to the South of France. I had never been to Europe and decided to go on my own, starting with London.

Hal asked me to take some American money to a friend of his who lived in London and then invited me to meet him in Villefranche Sur Mer, on the Riviera. I gladly agreed.

At dinner with Mike and Mother the night before I flew out, Mother was clearly nervous. Air travel was not as common then. Her one and only flight had been made with a stunt pilot for a picture in the silent teens. The pilot had taken her up to be shown the exact path he was to fly for her cameras. He landed to let her out. She started the cameras rolling. As the plane took off, its engine cut out and the pilot crashed in flames. She had not liked my learning to fly and now I was off halfway around the world.

Mike said, "Is custom to get father's blessing on trip."

Mother snorted but Mike, with a twinkle in his eye, was playing the role of the stern patriarch. Mike and I had never been close, or, rather, there had never been any demonstrated affection, but I fell in with the plot and knelt before him. He put his hand on my head. We were both hamming it up but, through the joking, I felt strangely reassured. I think he felt something, too. I have never forgotten that moment.

In London I stayed at the Savoy.

11

New Directions

The next day, Hal's friend and his wife came to lunch with me at the Savoy Grill. I secretly handed him the American money Hal had sent. I called the waiter and we ordered. This was shortly after the war and Britain was still on rationing, still trying to recover from her terrible ordeal. Hal's friend, who was an important industrialist, was fascinated with a menu that actually featured lamb chops. He and his wife hadn't eaten lamb in several years. They both eagerly ordered the chops and, at my urging, split another between them. I, coming from a country where people were concerned with keeping weight off, was impressed.

In London, at a cocktail party at the flat of Bebe Daniels and Ben Lyon, both former Hollywood stars who had been in London during the blitz and had their own radio show which helped British morale during those terrible days, I met Douglas Fairbanks, Jr. I refrained from discussing our onetime rivalry for the affection of his then-wife, Joan Crawford. I also met Cesar Romero and, at what seemed like a Warner Brothers reunion, Irving Rapper, who had been Mike's dialogue director when I first came to the studio and had gone on to direct pictures of his own. Also at this party, and extremely drunk, was Dane Clark, a star I had worked with many times at Warners and who, with Lon Chaney, Jr., had done *Of Mice and Men* for us at Laguna. An upper-class Englishwoman had seen us talking and asked, "Do you know that man?" I admitted I did. "Do you think it's proper," she asked, "when we'd just been introduced, for him to say, 'I want to fuck you?'"

I stifled a grin. Dane was a decade ahead of his time. That direct approach would not be considered polite until the sexual revolution of the '60s—not until the era of Vietnam protest and Free Speech.

11—New Directions

Cesar Romero and I toured Westminster Abbey with a guide who was interested only in getting Cesar's autograph and hearing about Hollywood. We were standing on a thousand years of history, the tombs of great kings and queens, poets, warriors, and he wanted only movie gossip.

I rented a car and drove down to Surrey, to the home of a friend of Mother's from her Australia days. Lady Barbara had seen me as a baby. She was now married to a baronet and their son, Richard, had just come down from Oxford. Young Richard took me back for a thorough tour of the university and also to Cambridge. For the first time, I regretted my dismal academic record. This would have been worth studying for. I reciprocated by introducing Richard to some of the Hollywood personnel then crowding London. Then I flew south.

In Nice, I was met at the airport by Hal's son, Brent Wallis, driving a huge Cadillac with top down and an American flag on the fender. Somewhat embarrassed, I proceeded down the coast looking like a visiting president.

Villefranche Sur Mer was lovely and, despite the huge rambling hotel where Hal stayed, still had the air of a small fishing village. I saw it again 40 years later and it had changed almost beyond recognition.

Revisiting Monte Carlo provided a similar disappointment. On my first visit to the impressive casino, it was still necessary to wear a dinner jacket. When I went back 40 years later, there were people in shirt sleeves, and slot machines lined the walls. Sic Transit Gloria Monaco.

From there I went to Rome and spent some time trying to find Mother's apartment on Via Vittoria Veneto, where she had lived in 1925 during the making of *Ben Hur*. I also did all the expected tourist things, including the catacombs, which were freezing cold after the broiling summer outside. I am not sure if it was that or something I ate but I was violently sick. The hotel sent up a doctor who spoke only Italian and a nurse who spoke German. I was able to make out a few German words and, for the rest, I described and they prescribed in sign language.

The flight home in a Constellation (state of the art in 1950) took 36 hours.

My next assignment from Hal Wallis was a story that went through a dozen title changes and came out *Peking Express*. It was an attempted remake of *Shanghai Express*, which Marlene Dietrich had done for Paramount years earlier. That had been a remarkable picture and Marlene's beauty was dazzling. Twenty years later, Dietrich returned to Paramount and was again starring in a picture. She saw the first day's rushes and was unhappy with the way she looked. The cameraman was the same one who had photographed her in *Shanghai Express* and she complained to him that he was not lighting her as well as he had before. "I'm sorry," he said, nodding his head in agreement. "But, then, Miss Dietrich, I was 20 years younger."

The leading lady in our version was, alas, no Dietrich. The leading man was Joseph Cotten and the evil Chinese general was Marvin Miller. I was allowed to direct the makeup and wardrobe tests of Miller. Such tests are done simply to show the producer and director how an actor will look in the part, makeup, wardrobe, etc. I attempted to make an impression by doing elaborate camera work.

Looking at the results, Hal shook his head. I had run up crew costs and wasted a lot of film. But he noticed. Instead of being given another writing assignment, I was allowed to stay with my own script on the set as dialogue director, to follow the whole production through from beginning to end. I was starting to realize that I wanted to direct and, for the first time, paid attention to camera angles, lenses, all the things I had avoided in earlier years.

While I was writing the story, I asked for a consultant on China and was given Weifan Hsueh, whose name everyone pronounced Shay. His name was Hsueh Wei Fan but, having gone to college in the States, he had done the usual thing and simplified it. After college he had married Evelyn, an American girl, and gone back to Shanghai to work for Standard Oil until the war. He was invaluable to me, both as consultant and friend. I went into my research mode and, besides reading all I could and absorbing all I could get out of Wei, I began Chinese lessons. I can still write a few characters of this incredibly difficult language but was never at a conversational level. I did, however, insist that Wei stay on the set throughout the entire picture. He had to teach the Chinese actors, mostly Cantonese, to use phrases in Mandarin. The two languages, though using the same characters in written form, are light years apart in speech.

Having already simplified his name from Hsueh to Shay, Wei was unable to understand why Dieterle insisted on rendering it as O'Shay.

On one very complicated scene in a railway depot under attack, bands of soldiers had to come charging from different streets and meet in the middle. It required split second cues to assure that the soldiers were moving when the camera panned from one group to the other. Wei was pressed into service as an assistant director and, at my signal, relayed from the director, had to send his troops, firing their weapons as they ran, around the corner to the rendezvous.

The shot was going without a flaw until Dieterle signaled me and I waved to Wei. One of his extras could not get his gun to fire and his frustration blocked the others. The camera arrived at the planned spot and there were no troops. "O'Shay!" Dieterle screamed over the loudspeaker, "O'Shay!" Then he exploded, "Oh, shit!"

A prop man fixed the gun and the next time the shot went perfectly but "O'Shay, oh, shit!" became a mantra for the crew.

Dieterle was as much a character as Mike. The two had great respect for each other but were both convinced that the other was unstable. "Mike," Dieterle would say in his heavy German accent, tapping his forehead with the white kid gloves, which were his trademark, against his forehead, "is very talented but has not all here."

Mike, for his part said that Dieterle was "a goddamn good director but, I think so, a little crazy."

Wei and I remained friends long after the picture was over. He and his American wife had two lovely daughters, one of whom later had an acting career. Wei had switched so completely to an American diet that he would rarely finish a meal without deep-dish apple pie à la mode. I am not prepared to assert that a change from a healthy Chinese diet to the junk food we eat was the cause but when I was in Australia Mother called to tell me he had dropped dead on a golf course in 1959. I wrote a eulogy which John McIntire, an excellent actor and friend to both of us, delivered. The Australian studio manager discouraged me from sending this by cable, saying that it might be garbled and would be extremely expensive. I had to make a call to my business office in Beverly Hills so he suggested I get one of the stenographers to take it down in shorthand and messenger it to McIntire. I did this and started dictating. The stenographer slowed me down, and finally admitted that she did not know shorthand. She slowly took the whole thing in longhand. The phone bill was astronomical.

But back in 1950, Hal Wallis went to Slapsie Maxie's one night. This club was owned by Max Baer, who had been a heavyweight champion fighter. Hal saw a comedy act—the team of Martin and Lewis. Recognizing their potential, Hal immediately signed them, got comedy writers and started production on a whole series of their pictures.

The Wallis Company had a large table in the commissary second only in size to that of the Cecil B. DeMille table where the great Biblical expert presided daily over his vast entourage. "The boys," as Hal called Martin and Lewis, would play practical jokes at lunch, have food fights, throwing butter at each other. Those of us at the Wallis table accepted these pranks with reactions ranging from amusement to disgust. But occasionally they were really funny.

One afternoon Jeannie (Dean's wife) called to tell him she was pregnant. Dean was late coming from his dressing room and Jerry took the call. He offered excited congratulations, hung up and swore us all to silence. "Watch Dean's reaction."

When Dean came in, Jerry said offhandedly, "Jeannie called. She wants to talk to you." He dialed while Dean sat down. "Jeannie?" Jerry said, "Here's Dean." He handed the phone over and gave us all a wink.

"Hi, honey," Dean said. He listened a moment while we all waited expectantly for his reaction of surprise and delight. Without a change of expression he said, "Whom do you suspect?" It brought down the entire table.

Hal went to New York to negotiate some complex deal with his partner, Joe Hazen. I was left without assignment and my contract option was coming up with a substantial raise. John Mock, the story editor, told me that they wanted to pick me up but at the same money. I was not thrilled about that, having delivered three pictures for them and asked what properties there were for me. He said they were concentrating on the Martin and Lewis stories. The first had been a huge success and, at the moment, they were all that Wallis Productions was concerned with. I knew how well I could handle drama and melodrama and preferred to stick to that field. It was not exactly that I felt it was demeaning to write slapstick but there was probably a little arrogance mixed in with my decision. I now had three feature credits and felt I was on a roll. To lose that momentum now might be bad. I thought long and hard about the matter and then made a very large mistake. I told my MCA agent, Wilton Schiller, that I had decided to get out of my contract.

Having made the decision, I instantly called Hal in New York. I interrupted him in a meeting and I told him there was nothing more for me to do with his company and I had to try my luck elsewhere.

"Wait until I get back next week," Hal said. "We'll work something out."

But I had wrestled so long with the problem that, having made the decision, I felt I had to be firm. I thanked him for everything he had done and quit.

Hal gave me one week of the pick-up salary so that my agent could quote the higher price when getting me other jobs.

I felt happy with myself. I had finally found my calling and I was off on my career. Hal did more of the slapstick comedies and then went on to do some of the finest "important" pictures of his, or anyone else's career. With patience I could have been part of that.

Marty Rackin, a writer friend who did work on the Martin and Lewis pictures, went on to become head of Paramount Studios.

At a later time, Mike made a similar mistake with the same person.

Hal offered him an equal partnership if he would leave Warners and come with him. Mike, despite his deep friendship with Hal, felt a loyalty to Warners, where he had worked for 20-odd years. Warner was dangling the prospect of Mike's own company on the Warner lot and it was dazzling. Despite Mother's urging that going with Hal would be an excellent move since it meant considerably more money and they worked perfectly together, Mike refused. He was loyal to the Brothers who brought him to America.

It was during this time that I married. I had met Joan on my first job as dialogue director at Warners, a very forgettable B called *The Gorilla Man*. She was born in Australia as Joan Marie Therese MacGillicuddy, had been a child prodigy and won the title of Best Violinist of Australia at the age of 13, defeating challengers twice her age. Her father, a doctor, discovered he had cancer and gave up his practice and took his family, wife Nell and daughters Joan and Mauricette, to London so that they

Charity cocktail party on the Warner Bros. lot on the set of *Navy Blues*. *Left to right:* Joan Winfield, Elisabeth Fraser, Bette Davis, and Faye Emerson (1941).

could have as much good time together as remained to him. In London, Joan studied acting at RADA—the Royal Academy of Dramatic Art.

Mauricette (Billie) went there, then moved to the Royal Academy of Music. She became a magnificent pianist. The two sisters were presented at court.

In 1938 the family went to New York to Joan's uncle, O.M. Bernuth, inventor of creosote, which was used to protect telephone and telegraph poles world-wide. He also owned a fleet of tankers that plied all oceans. At a party she attended in New York, Joan was discovered by a talent scout and brought out to Warners, where Jack Warner changed her name to Joan Winfield. The name had, if nothing else, the advantage of brevity. We worked on a couple of B pictures, went out for a while but then I was away for much of the war in San Francisco with the Office of War Information. After that, I was at the Playhouse in Laguna.

When Portia and I broke up after Laguna, Joan and I resumed our relationship. We went together for a long time before we decided, one night at dinner at the old Player's Restaurant on Sunset, to make it permanent.

Joan had been raised a Catholic and attended Mass regularly. She had never questioned her religion and this bothered me. I found arguments against her faith, citing my readings in comparative religions. The Communion was borrowed from the bread and wine of the Dionysian festivals. The Crucifixion was the death of the king to assure the spring harvest. That harvest was, of course, the Resurrection, etc. I had had a love-hate relationship with Catholicism. I was fascinated by the rituals but angered by the restriction—protest against authority.

Joan Winfield in a Warner Bros. publicity photograph (1941).

If, I insisted, you had to believe in something, try Buddhism. It is an offshoot of Hinduism and while it doesn't make sense, it makes more sense than any other religion. I saw the concept of the wheel of life and rebirth as something akin to Darwin's evolutionary theory. I no longer see that relationship. Perhaps I evolved.

There is a poem by the Hindu poet Bhartrhari which impressed me and which I often quoted to Joan:

> All we in one long caravan are journeying
> Since the world began.
> We know not whither but we know
> Time guideth at the front and all must go.
> Like as the winds upon the field
> Bows every herb and all must yield,
> So we beneath Time's passing breath
> Bow each in turn.
> Why tears for birth or death?

Finally Joan's Mass attendance stopped. I am not sure I ever fully unconverted Joan but I felt I had won my battle against un-reason.

On the night of our decision to marry, I took her home to tell her mother. Nell was watching television. As I made my announcement, I recognized a voice and saw my dead father's face on the screen. I am not sure what old movie it was but I took the event as a kind of blessing.

Joan and I agreed to fly to Las Vegas and be married simply and without any fuss. When I told Mother, who had been married three times in civil ceremonies, I got a totally unexpected reaction. She thought the idea terrible. Joan's mother, an ardent Catholic, would be heartbroken. Mother fought for a church wedding.

I found a lot to protest about in this idea but Fran Marion offered to call a friend and fellow author, Father Edward Murphy. He had published several books and was an ardent fan of Hollywood and its people. He flew out from his parish in New Orleans to perform the ceremony. I referred to him as the Black Market Priest because he was able to speed the time usually required to prepare mixed marriages. I found him a wonderful guy with a great sense of humor. He married us in Joan's church with my friend Harry Kronman, who had been a rabbi before he went into radio writing and producing, as best man. Fran was matron of honor.

The wedding reception was held in the beach house Mother and Mike had rented for the summer from Anatole Litvak, a director at Warners who had many excellent movie credits but none as memorable as his scene at Ciro's, one of the better nightclubs on the Sunset Strip. Hollywood tittered for days over the story of his drunken hard-core performance with Paulette Goddard on the dance floor, her dress pulled nearly to her waist and the conclusion of the event under the table in one of the booths. Whether the report was accurate or not was unimportant. It was scandalous in a town loving scandal.

Litvak's three-story house was built on the sands of Malibu. It had a dramatic spiral staircase connecting the various levels. Mike was so enchanted with it that he had his art director come down, take photographs and reproduce it as the climactic set in *Mildred Pierce*, where the shooting of the evil Zachary Scott takes place.

After the church wedding, Joan and I went back to the Litvak beach house where the wedding reception was held. Joan waited outside to greet some friends while I went into the tiled entry where a bar had been set up. The Brown Derby was catering the reception and Ted, the Greek waiter who always served us at the Derby, was tending bar. He greeted me, asked what I would like and had just mixed the drink when Joan entered, wearing her veil. Ted looked at her, stunned, then turned to me. "The wedding," he asked, "this one is for you?"

"It's for us," I said.

With tears in his eyes, he embraced me, then Joan. "Is beautiful," he sobbed. All afternoon he kept grinning at us as though we were his family.

Joan's sister, Mauricette, had married James Cassidy, who had produced several plays she starred in. The first was Ibsen's *A Doll's House* with Francis Lederer. Jim had changed her name to Dale Melbourne and they were living in New York. To ease Joan's mother's transition of Joan leaving home—of living alone—we took her back to visit her other daughter.

Nell had never flown before and was terrified but she agreed, running her Rosary beads the moment she hit her seat. It was a night flight and we had the forward compartment on a Constellation. Nell struck up a conversation with an aeronautical engineer, who was eager to learn about Australia. We had anticipated having to give her a lot of reassurance but after the engineer had fallen asleep, Nell stared out the window, very contented.

As we approached the East Coast, the sky was beginning to brighten. The flight attendant's announcement that we would be landing soon woke everyone. We congratulated Nell on her acceptance of flying. She smiled, saying that she had no fear as long as that other plane was flying alongside of us.

The engineer sat up quickly and followed Nell's look. What she had been watching was our flashing wing light.

"If," the engineer said with visible relief, "I'd thought another plane was flying that close, I'd have panicked." But it had reassured Nell. God flies in mysterious ways.

Returning from our New York honeymoon, I went to work at a number of studios, writing shows on a number of subjects. At Republic Studios, I wrote a Western that Allan Dwan produced. Dwan had been one of the great directors of silent films who, I later found when looking at my baby book, had given me a silver porringer for a birth gift.

Then I was assigned *King of the Wind*. In eighteenth century England, good horses were almost worshipped by the aristocracy. The Godolphin Arabian and the Byerley Turk were two of them. Marguerite Henry had written a book called *King of the Wind*, based loosely on the Godolphin Arabian, tracing the life of an Arab horse from its North African background to the English racetracks. That was the jumping-off place for the story. I got heavily into research and, for a brief period, I studied Arabic. I mastered some history but never got the alphabet straight.

Studios, in those days, had research departments staffed by very competent people. A writer had only to call and request a particular subject and his desk would be flooded with material. I began to do what I had never done in school. I read, studied, went far beyond the subject of horses to eighteenth century life. I finally realized that my work was providing my education.

Of all the work I did at Universal, what I remember most vividly was an assignment from Ross Hunter. Ross was the producer of many slick "woman's pictures" such as *That Touch of Mink* and *Pillow Talk*, all beautifully mounted and a tremendous success for Doris Day. So I was startled when he called me in to write a Western, something far afield from his most successful ground.

The studio had a commitment for a picture with Jimmy Stewart and wanted a Western vehicle for him. The story I came up with concerned an innocent man who had been framed with the reputation of a killer, a vicious gunman, on the run from the law, pursued by a posse.

I began research on all aspects of the West—guns and gunmen, the history of Western expansion.

This was in the '50s, the period of the original *Broken Arrow*, which starred Jimmy Stewart and Jeff Chandler. Jeff played Cochise and the broken arrow symbolized peace.

That picture made such an impression, and so much money, that Cochise and his Chiricahua Apaches were used in countless pictures as the standard hostile Indian tribe. It had been so overdone that I cast about for some new brand of hostiles. I came up with the idea of using the Yaqui, a tribe living mainly in Sonora, Mexico. They wore the traditional calzones blancos of the Mexican peasant but were fierce warriors. The novelty of the idea appealed to me as it did to Ross. So we had Jimmy Stewart dodging the threat of the savage Yaqui while the posse of his own people was also chasing him.

His mount killed, a kindly rancher gives our hero a horse called Tumbleweed that looks like the worst nag this side of the glue works but, when the chips are down, outruns the posse, saves the hero's life from the Indians and allows him, ultimately, to clear himself of the false charges.

There was one sequence in the script where the fugitive is chased into a blind canyon. He is exhausted; his water bag has been empty for days. He looks up at the black basalt cliffs, knowing the Indians are watching his helpless last moments. He no longer has the strength to move. His horse Tumbleweed is pawing at the sandy soil nearby. "Crazy horse," he mutters through thirst-cracked lips. He makes a couple of feeble attempts to shoo the horse away but the pawing goes on. Tumbleweed diligently digs in the bottom of the dry riverbed. Rifle cradled in his arms, the hero tries to keep watch but his head nods in sleep. He is awakened by a strange, slurping sound. Tumbleweed has found water beneath the sand. He crawls forward and the horse relinquishes his position to allow the man to drink. When I dictated this scene, my secretary had called in sick with a bad case of flu and the stenographic department had sent me a substitute. She took down my dictation very efficiently. I did not have to slow down and finished the entire sequence in one afternoon. What I got back made me laugh hysterically, reminding me of my first experience as a junior writer at Warners. My script now described the hero looking up at the black bath salt cliffs rimming the blind canyon. The secretary heard me and, laughing, came in. "It's nothing," I told her. Then, among my other changes, I turned the cliffs back to the black volcanic *basalt* I originally had in mind.

Several things happened after the script was finished and ready to shoot. I cannot remember my original title but it was changed to *Tumbleweed*, which sounded like a Gene Autry Western. Then the studio lost its commitment to Jimmy Stewart. After a frantic search for a suitable star replacement, someone in the front office came up with the idea of using Audie Murphy, who was under contract and being paid whether he worked or not. He had been signed for his publicity value. Audie was a genuine hero—the most decorated soldier of World War II. He had been awarded 33 medals, including the Congressional Medal of Honor. If anyone was ideal for the part, it was the type of man Audie was. The problem was that he was small and had a baby face—not at all the image of the Hollywood hero.

I was working on another script when I heard about the casting. An executive decision of casting was not to be challenged so I begged to be allowed to rewrite scenes to account for the radical change in the appearance of the hero but the cameras had already begun to roll. So the opening scene, where the hero walks into a bar and all the customers back away from him in terror, made as much sense as little Shirley Temple holding up a bank.

I went to the set and found some very strange-looking Indians who were supposed to be Yaqui. On inquiry, I found that the wardrobe department had found a bunch of Navajo costumes at Western Costume at a bargain price and decided to use them. It still might have worked with Navajo hostiles except that many scenes had already been shot where the Indians were referred to as Yaqui. I was informed that there was no change possible. So we had gotten away from the convention of savage Apaches by using Yaquis who dressed like Navajos. The ultimate capper arrived when the ad for the picture came out. It showed Audie holding two six guns. Underneath was the legend SINGLE HANDED, HE FACED THE APACHE TERROR.

I had an idea of a novel I wanted to try, set in Taos, New Mexico, where three cultures meet—Indian, Spanish and Anglo. Joan's first pregnancy had a few more months to run and I was going to drive to Taos with Walter Rathbun, the friend who had suggested the Laguna Summer Stock Company. He had just been diagnosed with leukemia and knew he did not have a great deal more time. He wanted to see Taos and I wanted to do some preliminary research on the novel. The night before we were set to leave, Joan went into premature labor. Our daughter Elizabeth was born the next day. Extremely premature, she was put into an incubator, where she stayed for several weeks. Taos was put on hold.

Elizabeth was brought home with a nurse and we had a special room prepared for her with a screen door. Only her mother and I were allowed to enter. The nurse stayed for a couple of months. Then we got Nanny Banner. "Nanny Banner" was how she introduced herself and that was the only name ever used. She was middle-aged, very short, stocky, with an Edinburgh accent. She had worked as a nanny in the U.K. before being brought to the United States. She had last cared for Barbara Stanwyck's son, Dion, who along with "Prince Charles" and "wee Princess Anne" became our children's role models. Nanny was constantly telling our children, "You mustn't toy with your food. That's no' the way Miss Stanwyck's Dion acts." If they fidgeted when being introduced to adult, "That's no' how Her Majesty's children would behave." Despite the fact that our children soon learned to outwit her, Nanny was wonderful and stayed with us for many years.

When we had had to cancel our Taos trip because of the birth of our daughter, Walter Rathbun, Bunny, an ardent amateur photographer, was consoled when Dr. Lusk, who did the delivery, used his camera to shoot pictures of the baby and her mother in the delivery room. I promised Bunny we would make the Taos trip the next year. Unfortunately, he died before the year was up.

There were many writers working at Universal at that time. Writers

John watches as Mike holds granddaughter Elizabeth MacGillicuddy Lucas (1953).

were hired on a weekly salary and worked as long as was required or until fired. Today scripts are either done on spec—written without an assignment in the hope of a sale—or writers are hired to do a specific job for a negotiated fee. I would later return to Universal to direct but, in my days there as a writer, I had a small bungalow. Universal was one of the oldest studios and rambled over hills and dales. Where the great hotels, theaters, rides and shops are now, sheep then grazed on the hillside—this as late as 1950. Long before that, the bungalows had been built for important stars. In the bungalow next to mine was James Moser, who created *Dragnet* with Jack Webb. Jim and I talked and took walks around the back lot, with its multitude of sets, and watched the sheep on the hills. It was a pleasant place. By contrast to Columbia where I went next, it had been Heaven.

Columbia was an old studio in the middle of Hollywood with no back lot, no standing sets, essentially buildings and stages. The first of the unimportant films I wrote at Columbia was *The Return of Captain Blood*. It was assigned to me by the producer, Harry Joe Brown, who had been Fran Marion's production manager when she was producing the Fred Thompson Westerns. With *Captain Blood*, I was still in the shadow of Mike. But this starred Louis Hayward instead of Earl Flint.

The studio was presided over by Harry Cohn, the ogre of the film industry. One of his favorite tricks was said to be calling a writer into his office, throwing the writer's script on the floor and asking, "What's this shit?"

This never happened to me. Perhaps I was lucky; perhaps my assignments weren't important enough to warrant the effort.

Years later, on Cohn's death, the funeral service was held on one of Columbia's sound stages, with the coffin on a dais and the eulogies delivered over a microphone. The service was packed, leading one writer to say, "They complain about poor box office attendance but you give people what they want to see and they'll come out in droves."

At about this time, Joan joined a group of women, at first wives of people in show business, later women in the industry in their own right. They worked to raise money for the Exceptional Children's Foundation, a charity serving children with developmental disabilities and brain injuries. They called their organization SHARE and produced a yearly show—first at Ciro's—one of the two large nightspots on the Sunset Strip. Big-name singers, actors and comics did spots or emceed. The SHARE ladies acted as a chorus and did dance numbers and songs, choreographed by such talents as members Marge Champion (wife of Gower), and Miriam Nelson. They were so nervous about their first appearance in a cowboy number that a fence was built on stage so the trembling women could lean on it. Over the years the SHARE show moved to ever-larger places and became a regular media event.

I was writing a lot of television scripts—*Topper*, *The Loretta Young Show*, *Mr. and Mrs. North*.

One weekend, I was spending time with the family at Malibu when I got a call from Jim Moser. When he broke up with Jack Webb, they had, besides *Dragnet*, a medical series idea. Jack got *Dragnet* in the settlement and Jim walked away with the other show, which he called *Medic*. He had just gotten the go-ahead for production and asked if I would write one for him.

Medicine had always held a fascination for me so when, Jim Moser offered me the chance to work on *Medic*, I quickly said yes.

Medic's offices were at the old Goldwyn Studios where Mother had gone with Darryl Zanuck when he first left Warners and before he took over the Fox lot to make it Twentieth Century–Fox. There she wrote *Folies Bergere* with Maurice Chevalier and *The Mighty Barnum* with Wallace Beery. She was given a novelist as co-writer, Gene Fowler, whom she taught the art of screenwriting.

I seemed to be following my parents from studio to studio and never catching up. I wrote several of the *Medic* scripts and finally got what I had always really wanted—I was able to direct.

The Los Angeles County Hospital let us have an unused wing and many of our first shows were shot there.

The first script I wrote involved epilepsy. We had an advisory board composed of physicians of the Los Angeles Medical Association. A physician in the particular field a script was dealing with would be chosen to give technical advice during the writing and one would be on the set during shooting to assure authenticity.

We cast a young boy, Dennis Hopper, to play the epileptic. I took him over to the Veteran's Hospital in Sawtell. Epi-Hab (epilepsy and rehabilitation) occupied old buildings of the Spanish American War period. Dennis watched seizures, talked to patients. One old man came up to us and, speaking in unintelligible guttural gibberish, pointed to the ceiling and walls of the building. We were trying to be polite but at a total loss when the doctor who was conducting our tour spoke to him and led us away. He explained that the man, an epileptic who had had several strokes, had been confined here for many years. He had been a contractor and had constructed this building and constantly tried to get that message across to whatever new faces came through the institution. He had, in effect, built his own prison.

Dennis absorbed what he had seen all too well. On a day of location shooting, the doctor assigned to the set was unable to come and had a substitute cover for him. The substitute doctor arrived in the middle of a take while Dennis was acting a grand mal seizure. The take was spoiled because the doctor rushed in to treat him. Dennis got his first really big break in *Easy Rider* and went on to a very successful acting career, got through a lot of severe personal problems and is now directing as well as acting.

The next script dealt with manic depression. This was a touchy subject because there was a good deal of controversy in the medical profession over methods of treatment. Instead of the usual single doctor assigned to work with me, the advisory board insisted on two. The first doctor was a typecast Viennese Freudian psychoanalyst who had a slight accent and a Van Dyke beard. The second was a man who, years later, almost married Joan's sister. I did not introduce them and have no idea how they met but, when I worked with him, his professional approach to manic depression was not to listen to a patient's dreams, his problems or his early life. Patients were simply to come in and submit to insulin shock—somewhat like electro-shock therapy, which I also watched. It is frightening as it convulses the patient and knocks him out for a time. Somehow I had to resolve these two diametrically opposed differences in treatment and come up with a workable story.

My first meeting with the Freudian doctor took place at Lucy's, a restaurant opposite Paramount studio that was very popular then. I came at the appointed hour and the doctor was not there. I had a drink and waited. After having my fill of the delicious Italian bread served, I was just about to phone and see if there had been a misunderstanding when he came in breathlessly. "I am sorry," he said. "But my son just had an orchidectomy [surgical removal of the testicles] and you can imagine the guilt I feel." That will forever stand out in my mind as a truly Freudian statement.

Foreshadowing the work of Henry Kissinger and using shuttle diplomacy, I got the two men to agree, point by point, on the line of the story. At any rate, the script was finished and Lee J. Cobb did a memorable job with it.

Then I had to take a brief break.

Long before Joan's sister's affair with the chemical psychiatrist I had dealt with on the show, she was married to Jim Cassidy with whom Nell, Joan's mother, had gone back to stay after our wedding. Billie, born Mary Mauricette MacGillicuddy, was six years older than Joan.

Her husband, James B. Cassidy, was also brilliant—as a con man. He put together a touring company of Ibsen's *A Doll's House* by telling Actor A that he had signed Actor B, who loved the play and wanted to work with Actor A. Then he would tell Actor B that he had signed Actor A, who wanted to work with B. Both were flattered, both signed. Billie played the lead opposite Francis Lederer. Cassidy also changed her name to Dale Melbourne. The confusion between her given name, Mauricette, and Billie, the family's term for her, and now Dale never seemed to bother her.

They were married in the Lady Chapel of Saint Patrick's Cathedral in New York. I was shooting and we could not attend.

Just a year after the wedding, and not many months since we had taken Nell to visit them, Billie called to say that Jim had died of melanoma. I do not remember what picture I was finishing but I will never forget what followed. The shooting ran late. Joan met me at the studio. We drove directly to the airport and took a night flight. I was exhausted. When we got on board, I took a sleeping pill, knowing how stressful the next day would be. Joan, as she usually did on planes, knitted. I do not actually remember the incident but she told me that, about two hours into the flight, I opened one eye and muttered, "There's something wrong with the number three engine." Then I went back to sleep and was unwakeable. A few minutes later the captain came on the intercom and said that we would be making an unscheduled stop in Dallas as a safety measure because of a slight mechanical problem. I woke only when we were on the ground and being transferred to another plane.

The funeral mass was in the Lady Chapel of St. Patrick's on the same spot where Jim and Billie had been married just a year before.

12

Test Patterns

    The burial was to be in the small town in Massachusetts where Jim was born and where his family still lived.
    The rain was torrential as the hearse and our limousine started the long drive north from New York. Joan, Billie and Jim's sister, Jean, were in back. I sat on the jump seat. The limousine driver lost the hearse in traffic. Then he missed the turnoff and finally lost his way entirely.
    We were driving muddy back roads in an almost biblical deluge. Jagged lightning lit the sky. Thunderclaps were like an artillery barrage in our ears. At last the driver had to confess that he was hopelessly lost. We found a tiny gas station and stopped. The driver carried his map inside to get directions while the gas tank was being refilled. We were already an hour late and a large crowd, including the mayor, were waiting for us. Joan and I decided we had better go in and phone to let the funeral home know where we were and our expected arrival time—still over an hour away. As I hung up, the driver was still poring over his map, looking confused. I started out and witnessed something I had read about but had never expected to see. It was fantastic. A ball of lightning landed just outside the door where I stood—a fuzzy round ball of dazzling light. It rolled between the gas pumps toward the open door of the limousine. Billie and Jim's sister saw it coming. It touched the car and exploded with a tremendous sound but did no other damage.
    It did, however, completely unnerve the two women. They lost their hard-fought composure and sobbed all the long drive to the rain-drenched burial.
    Most of all I remember the mortician, a fat, pinkish man who had been Jim's boyhood friend. He was so proud of the job he'd done. "We

had to tuck his clothes under him," he said before the lid was closed for the last time. "The cancer had ate him all away. But don't he look good now?"

As soon as possible I returned to the Coast and *Medic*. After writing several scripts, when I felt I had made myself, if not irreplaceable to *Medic*, at least desirable, I told Jim Moser I wanted to direct my next script. The idea was as not greeted with whole-hearted joy but was finally agreed to. This was a period in the Cold War when the Russians had the A-Bomb, the early '50s, when everyone was building, or wanting to build, bomb shelters stocked with survival rations, waiting for the Big Drop. All sorts of Civil Defense Units were being formed. I chose the theme of a volunteer medical team with its support group, reacting and setting up an emergency medical station after a nuclear attack. I called it "Flash of Darkness." We explained the necessity of triage—doctors working on those who might be helped, simply holding those exposed to too much radiation to live. We got a lot of reaction, much favorable and a lot claiming we were scaring the hell out of people.

Another traumatic experience was a story I did for *Medic* on polio—then called infantile paralysis. This was before the time of Salk and Sabine. Our set needed a lot of large iron lungs, which were the only treatment then. Patients were put into these huge iron cylinders with only their heads showing. The suction and release of air within the machine would force the patient's lungs to inflate and deflate, causing them to breathe. The patients had mirrors above their heads into which they could view their limited world.

My medical consultant was a woman doctor who had had polio, a case not as severe as most but she had spent time in such a lung. Many less fortunate remained in them until they died. The script I ended up writing was mostly this woman's experience.

The lungs for our set were loaned to us by Rancho, a large center for polio treatment. The extras were put into them. I had rehearsed the first scene. We were about to shoot when I saw our assistant director in the middle of the set crying. I went to him. He had recognized the serial number on one of the loaned iron lungs. It was the one in which his wife had been confined for over five years until her death. I told him to go outside and take a break. But he was gutsy enough to refuse. The show was hell for him but we got a good one.

The star of *Medic*, Richard Boone, later was to star in the very successful series *Have Gun—Will Travel*. He and I got along very well, became good friends and exchanged our children's birthday parties. For me, the most important thing was that I was directing, and doing it my way. In the first episode I elected to cut in the camera—that is, not give an editor a lot of different angles to work with. From beginning to end, I used master shots, moving the camera and actors in and out of close-ups as the action required. The whole film would be my vision with no possibility of change. I gave them no film to change a frame with. Hitchcock used a similar technique in *Rope*.

Fortunately my version worked and I was a hero to the company. I never again, however, shot a picture that way. Having left myself no possibility of second thoughts, I realized the advantage of having film enough to work with if you weren't quite as good as you thought. But I had made my point, at least to myself. I had mastered the craft.

The vacant wing that the Los Angeles County Hospital allowed us to use had operating rooms, wards, private rooms and endless corridors.

One memorable episode I shot there was a true story which had happened at this same hospital. An infant, who was now seven years of age, had been in and out of the hospital most of her life. Her only relative was her grandmother. The mother had killed herself after feeding the baby lye. The grandmother had rushed the child to the hospital and over a period of years there had been a series of some 14 operations. Being black, the baby had a keloid tendency—a heightened propensity to form scar tissue. Each time the throat or the intestines would scar shut, more surgery would have to be done to save her life, creating more scar tissue, necessitating more surgery. It was Catch 22. The child was wonderful and was adopted by the staff of the hospital. There were constant small presents and, between surgeries, special parties for her. This being a teaching hospital, the staff was constantly changing so her grandmother was her only true link to the world outside.

We had endless readings before we cast the girl but, unexpectedly, the really tough role was the grandmother. We read every black woman over 60 who claimed to have acted. In those days there were so few parts for black actors that not many had had any experience. If they had, they were generally too young. We were desperate. The casting director had run through all known contacts. Then, like a miracle, the perfect woman walked in. She was old, wrinkled, stooped beneath a mass of gray hair. She looked ideal. I prayed she would be able to handle the lines. The entire show depended on her and the child. She sat down and, taking out her spectacles, read as though she had been born for the part. I was delighted, and signed her. Then, for the first time we were introduced. She was Madame Sul-Te-Wan and she addressed me as Director Lucas. "You know, Director Lucas," she reminisced, "I worked with Director Griffith in *Birth of a Nation*."

12—Test Patterns

I was stunned. I was in the presence of living history. This woman had worked with the legendary D.W. Griffith. "What did you play?" I asked.

"I played a slave," she told me. "It was a character role."

That had been several years before my birth. My God, I wondered, how old could Madame be? But I was so happy to find her that nothing else mattered.

On the appointed day of shooting, she arrived at the hospital with her "makeup woman." I wanted no makeup on that wonderful face but the makeup woman's job, it developed, was to carry Madame's chair from place to place and see to her other needs.

Then came the first scene. The actor playing the doctor reported on the baby's condition. Madame spoke the opening speech and then went blank. Take Two. At almost the same place she dried up. Madame, it seemed, with her glasses, could read. When the script was given to her to study between takes, she was word perfect. Unfortunately, there were no spectacles for her memory. She could barely remember one line at a time. I had the script clerk feed her the lines, one by one, with the camera rolling and she would repeat them. The cutter would have to cut away to make the transitions work. We exceeded the entire episode's budget of film that first day. It was miserable. I was constantly saying, "Cut, print. Pick-up." Then the other actors began to blow their lines. It was infectious. Only Madam Sul-Te-Wan was unruffled. We went on through the entire episode getting one line at a time out of her. I shot many things to cut away to, the baby, hospital staff, so the cutter would be able to piece together a performance. It worked. When the picture was edited, Madam Sul-Te-Wan came off with a heart wrenching performance that was built frame by frame by an exhausted film editor.

While I was shooting, hospital staff would sneak up to watch. They would inform me when some especially interesting surgery was to be performed and, when possible, I would sometimes stay after the company had gone home. My love of medicine re-asserted itself. I was fascinated but knew it was not for me as a career. I was settling into my role as professional dilettante. Such education, even though it was not very deep, was giving me a wider view of life.

Medic worked on very tiny budgets but I did manage to write and direct some impressive shows, including one on a hospital ship. The Navy gave us, without charge, the hospital ship *Hope* with her full complement of deck officers and crew. We had helicopter landings at sea, etc. On a hospital ship there are endless beds and many rooms. The entire crew lived aboard while shooting.

At the after end of the ship was the helipad where we were filming a helicopter landing a barely-alive patient for surgery. The *Hope*'s second officer stood beside me at the camera and when I asked that we turn left to keep the buildings of San Pedro out of the background, he would call the captain on the bridge and say, "Mr. Lucas requests come to course 279 degrees." That made me feel very nautical. I also had a mini-reenactment of Mike's reversing the course of the task force of the *Enterprise* on *Dive Bomber*.

I used the captain and the bridge crew as actors—playing themselves—and that gained me considerable Naval popularity.

It also started my lifelong love of location shooting. At the major studios, even at this late date, in the '50s, sets were built on the huge sound stages, even exteriors of houses, with driveways and streets. It had originally been done due to the technology of the day. Costs were less. It had been cheaper to build sets than to take a company beyond the confines of the studio and the light was more readily controlled. There was also the matter of amortizing the cost of the studios.

Movies had started by shooting outdoor locations and I felt they should go back to their beginnings, employing the technology we had acquired along the way.

In this period came the birth of my second daughter, Victoria. She also was premature. We rushed Joan to the maternity ward and, before they could get the epidural block in, Victoria was born. Joan's friends in SHARE told her that, if she could get the delivery time down to six months, they would be willing to try it.

At the conclusion of the first season of *Medic*, Dick Boone was approached by a producer who wanted to do a feature in New Zealand. The script concerned the first contact of the Europeans with the native Maoris. Dick wanted me to direct it. I had other commitments and said no. Big mistake. Another such one came in the same period when Sam Goldwyn, Jr., wanted me to do a story on narcotic addiction. Starting our research, we met with the head of the Los Angeles Narcotics Division. He was a nice, though somewhat rigid guy, eager to be part of a motion picture and almost burying us with recitations of case histories. His cooperation ended abruptly when I asked what would happen if all drugs were legalized. I told him I knew it would not stop addiction but would take the immense profit out of drugs, eliminating the criminal dealers and preventing them from deliberately addicting children. The detective became apoplectic. I explained that the question was asked only to explore all aspects of the narcotics problem but that made little impression. Either he felt I was suggesting he be put out of a job or was simply too emotional about the matter to be rational. At any rate, the picture was never written, never made. It is a shame because some time later *The Man with the Golden Arm*, starring Frank Sinatra, came out and was extremely successful.

Mother called to tell me that her Great Dane, Mike, had died. We had had a series of Danes. Stanley was the first, named after the American journalist who discovered Dr. Livingston, the medical missionary who was presumed lost in Equatorial Africa. I named him Stanley because he was a gift from Dr. Steele Livingston, our family vet. Steele gave him to us after the death of our collie, George. George had been presented to Mike by Rudd Weatherwax, owner and trainer of Lassie and the many other dogs who doubled for Lassie in the films.

Cappie, my favorite Boxer, whose flatulence so enlivened many nights in our projection room, had died and taken his place in the animal cemetery Mother had on the hill, some distance from the house. She had coffins made for all the deceased pets and bronze markers with their names and comments like "Gallant Friend."

The problem is that, with the death of Mike, our third Great Dane, the marker read "Mike, Loyal Companion."

My stepfather had not seen the marker until it was in place on the grave. He came angrily down to the house. "Goddamn, Besky, take away that thing."

"What's wrong?" Mother asked.

"People think is me."

He would not be laughed out of it or consoled until Mother agreed to have a new one made using her own name. It read, "Mike Meredyth, loyal companion." Giving the deceased dog her name removed her husband's objections.

After *Medic*, I went back to Columbia—this time as a director, to do many segments for Screen Gems. I worked with George Brent and Ann Sheridan, big stars from my Warner days, now doing television. We recalled how we had spent December 7, "the day of infamy" that plunged us into war, listening to the radio together.

George had been the star of *Gold Is Where You Find It* and many other pictures I had worked on with Mike. Annie had worked with Mike on *Angels with Dirty Faces*. On both shows I had been script clerk. Ann had been billed as the Oomph Girl for some reason known only to the publicity man who coined the phrase but she was a G.I. pinup girl through World War II and one of the big stars at Warners. Now, 15 years later, both were doing television for me.

My first Columbia directorial job was a humbling one. Charles Bickford was the star. He was an excellent character actor whom I remembered seeing on Mike's set when I was perhaps ten years old. It was a Saturday night and we went to pick Mike up for the trip to Laguna.

A vast snow bank had been constructed on the stage of the old Warners Sunset Boulevard studio and Bickford and another actor were lost in a blizzard created by batteries of wind machines and prop snow. It was one of the few sets I had actually paid much attention to. Companies then shot six-day weeks with Saturday night usually late because on Sunday the cast and crew could spend the whole day recovering. Bickford, I believe, perished in the storm. At any rate it was still vivid in my memory as I directed him for the first time. Or, as it turned out, he directed me. He was a cop and was required to chew out some juvenile offenders. After the first take which was fine, I decided to experiment and went up and quietly suggested that, for the next take, he try coming on a little stronger to the kids.

"I have come on as strong as the scene requires," he said in a voice low enough not to carry to the crew but that brooked no contradiction. I backed off, feeling stupid. I ordered the scene printed and let him set his own pace from there on. He was right, as his performance proved. It was also a lesson. Do not needlessly meddle with a performance. Study what the actor has to give and intervene only if it is wrong.

Another memorable Screen Gems episode, *Adventure in Iraq*, was shot on the Columbia backlot in the Valley many years before Saddam Hussein. The script called for Peter Graves to be building an oil pipeline in the desert. Ann Sheridan was the female lead. The script called for desert heat so intense that men were dropping, dying of heat exhaustion. The problem was that we shot this in mid–December. While Peter, with makeup oil simulating sweat covering his face, was talking of getting help for the men dying of heat, it was so cold that steam was coming from his mouth. We tried holding ice cubes in his mouth until just before the take. It would work for half the scene. Then the steam would restart. Television timetables were inflexible. The scenes had to be shot. Finally I got the idea of having him smoke a cigarette (this was before cancer warnings, when smoking was still chic). The device worked for Peter but all the other actors had steam streaming from their mouths. Still the schedule called for the scenes to be shot that day. Ultimately every single actor had a cigarette going. The Reynolds Company must have loved that picture.

I did many pictures at Columbia.

Then came the interview. A reporter from *Variety* interviewed me over lunch at the Brown Derby and kept asking about the difference between features and television. In an unguarded moment I told him how much I preferred shooting on location. "We should set fire to the studios and go make pictures," I told him as a joke but it was not so reported. My employers at Columbia chose the worst interpretation. I was called into the front office and asked about it. The studio heads were indignant and wanted no part of an explanation. They insisted I write a letter to *Variety* demanding a retraction. "Or else" was not said but its ghost hung between us, the implication clear. I wish I could say that I told them what they could do with their retractions but I did send a letter to the reporter, explicitly explaining my intent and assuring him that I intended no actual arson.

It was not the time for valor. The McCarthy era was in full swing. Innocent people were being persecuted right and left. At one point the psychotic senator even forced President Eisenhower, whose loyalty to the American Way could hardly be questioned, to back off from protesting McCarthy's accusations of disloyal Commies in his administration.

After every casting session we conducted, the producer would have to pick up the phone, call a secret number and ask if the actors we had chosen were all right to use. No one was sure, from day to day, who was blacklisted. This situation existed all through the industry but I felt that Columbia was being more cooperative and authoritarian than need be. I went elsewhere.

Mike, meanwhile, was at Paramount making *White Christmas*, starring, besides Bing Crosby and Danny Kaye, Rosemary Clooney and Vera-Ellen. I had done *Brigadoon* at the Laguna Playhouse with Vera and we had developed a relationship so I went to Mike's set when I had available time.

Mike got a letter from Gabriel Pascal, thanking him for helping him secure Claude Rains, with whom Mike had done many pictures, for the role of Caesar in George Bernard Shaw's *Caesar and Cleopatra*. He complained of his difficulties, when he first started producing, of getting the proper financing and approval from bankers—the usual problems of film production. Then he went into:

> Have you forgotten, dear Mike, our conversation about your coming to England? I was thinking of our old dreams when, in 1924 (or was it 25?) we walked along the Boulevard des Italiens and the Champs Elysee, about the day when we should work together like two brothers, you as Director and I as your Producer. You are now the greatest director in America and I am supposed to be the top Producer in my country since Alex became a Metro executive. I think we should realize our dreams and that you should have the courage to accept my offer which I gave you last September and come over, not only as a Director, but as a real brother.

> My situation is as follows: Mr. Rank is financing the whole negative cost of my pictures. I get an adequate salary as Producer-Director. I am directing the actual vehicle myself. I have a very nice Irish chap who was Forde's [meaning John Ford] assistant director in Hollywood, Brian Desmond Hurst, as my co-director and I get 50% of the profits. If you decide to come over next September, I will arrange for you to get a top salary and I would give you half of my 50% of the profits from all the pictures you direct for me.
>
> But this is only if you have really decided to leave Warners, because I have too much consideration for Harry and Jack Warner to steal you away from them. So my offer is only if, for some reason, you have decided not to continue your relationship with that clever family. You tried so hard years ago to convince Jack that we should make together for him *Devil's Disciple* and, in his boyish vanity, he did not realize what he missed, so maybe we can do it in England.
>
> Give my love to your sweet lady, and talk it over with her. She has so much more common sense than we with our horse brains together, that I would like to know what she advises you to do.

He went on to promise to send the script and asked Mike's advice on a montage sequence he had "invented." Then he closed with:

> God bless you, my dear brotherly friend.
> With affectionate regards,
> Gabriel

That was another offer Mike did not take. Whether Warners heard about it or not, they renewed their promise of his own production unit on the Warner lot.

I was doing a great many things then, writing for *Mr. and Mrs. North*, *Topper*, *The Loretta Young Show*, *The Thin Man*, etc. I worked at almost every studio in town.

The vital importance of casting was impressed on me when I wrote up an idea for a television series featuring an old priest, Father Francis Darling, frail, seemingly helpless—a sort of clerical Miss Marple. He gets involved in various situations, murders, juvenile gang problems, mysteries of all kinds. While he seems to be overwhelmed with whatever he's involved in, it always gets done, solved, rectified. The audience may decide for itself if it is pure dumb luck, a crafty intelligence or divine intervention.

The agent I had then suggested that, rather than shopping the idea around, we take it to *The Loretta Young Show*. I had written several scripts for Loretta and, as a devout Catholic, she might well be interested. We would then have a demo show to take to the networks for a series pitch.

We showed the script to Loretta. She was enthusiastic and agreed. Our lawyers drew up a contract, giving her this one script but retaining for me all rights to the characters and situations. This was before I was directing so I left it in what I assumed were the capable hands of Loretta's company.

When the show aired, I was stunned to see that Father Darling was a young, vigorous priest who looked as though he might have coached the football team at Notre Dame. The whole concept was out the window. There was no surprise, no fun. In God's name, why?

Later, when I was directing, I paged through a casting book with the casting director of the show I was doing and happened upon a picture of the actor who had been cast as Father Darling. He was the only one in the book who was pictured in a Roman collar. It made somebody an easy choice and probably cost me a series.

Jack Webb, who was in *Dark City*, the first picture I did for Wallis, was shooting *Dragnet* at the old Republic Studio, and asked me to write some of the episodes. It was a kind of reunion. Jean Miles, who had been Portia's friend and roommate at the Pasadena Playhouse—they came from the same town—had been Mother's secretary and was now Webb's executive secretary. After doing many of the *Dragnet* episodes, Jack had me write for a series he was starting called *Noah's Ark*.

Jack loved gadgets; he loved all the newest developments in filmmaking and had come up with a technique for *Dragnet*—which was shot mainly in close-ups—using TelePrompTers all over the set. He and the other actors were not required to memorize lines—if you were talking to someone, you simply looked over his shoulder and read your lines off the TelePrompTer while the other actor was reading his lines from the TelePrompTer over *your* shoulder.

It saved time and film and worked perfectly for *Dragnet*. But *Noah's Ark* was not *Dragnet*. It was the old doctor–young doctor theme—the *Dr. Kildare* formula that Lew Ayres and Lionel Barrymore, as Dr. Kildare and Dr. Gillespie, had done so successfully as MGM features.

But Webb's doctors were veterinarians. There were animals all over the place. A receptionist-nurse provided the love interest. Nothing could be more warm and fuzzy.

Victor Rodman, playing the old doctor—the Lionel Barrymore role—was an actor who was really confined to a wheelchair. He and Paul Burke, the young doctor, were both terrified of Jack, who could be very demanding and brutal. The TelePrompTers were in use. Jack was directing all the shows.

On the second script I wrote for him, he told me he'd like me to direct but said he hadn't found the right tone for the show yet, hadn't set the style. I tried, tactfully, to suggest that this wasn't *Dragnet* and the staccato style that made that show so great wasn't appropriate for this one. I didn't get through. He wouldn't give up. He had to solve the problem his way.

Revue Productions (an arm of MCA), which owned the studio, had built Jack a separate building with offices and cutting rooms on the ground floor. Above these was a luxurious suite where he lived with his wife, singer-actress Julie London. He would have me up for drinks and talk about various aspects of moviemaking. It was a very friendly relationship. But I once mentioned *Medic* and he went into a diatribe about Jim Moser, who had created *Dragnet* with him. Their parting had not been amicable. Moser had often reacted in a similar fashion, but with less venom, when Jack's name came up.

I continued writing scripts, Jack continued directing them with the cast getting ever more uptight.

When I turned in the eleventh script, he asked me to direct it.

I arrived early on the set and ordered all the TelePrompTers removed. When the cast came in, I said, "I'm sorry to do this to you but we're going to sit down while the crew is lighting for the first shot and learn lines." I am sure someone quickly phoned Jack about the heresy but he did not interfere. For the rest of the day we *played* scenes instead of reading them. Nervous at first, the cast settled in and began to give performances.

On the second day (these were three-day shoots), the cutter came down to the set. He had just run the dailies and was ecstatic. He said they were the best he'd seen. Many people in the company came to congratulate me. I had to explain that it was no act of genius. I simply had made the cast members feel they were working together.

Toward the end of the last day, Jack came onto the set and shocked everyone by announcing that this was the final show. He was canceling *Noah's Ark*.

I later found out that the network had decided to cancel after the contractually agreed 12 shows. The series' ratings had been dismal. I am sure Jack had known that when he gave the eleventh show to me.

Contractually, the network could not pull the plug until the twelfth show but Jack was so furious he said, "They can't fire me. I quit."

His pride was so damaged that he pulled out with just 11 shows, not enough to go into syndication and recoup his losses. There was nothing that could be done with 11. God knows I had done things just as stupid and stubborn but not as instantly costly.

Much later, when he was doing another series and looking for directors, my agent suggested me but was told Jack didn't like my work.

12—Test Patterns

Warner's promise had finally come true and the Michael Curtiz Production unit had been set up on the Warner lot. Mike's offices were the old Marion Davies bungalow, actually a fair-sized house, that Hearst had built for her on the MGM lot when he had formed Cosmopolitan Productions to showcase her talent. She had been Hearst's mistress for many years and he was determined to make her into a great star. She had a fine comedic talent but he would not permit her to display it. He wanted her in historical, "important" parts.

Then came *Citizen Kane*. Orson Welles made a classic picture, his first, which greatly resembled the life of William Randolph Hearst and his affair with Marion Davies. For her and for his own pride, he used the vast power of his press in an effort to destroy Welles.

There is a poem about this bungalow Mike inherited, written by Dorothy Parker, poetess and great wit, who occasionally worked in films. She had been a guest at San Simeon, Hearst's castle. Because Marion Davies was an alcoholic, Hearst was strict about drinking. One cocktail was allowed his guests before dinner. Parker had more, probably having brought her own supply.

Marion herself had a magnificent perfume collection in her bathroom, many of the bottles filled with booze to avoid scrutiny.

At dinner, Parker not only overdrank the limit but she lit a cigarette at the table, a definite no-no. She was asked to pack her bags and leave. One story has her writing the poem in the guest book on her way out. The other version has her walking on the back lot at Metro, where she was briefly employed, and spotting the Davies bungalow in all its Spanish splendor with religious ornamentation appropriate to its period. At any rate, the poem pointed out the hypocrisy of Hearst and Davies:

> Upon my honor I saw a Madonna
> In a most peculiar niche
> Above the door of the well known whore
> Of the world's worst son of a bitch.

Mike now had that historic building as his offices. His company was going into production so I went to work for him as a writer, making it a family affair. Mother was acting as story editor and had persuaded Frances Marion to write for them. Mike chose as his producer a wonderful film editor who had cut some of his best pictures, George Amy, resourceful, a genius for effects. In our first production, *The Unsuspected* with Claude Rains and Joan Caufield, he used rear projection to create a fabulous illusion with a set consisting of only a corner of a building and two open entrances backed by process screens. In one entrance, a taxi pulls up in

Michael Curtiz (back to camera) at a production meeting for *The Unsuspected* (1947). Included are Claude Rains (center), Fred Clark (second from left) and John Meredyth Lucas (right).

front of a screen showing the traffic of Fifth Avenue. A man gets out and rushes into the other entrance in front of another screen showing the busy interior of Grand Central Station.

With today's techniques of blue screens and computer aids, the effect would not be exceptional. In its day it was a revolution. You would swear you were at Grand Central Station.

George, unfortunately, was not a businessman and couldn't cope with the wiles of the Warners. Mike, loyal as ever, would not. Warner bookkeeping was almost beyond understanding, even by expert CPAs.

Like Hal Wallis when he started his own production company, Mike began to produce inexpensive pictures to build a cash flow. Marty Melcher, an agent who was married to one of the Andrews Sisters, one of the hottest singing groups during and after the Second World War, brought in a girl called Doris Day. Mike tested her, put her under contract and did three pictures with her. Marty, her agent, married her as soon as he could divorce the Andrews sister (Patty) he was married to.

12—Test Patterns

I functioned as dialogue director on the picture. My future wife, Joan, had a friend, a girl who had worked briefly in the Warner Music Department. She had divorced her husband and was broke. Joan took her in to her apartment until she could get on her feet again. As a musician, this unfortunate girl decided Doris Day needed a lot of work. Her phrasing was wrong and she needed voice lessons. She became loud and insistent one night to Mike, who looked astonished, but said nothing. Fortunately, he also did nothing. Doris Day's singing style was left alone to bring her fame and fortune. Joan's "friend" had not only been using her apartment and eating her food but frequently borrowed her car, ostensibly to look for work. One day when Joan had gotten it back, a car raced into the intersection in front of her. Joan slammed on the brakes and a whole family of empty pint vodka bottles slid out from under the seat. The "friend" found a new home.

All Mike's Doris Day pictures were moneymakers although the Warner books showed a loss. Besides functioning as dialogue director, I did several other scripts. One was an adaptation of James Cain's bestseller *Serenade*. It concerns a bisexual who, in Mexico, regains his masculinity and his great singing voice through a relationship with a Mexican peasant girl. The very hint of homosexuality was forbidden in those days and several studios had tried to find a handle that would keep the elements of the story but avoid the censorship problem. Cain wrote me that of all the scripts done from his book, he liked mine the best.

Compliments among writers is one thing, getting a picture on the screen another. The studio fought against it, claiming it was uncastable, making various other excuses. It was never made. Another script I did, *The Other Woman*, was done only after Warners got back the rights to all of Mike's properties.

The evil of studio bookkeeping is not a new thing. But with a combination of that and other efforts, Warners was finally able to put Mike in a position that was untenable. They offered to buy the company from him, tendering what they called a generous profit to buy out all his rights including Doris Day's contract. Day, they told him, was worthless. They were going to let her go. Mike reluctantly signed the agreement.

The Warners had Doris Day's contract and had a superstar. Her career is history. After that, Mike finally lost his loyalty to the Warners and left.

I went back to freelancing. At Republic studio I directed many episodes of *The Crusader* with David Brian. One day I got a call from my agent. Would I go to the Walt Disney Studio and talk to the producer about making a promotional film for *20000 Leagues Under the Sea*, which was being shot on the Disney lot? I told him I did not do commercials.

"This isn't exactly a commercial," he said. "They're offering exceptional money. It could only cost an hour to listen."

Reluctantly I went to meet with the producer, Card Walker. I had never heard any names on the Disney lot except Walt's, who played polo with Mike a few times.

Disney's was like no studio I had ever seen. It resembled a small Midwestern campus, lots of green lawns, a very relaxed air, none of the bustle and stress I was used to.

Card Walker explained that Dick Fleisher was directing *20000 Leagues Under the Sea* and the company had spent a lot of time in the Bahamas on the underwater sequences. The 16mm cameramen assigned to the picture had filmed the making of the picture (a usual promotion now, a totally novel idea then). They had 12 hours of film showing fish, the submarine and company underwater, etc. They wanted to make a half-hour show of this for the new *Wonderful World of Disney* show that was going on ABC. Disney was wonderful indeed. He was using the time paid him for a television entertainment show to advertise his motion picture. I was still reluctant. It seemed too much like the advertising business but I agreed to screen some of the film and decide.

I ran only an hour or so and I was enchanted. The film was excellent. I could see a way of handling it and told Card I'd give it a shot. I was given an office in the main building. I was assigned a secretary who turned out to be the younger sister of Camille, the cabaret singer of my brief UCLA days. I was also assigned a film editor.

With the editor I picked out certain shots I liked, then I wrote a script. I wanted Disney's approval on the script before I made a final edit on the film so I sent the script to his office and awaited his reaction. I waited. Two weeks passed. I called Disney's secretary. Yes, the script was there. I waited another week. Nothing.

I called my agent. "Don't worry," he said. "Disney does things differently. Anyway," he added, pleased, "the checks come on time each week."

Two weeks after that I called the office of Walker, the producer who hired me. He was out of town. Finally I went to a friend, Bill Walsh, who had worked in publicity for Maggie Ettinger before moving to Disney and had finally forgiven me for the Ruth Roman affair. He was later to produce *The Mickey Mouse Club*. I explained my problem.

"You sent in a script!" Bill laughed. "Walt never reads scripts." He explained that the usual procedure was to prepare storyboards with sketches Walt could follow while the idea of the story was being explained. I said that the producer had not told me this.

"What producer?"

"Card Walker," I told him.

He laughed again, explaining that Walker was not a producer. He was head of publicity.

I called my agent again and explained the circumstances. "Maybe Walker hadn't the right to hire me."

"Checks are still coming in," the agent said.

I later learned that almost nothing goes in the usual way at Disney.

I was assigned a storyboard artist. He translated my script into innumerable drawings, which were tacked onto two large storyboards.

Then, feeling like an idiot, I had the storyboards set up at the front of the main theater and, when Walt and his entourage came in, I stood there with a long pointer in my hand, indicating the pictures, one by one. "And here's where the fish first sees the submarine" for 30 minutes. Walt loved it and wanted the show expanded into an hour.

While working on the new, expanded version (it was later to win an Emmy), he asked me to do a show on *Lady and the Tramp*, an animated feature he had in production. I had not yet finished with the first assignment so I was given a second storyboard artist.

We had not yet completed that when Walt wanted to do a half-hour on the actual shooting of the attack of the giant squid in *20000 Leagues*. The ship and the mechanical squid were in a huge tank built on a sound stage. I was assigned a 16mm cameraman to photograph the event. The segment was to contain, besides the battle, the history of giant squids, their mention in literature, etc.

I took my cameraman to the stage, promising Dick Fleischer, the director, I would try to keep out of his way. We shot the squid attack, including the crew and cameras shooting the feature. My cutter assembled it. Walt was happy. It would fit well into the format of *The Wonderful World*. Then he wanted to do a show on the history of the submarine, from Civil War days to the present.

I said I'd start research on the project right away. "I've taken care of that," he told me. "I got a guy called Willy Ley to help you."

"Willy Ley," I said, stunned. "The German science writer?"

"Yeah," Walt said. "I've got a couple of other ideas to do with him, too."

From the time I used to be sent to Auntie Vi's to get me out of the way on party weekends, I have loved science fiction. A drugstore two blocks from Auntie Vi's house, where I used to walk to get ice cream cones, had a large magazine rack. One day I finished my cone quickly and started to browse through the magazines. I found *Science Wonder Stories*.

I read the first one sitting on the floor of the drug store, ran back to Aunt Vi's to get the extra money to buy the magazine. From that moment, I was hooked. I read every issue of *Science Wonder Stories*, *Amazing Stories*, then *Science Fantasy*. I looked forward to the time when the extra thick *Amazing Story Quarterly* came out. I was fascinated by a column called "Science Fact," which was written by Willy Ley. So, years later, when Disney actually offered me my hero, I was speechless.

Willy Ley, a rotund man wearing thick glasses and looking much younger than I expected, sat across the desk from me. Imagine how a teenage girl would feel if Elvis gyrated into her living room. I gradually got over my shyness and found Willy a wonderful man with a sense of humor and an eclectic interest in life. We spent a lot of time together, in and out of the studio. He was married to a ballerina, Russian and gorgeous. They had two children.

We became great friends and I found him even more amazing than I expected. Once when walking on the beach of our Malibu summer house, his daughter, aged five, looked at a hermit crab in the tide pool. "What's it good for?" she asked.

"That," Willy told her sternly, "is enough of that anthropocentric nonsense. It fulfills its own purpose."

The five-year-old not only accepted the rebuke but understood its meaning. That was Willy Ley.

13

Foreign Accents

Willy and I worked out several shows on the development of the submarine and rocketry.

Wernher von Braun was also brought briefly to the studio as an advisor. Willy had sponsored him into the German Rocket Society where, during the war, he developed the V-2, the dreaded ultimate weapon used against England toward the end of World War II. He and most of his assistants were captured and he became one of "our" German scientists, competing with the Russian German scientists, who had been captured by our then-allies. Von Braun later took over our American development of rockets and intercontinental missiles at the Redstone Arsenal, ultimately landing us on the Moon.

One day we three were having lunch together at the Disney commissary and were discussing the smog, which was just becoming a problem in the Los Angeles Basin. I mentioned the formation of the basin and the atmospheric inversion layer that held the smog down until it backed up against the surrounding mountains and couldn't escape. "Then," von Braun said with Teutonic dispatch, "you blast a hole in the mountain." I've always wondered if it would work.

I had been hired at Disney to do what amounted to a commercial. Now I had five shows in various stages of completion, a secretary, two storyboard men, a cameraman and a cutter. I had an entire production unit. Then came the day when I showed Walt a rough cut of the submarine show. I had recorded Willy doing the narration.

We did not get far into it when Walt asked, "What the hell's he saying?" He turned to me. "Why the hell is he doing the narration?"

I said I thought it made the show sound interesting and authentic. "Well," Walt said, "that's what makes horse racing."

The phone was ringing as I got back to my office. I had been fired.

In retrospect, I should have known better. Walt had a TV series, *Robin Hood*, shooting in England with Richard Greene in the lead and many British actors. I had sat with him a few times in the projection room watching dailies. At almost every other line, Walt would grumble, "What'd he say? I can't understand those damn Limeys." After that I had made the mistake of putting an accented narration on a Disney film.

Having been ejected from Disney and done a couple of pictures at another studio, I got a call from Disney to come back and write for the *Zorro* series, which was just starting on *Wonderful World*. I had mixed feelings but I finally went. Walt greeted me as though nothing had ever happened and told me excitedly about the authentic sets he had had built. Walt was fascinated with early California.

Norman Foster, who had been an actor and director, was married to Loretta Young's sister. He was directing the series and also acting as producer without title. Nothing went normally at Disney. Norm had gone through the same experience I had. He had done scripts on the outlaw Joaquin Murrieta, a sort of a Robin Hood of Spanish California, and had been trying for weeks to get Walt's approval to go ahead with the project. He finally followed Walt into the toilet and, standing beside him at the urinal, in effect holding him captive, told Walt the idea, got him to say it sounded promising but he hadn't studied it. When Norman got back to his office, there was a message to call Walt's office. He did. The secretary told him he was fired. Later Norman, rehired, did that same Murrieta story for Disney.

Mother's last picture for Darryl at Fox was *Mark of Zorro*, starring Tyrone Power. That was in 1940. Now, over 15 years later, I was writing *Zorro*, the series. After doing several scripts, I began directing them.

Directing, true to the Disney tradition, was different and strange. First, I found that the main sets had not been built with wild walls. These are walls that can be easily moved and then put back to accommodate camera angles and lighting. The Disney walls were solidly and permanently built, like a house.

Then, at production meetings, customary before each shoot, where all the elements required for that episode are discussed and the director requests certain equipment, camera lenses not normally carried, dollies or camera cranes and the like, there is generally an attempt to keep the director's requests within financial reason. Here I found that anything I asked for was readily granted. It was unnerving. Everyone was so friendly, all striving to help and please. They still operated as an animation studio— unused to the procedures of live action. That, however, was to be changed.

I finally felt at ease when I met with a newly hired unit manager whose job it was to watch the budget, see that there were no overruns. I met with him and my assistant to go over the shooting schedule. One look at his sad Jewish face, frozen in an attitude of perpetual anguish that implied that anything requested was impossible, and I was reassured. This was the picture business I knew.

As silly as it was, *Zorro* was a popular show. Kids seemed to love it. When my younger daughter, Victoria, was in nursery school, the teacher was having a discussion about jobs, asking the children what their fathers did. Various kids said banker, doctor, pharmacist, architect, etc. Victoria was silent, turning her head away. When the teacher got to her she refused to answer. When pressed by all the other kids, she began to cry. "Mummy said my Daddy is going to shoot Zorro," she sobbed.

When we had finished our season of *Zorro*, Walt called me in to discuss a project especially dear to his heart. During World War I, though underage, he had run away, joined up and served as an ambulance driver in France. He carried with him a book titled *The Gray Seal*, which he read and reread. It was a sort of early Superman-Batman. The Gray Seal was a rich young man whose hobby was stamping out crime. The gray seal (as in sealing wax) was his signature. It was pretty unbelievable, even for a children's show, and as diplomatically as possible, I told Walt so. He would hear of no argument, insisting it was a wonderful character. Walt had such an instinct for what would please an audience that there was only so far you could logically disagree. His secret of success was that he had a truly childish enthusiasm.

One Saturday I had to go into the studio to see a rough assemblage of footage my cutter had made. Joan and I were going to a party later in the afternoon and I took her with me and I told her she could go to my office and read—I would just be an hour. We passed a room on the lower floor where a huge tabletop scale model of the future Disneyland was set up. Walt would, from time to time, examine the models and change things even while the ground was being broken and some of the foundations laid. It was his baby.

I saw my cut with the editor and made my changes, which took longer than expected, then went to my office. Joan was not there. I searched around and finally found her down with the Disneyland model. I apologized for being late.

"That's all right," she said. "That nice man over there has been showing me all the rides." She indicated the man. "He must have spent an hour."

"That nice man," I told her, "is Walt Disney." I formally introduced them.

After many episodes were roughed out, *The Gray Seal* was, as had been clear to me at the beginning, a waste of time. Walt hated to give up on anything but he finally did.

While I was in one of our many conferences, my son Michael was born well over a month premature. Walt's secretary had strict standing orders that he was never to be disturbed for any reason during story conferences but Mother got on the phone and explained that the doctors said my son's heart had a potentially serious problem. That did it. She burst into the conference and told me, expecting Walt's wrath. Instead, Walt sympathized, insisted that I go to the hospital at once and asked if there was anything he could do. The secretary was dazed.

I went.

The valve problem in Michael's heart recovered over the next few days and he had a normal development. But *The Gray Seal* died.

I did, however, learn one fascinating thing while I was at Disney. From the first day I wondered at the arrangement of the main executive building. It was laid out as a series of separate wings. At the entrance of each wing was a long counter. Past the counter there were a couple of large offices, then an open oval with smaller offices opening all around the oval. I started working in one of the smaller ones. Then, as my projects expanded, I needed more room and graduated to a large office. But I kept wondering at this arrangement, which I had never seen before. I finally decided that it must be because Disney had started as an animation studio. It was only lately that it had branched into live action. Probably, I thought, the drawings and cells went to the counter and were distributed from there. None of the people I asked could tell me how it worked. But these people were not animators. I asked Walt.

When he had built the studio, animation was a small enterprise, almost a garage industry. He had trouble getting a loan for such a structure as he envisioned. Bank after bank considered it too risky. There was, however, one thing this end of the San Fernando Valley needed—a hospital. They lent him money to build a hospital. Then, when his business failed, the bank would have a readily usable property.

The long counters were nurse's stations; the large offices were wards and the small offices private rooms.

Disney did not go broke and, ultimately, to meet the need the bank anticipated, St. Joseph's Hospital was built directly across the street from the Disney Main Gate.

In 1956 I worked with Mike once more at Paramount, writing a story that was finally titled *The Scarlet Hour*. Paramount had a contract that Mike couldn't get out of and they had a couple of unknowns they expected Mike to make stars of. He was indeed a starmaker but to make a star you need some sort of quality, not necessarily acting ability but beauty, personality or some special attribute. None was forthcoming in this cast.

Mike, by now, was getting older. It had been awhile since *White Christmas*. He had done other successful films, *We're No Angels*, *The Vagabond King*, *The Best Things in Life Are Free*, *The Helen Morgan Story*, but none had been a real blockbuster. The one that should have been a really big was *The Egyptian*, which he'd agreed to direct for Darryl Zanuck. It was from a best-selling book and had a role ideal for Marlon Brando, who had been signed.

But when Darryl insisted that his current mistress, Bella Darvi play the female lead, Brando balked. Darryl had somehow convinced his wife that Bella was simply an innocent actress who, being new to this country, needed their help. The girl was charming to Virginia and actually moved

Mike sets a shot on the set of *The Egyptian* (1954). Actors include Joan Winfield (background, center), Edmund Purdom, Victor Mature, with Michael Wilding as Akhnaton and Anitra Stevens as Nefertiti.

Joan Winfield and Peter Ustinov relax between takes on the set of *The Egyptian* (1954).

into their house. Despite Brando's contract and interminable negotiation, Brando was inflexible with, as it turned out, good reason. Darvi was beautiful but nothing else.

Darryl set out to convince Mike that he would be able to get a great performance out of Darvi. Friendship was a fault of Mike's.

With Brando gone, a search was on for a replacement. It was not easy to find a big male star willing to play under Zanuck's rules. By default the prize finally went to Edmund Purdom. There were some good things in the film—Victor Mature, Jean Simmons and Peter Ustinov. But Purdom and Darvi did not twinkle into stars. The only one to benefit from the exercise was Ustinov. He afterwards made a career of quoting Curtizisms at dinners and on talk shows.

Mike cast Joan in a small part as nurse of the Pharaoh's children so I finally drove to Taos alone. Joan was to meet me there as soon as she finished her part. I went to write a novel set in New Mexico, the meeting place of three cultures, Anglo, Mexican and Indian.

I rented the Taos art gallery of Eulalia Emetaz. She was going to Colorado for three months and she let me have her home, one half of which was art gallery, the rest living quarters. It was the oldest house in Taos, built in 1620, with adobe walls four feet thick so that the windows were deeply recessed. It was cool in summer, relatively warm in winter, when temperatures could suddenly drop to 20 below.

One problem with an adobe house built in 1620 was that the roof was covered with a layer of dirt to seal the branches and thatching. At all times, dust fell in a gentle misty rain. In the dining area of the main room, it was necessary to bring covered dishes to the table and eat quickly before the dust made the food gritty.

I did a lot of reading, research and visits to the Taos Pueblo. Visitors were welcome at the ceremonial dances but not in the living quarters. These are multi-storied apartment complexes that have remained virtually unchanged since they were built 800 years ago.

The ceremonials were fascinating. The drums were in the kivas—underground ceremonial rooms—and their beat could be felt through the earth, through the soles of your feet. After hours of it, you retained the feeling long after you went home, as one still feels the motion of a boat after coming ashore.

As soon as she was through with the part she had played in *The Egyptian*, Joan joined me in Taos. *The Egyptian* had been a troubling experience for her. Mike's current mistress was also on the picture. The crew knew. Eli Dunn, under whom I had worked at Fox, was the assistant director. Was Joan being disloyal to Mother by working with that girl? It raised all sorts of questions.

We stayed in Taos for another month, spending a lot of time at the pueblo. We had retained the services of Eulalia's Indian maid, who lived in the pueblo. I had made friends with her husband who had a ceremonial post at the pueblo. He got us into places where tourists cannot go. It was fascinating research but the novel never got written.

We returned to Hollywood and I directed a bunch of shows at the Hal Roach studio for Ben Fox, producer of *Code Three*. One day he called and asked if I'd like to go to Australia for a year as assistant producer and director on a new series to be shot in Sydney. I was also to write as many scripts as I could manage.

The series was to star Peter Graves, playing Christopher Cobb, an actual historical character, an American who failed to strike it rich in the California gold fields in '49 and, went to Australia when their gold rush happened a few years after ours. The Australian gold strike had many incredible parallels with ours. Chinese coolie labor was imported with the same ugly race riots which had occurred in California. Cobb went to try his luck in Australia. But, this time, he did not dig for gold, but set up a stage line, Cobb & Co.—a Down Under Wells Fargo. It made him more money than he could have pulled out of the ground.

I told Ben I'd think about the offer.

What I did was write a treatment called *Dance Out of Darkness*. This was the Alicia Alonzo story. I had been contacted by Alicia's companion and advance woman who told me Alicia's incredible personal story. She had danced with the Ballet de Monte Carlo, the New York Ballet and others. She had danced all over Europe—all over the world. Small, beautiful, with sharply defined features, she was Cuban and had her own ballet company in Havana. But more important, from my standpoint, was her personal story. She had a detached retina at a very young age. Several surgeries. When she continued to dance, the retina of the other eye detached. She had very narrow slits of vision in both eyes, like peeping through an almost drawn curtain. While she was confined to bed after her various surgeries, she used her fingers on the coverlet, to learn the steps of the many ballets she wanted to dance. Her fingers were fascinating to watch.

She was married to her choreographer, had children and was still dancing. I went east to meet her at the old Met in New York while she was dancing the *Swan Lake* pas de deux with Igor Youskevitch.

Her vision was so bad that she had men stationed on either side at the rear of the house with red flashlights to give her points to fix on so could stop her turns at the precise spot required.

While we were meeting together, I was backstage several times at the old Met and found that the iron staircases that go up to the top dressing rooms make a fantastic vantage point from which I could see the stage area and backstage at the same time. From there I watched *Graduation Ball*, a lovely ballet, which had been choreographed by David Lichine and opened in Australia. From where I stood, I could see the dancers in the set onstage and, in the wings, unseen by the audience, Lichine, dancing the part of the Old General, then of the other dancers, step by step. God, how I wanted to find a way to use that scene in a picture.

Alicia was dancing in Los Angeles soon after I had finished the script. I made a contract with her. Alicia had a ballet company in Havana. We would use that for the dancing and shoot the scenes of her early life there. I would direct the picture. I got Harriet Parsons, daughter of Louella, as producer. She had brilliantly started her career by producing *I Remember Mama*.

Harriet had every reason to remember Mama. She was around the Venice beach house Mother shared with Maggie and Louella Parsons when I was quite small. Harriet, who was probably in college at the time, gave me my first camera—a Kodak box camera. She later told me that, at

Mike and John stand with Alicia Alonso and Guy Madison during a cocktail reception for the Cuban ballerina at Encino (1958).

the age I was when she gave me the present, she was clearly more literate than her mother believed. She remembers Louella telling a friend in her presence, "Harriet isn't very p-r-e-t-t-y but she's s-m-a-r-t."

We met with Natalie Wood, whose career was just taking off. She was a dancer and could handle the close shots. Alicia, wearing a Natalie Wood mask, would dance the longer shots and the complex steps. I threw a huge party with Alicia, the Cuban Consul, most of the Hollywood press, stars including Cesar Romero, who was Cuban and whose grandfather had been Jose Marti, the hero of Cuban independence. Everything looked bright. The picture could be shot on a low budget because of Alicia's Cuban involvement. She had been declared a national treasure.

Then came Castro. The Battista government fell. The United States did not favor Castro or allow any connection with his government. Our Cuban partnership was no more. *Dance Out of Darkness* was never made.

Ben Fox was pressing for an answer to his Australian offer. I now gave it serious consideration.

Mike went on to direct *The Proud Rebel* with Alan Ladd and Ladd's son David, a beautiful picture but not a blockbuster. Less than two weeks before shooting was to start, Mike woke in the night with a terrible pain. He later admitted that he had had it for some time. Dr. MacDonald came out to the house and diagnosed acute appendicitis, on the point of rupturing. Mike needed surgery immediately. An ambulance was called.

Mike was horrified but stubborn. He was about to shoot *The Proud Rebel*. He adamantly refused to go to the hospital until I had called Sam Goldwyn, Jr., my friend and producer of the picture, in the middle of the night and got his dazed assurance that the production would be pushed back. Only then did Mike allow the waiting ambulance to take him.

While in the hospital, they detected a nodule in his prostate and biopsied it. He was told there was no problem. With his usual incredible energy, he was out of bed in less than a week and, despite doctor's warnings, back at work in two. The picture's schedule lost only one week.

An unkind reviewer praised *The Proud Rebel* but added, "At last Alan Ladd has contributed something to the screen—his son."

Mike did a picture with Wallis at Paramount—*King Creole* with Elvis Presley. Another excellent picture. Mike and Elvis got on very well together and Mike got a real performance out of him. But this picture, while doing very good business, was not an epic.

He did, in quick succession, *The Man in the Net*, *The Hangman*, *Olympia* and *The Adventures of Huckleberry Finn*.

Mike was beginning to be concerned with his career, with intimations of mortality, and was very concerned with Mother's rate of spending. The house was bursting with servants, and her gifts to all her friends and people who worked for her were wildly extravagant. There were 50 and 100 dollar tips to the hairdressers and manicurists who came to the house. This had apparently led to some hard words because I have a letter he wrote her—probably sometime before December 7, their anniversary. It reads (with his spelling):

> Bess Darling,
>
>   I'm terrible sory tath the last 2 week bote so many unplesent problem our life wich disturb our anniversary. But you should know that this problems ar not mine alone. I'm try to think for our future only in our interest thath we shuld live without financial trouble.
>
>   Hoppe you forgive my nervises and hope we have many years to comme together in happiness. Belive my sincerity and apriation to you. For ever Much love,
>
> Mike.

Elvis Presley and Mike confer on the set of *King Creole* (1958).

I was not aware of these domestic problems when I talked over Ben's Australian offer with Joan, who had been born in Melbourne. "I'm going to take you back to your people," I told her. We decided it would be fun and educational for the kids. I arranged to take Joan, Elizabeth, Victoria, Michael and their Mexican nanny, Paula, who spoke almost no English. Michael, well over his birth problems, was healthy now and almost two years old. Aside from his age—I had been taken to Australia at less than a year, this was a replay of my own experience.

We were all to go together but Joan developed a gall bladder problem that required surgery. I waited to see that come out all right but could not wait for her full recovery. Time was pressing so Ben and I flew out two weeks in advance to get housing and set up the company. Then Joan followed with the kids and Paula.

The state of the art in flying then was the civil version of the B47, one of the early jets. It was 17 hours' flying time with stops in Honolulu and Fiji for refueling.

Before boarding the Qantas flight, Ben discovered an insurance booth at the airport where you could buy a million dollar life insurance policy for the round trip for some very reasonable price. I got one, too.

A Western townsite had been built for us near the Artransa Studios outside of Sydney. Artransa was not what we would call a studio although they did have two stages. The studio was

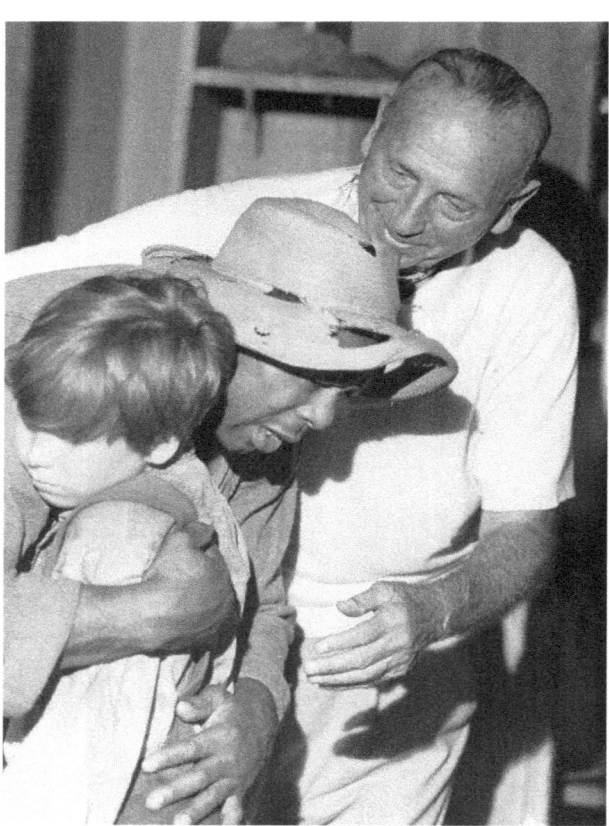

Mike sets up a scene with former boxing champion Archie Moore and Eddie Hodges in *The Adventures of Huckleberry Finn* (1960).

in the middle of nowhere and was bordered on the west and south by a huge eucalyptus forest, trees 90 to a 100 feet tall. While we were discussing our crew, which was to be all Australian, we heard sounds like cannon going off. We rushed outside and were engulfed in smoke. We could see gigantic flames licking up the tall trees. When they reached the tops the fire would crown—explode like the Fourth of July, spewing fire in all directions and catching the adjacent trees.

The studio personnel, used to these problems, rushed to man hoses, trying to keep the flames away from the studio.

I wanted a camera. God, with a spectacle like that, I would write an episode to use it in. Our cameraman had not started work and could not be reached by phone. I kept bugging the busy firefighters. Wasn't there anyone who could use the cameras in the department? There wasn't. I am fine with a still camera but I knew I could never manage a large motion picture camera.

While the battle to save the studio went on, I went through lists in the studio manager's office, calling cameramen. I got one who promised he would come "straightaway." I was delighted until I learned he lived in Hornsby, at the very end of the North Shore railway.

My mind was already developing a story of our stagecoach caught in a catastrophic fire. When the cameraman finally arrived, the studio was safe and the fire had nearly burned itself out. We could see flames in the distance and smoldering stumps in the foreground. I never got my fire episode.

The next problem was housing. Ben, Peter Graves and his family, Peter Maxwell and Kathleen chose houses at Whale Beach (pronounced *wile*). I needed a school for the girls and a large house. We finally found one far inland and distant from the others, in a town called Wahroonga.

Because of time and film delivery dates, we had to start shooting before my family arrived.

Our first location was up the Hunter River at an old hotel built in the last century by convict labor. The British used Australia as a prison colony. The hotel had two guest rooms, one with a bath. We put Peter Graves and his family there and got trailers (called caravans in Australia) for the crew. Ben and I decided against sharing the hotel and its lack of conveniences. We rented a cabin cruiser and went up the Hunter River to dock beside the hotel and live aboard.

It was 40 miles up a river full of sandbars. We went aground twice and arrived late. I had planned to have a swim before dinner but we had to forgo that. Taking our dinghy, we rowed ashore and managed to catch dinner before the dining room closed.

When I told the owner of the hotel of my disappointment at not having a swim, he went white. He had lost two hotel employees in the river that year—to sharks. It turned out that the mouth of the Hunter, where we rented the boat, was the breeding place for sharks all up and down the coast of New South Wales and the Hunter River is tidal even 40 miles upstream. Australia is a shark's paradise. There was no swimming by us for the duration.

We said good night to the crew, got back to the dinghy, rowed out and could not find our boat. Finally, through the weeds, I made out a flickering light almost at water level. We approached. It was our masthead light. The tide had gone out and the boat we had rented to live on in comfort lay on its side in the mud. I managed to wedge myself into my bunk, actually lying on the bulkhead. Near four o'clock in the morning, the tide came in. With a series of startling groans and heaves, the boat finally righted itself. It remained anchored in midstream for the rest of the shoot and we rowed very carefully back and forth.

On the first day of shooting, Joan, Paula and the three kids arrived at Kingsford Smith airport in Sydney. The studio manager had the press there to greet a former Australian actress who was returning with her family for the first Australian international television series. The kids blinked at the popping flash bulbs.

"Mummy," Elizabeth asked, "Are you famous?"

Joan shook her head

"Then why are they—?" Elizabeth began.

Robert Lord, the studio manager, kindly intervened. "There's a difference," he told the children, "between being famous and being important."

I had rented the house in Wahroonga (a wonderful Aborigine name, translating roughly as Our Home) on the North Shore Line where there are a series of villages resembling English Railway towns, all with aboriginal names. I also arranged to have the house fumigated. Australia has more poisonous animals than any place I have ever heard of—spiders, ticks, snakes. There are two varieties of snake that are non-poisonous. The rest range from rattlesnake-like to almost instant death. The Australians have a very *laissez faire* attitude about these dangers that share the continent with them. They feel that, if left alone, the animals will leave them alone. As a foreigner, reading the horrifying posters the government put out for travelers and thinking of the children playing in the yard, I had the feeling that every misstep would be our last. So I had the house and grounds fumigated before the family arrived.

I had myself driven back from the location the night their plane got in. After shooting all day and driving three hours on miserable roads, I walked into the house, found the children asleep, Joan in bed. I went to the kitchen for water and found a large tarantula-like monster in the sink. It escaped. Exhausted, I went upstairs and found another on the landing. Determined to know what risks we were facing, I got a glass and captured it, put it on the back porch for later identification. A quick check partially reassured me that the children's rooms were clear of danger, then I grabbed a few hours of sleep before my driver arrived at five to take me back to the location. I showed him the monster I had captured and he smiled, " No fear, mate," he said. "Tarantula. They eat the redbacks. Mind the redbacks and the trap doors, they're the worst." So what I had taken for the enemy was really on our side. On the drive back I got a lecture on letting things alone. Spiders have their life in the cellars and underground burrows. My cleansing fumigation had simply flushed the survivors up into the house. The driver did, however, warn me never to put on shoes without shaking them out. "Scorpions."

Later, while shooting on our townsite, which was brush-covered, I almost lost my fear watching our crew deal with snakes. They would grab the tails and snap them like a whip, breaking their spinal cord. They would then casually throw them over their shoulders and get on with their work.

We became quite a family, Peter and Joan Graves, Peter Maxwell (the Hungarian-British director) and his wife, Kathleen. Ben, Peter and I were American. Australian law required British Commonwealth Content in any picture shot there. That meant that, besides actors, we must have a British director. Peter Maxwell, born Hungarian, was a British citizen, had gone to what he described as "a rather good public school." He filled the British requirement. I, as associate producer, alternated with Maxwell, directing every other show.

Our shooting took us all over Australia, to Canberra, the capital, to Melbourne, where Joan and I toured her childhood home and school. Then to Adelaide on the southernmost tip of Australia.

From Adelaide we flew 1,500 miles north to Alice Springs. There we shot parts of six different shows using aboriginal tribes and the fantastic landscape surrounding Alice Springs, which is in the dead heart of the continent. The Aboriginal tribes were as unspoiled by civilization as it was possible to find. They were fascinating. They really do the miraculous tracking you read about, can tell whose footprint they see in the dust, even the walker's state of health. They can dig in the baking desert sand and water will seep into the hole. But then, they've had God knows how many millennia to practice before Europeans came.

We worked from the splendor of the Alice Springs Hotel, the only

On an Australian outback location for the series *Whiplash*, John directs Peter Graves and native Australian actor Robert Tuddawalli (1960).

hotel in town. It was of cement—all bare cement, lobby, halls, rooms. We had one of the few rooms with a private bath. In the center of our large bedroom hung a single light bulb on the end of a cord. The bathroom contained the requisite washbowl, toilet and shower. The odd aspect of the shower is that it had no enclosure. Water came out of the showerhead and spurted all over the bathroom, basin, toilet—everything. The bathroom being a step up from the bedroom, surplus water ran down onto the cement floor beneath the bed where a drain had been provided for that problem. The hotel food was god-awful. Australia had recently relaxed its white only immigration policy and had begun to let in southern Europeans so excellent Greek and Italian restaurants were beginning to spring up. We found a small family-run Italian place and ate there whenever possible.

One of the episodes we shot concerned an outbreak of hoof and mouth disease and the heroic efforts to stamp it out. We were shooting on the station (ranch) of a man named Bob Darkin who owned 120 square miles of land and considerable cattle. One of the scenes called for the killing of an infected steer. I explained the scene to Bob and asked him to get his vet over with a tranquilizing gun so that, with proper cutting, the animal could appear to be shot and fall to the ground. "No fear, mate," he reassured me. "She'll be right."

On the appointed day we were ready for the scene and I asked Darkin where the vet was. He shook his head at my stupidity and picked up his rifle. "No need to trouble the vet. It's only a bloody steer, mate." We were pressed for time and I reluctantly gave in to local custom. At the appropriate moment I signaled and the owner shot the animal neatly through the heart. That was on a Friday afternoon.

Saturday morning Darkin popped into the hotel while we were having what passed for breakfast. He ordered a pint of beer, followed by many more. Then he invited the entire company to a barbecue at his station that night. At noon, after consuming rivers of beer but showing almost no effect, he rose and announced that the meat was aging but he would have to see to the "barbie."

Arriving at the station, we found he had felled several trees to make benches for us in a dry streambed. Overhead, far from the lights of any city, the entire sky was ablaze with stars. I could make out the Southern Cross but the other constellations, being hidden from us in the northern hemisphere, were a spectacular mystery. Darkin had had four stockmen (cowboys), two of them aboriginal, build a huge fire over whose glowing coals yesterday's unfortunate actor turned on a spit.

"Time for grog," our host told us and led us to an incredible array of liquor and vast barrels of beer. By the time we had spent an hour or so making inroads into this liquid hospitality, no one had any scruples about eating the steer. It was delicious. We sang. Some made an effort to dance in the sandy soil of our improvised restaurant.

That period in Alice Springs was the most memorable of all our time in Australia.

In those days it was not possible to fly from Alice Springs to Sydney. We had to go south again to Adelaide and then north-northeast to Sydney, adding many thousands of miles. But our crew filled an entire plane when we left. Being Australia, there was a lot of grog on board. We drank freely. At one point, Peter Graves sat the stewardess down and went up and down the aisle with the liquor wagon, passing out drinks. An hour out of Alice Springs, we had to make an emergency stop to refuel, not the plane but the bar. By that time we could have flown to Adelaide without the need of a plane.

In Sydney, when there was not a party at one of our homes, we would celebrate Saturday night with Peter, Joan, Kathleen and Peter Maxwell at a restaurant in King's Cross—the Chelsea.

Casting for the series was difficult because the Australian accent, particularly in women, was grating on American ears. We were amazed and delighted the first night at the Chelsea as we listened to the singers, beautiful girls with great voices and no Australian accent. We thought our casting problems were over. But, when they were brought over to the table to talk, out would come "Ow dja do?" They bought American records, listened intently and precisely copied the intonation and accents of the songs.

We settled, finally, on radio actors. They were used to playing with a number of accents. We had them use English North Country. It sounds foreign but easily recognizable to American ears and lacks the harshness of the Australian product. At one early casting session, Ben Fox asked an actor if he could lose his accent.

"Mr. Fox," the actor reasonably replied, "I don't have an accent. You do."

We flew from Sydney to Melbourne, where Joan had been born, to check locations. Joan's mother had had several properties there as well as their home, St. Roche, that Joan wanted to see again. We sat in the airport. Our flight was delayed because a terrible storm raged outside, sheets of solid rain and lightning. We learned our plane was to be a Lockheed Electra. On the airport newsstand was a copy of *Time*. On its cover was a picture of an Electra, which had crashed in New York, killing all aboard. Chairs, plane parts were scattered widely. Even with the bodies removed, it was an unnerving sight. I didn't like the weather and the delay was going to get us into Melbourne too late to do any scouting. Joan interrupted my pacing and asked if I was nervous. I said "no," not very convincingly.

She had read the astrology column and under Taurus, which is my sign, it said, "If you feel nervous today, do not travel."

I told her astrology was a lot of nonsense. I am not sure if I convinced her. I did not quite convince myself.

The rain slackened and our flight was called. We made an extremely turbulent takeoff but after a few minutes we climbed above the storm and the flight was smooth and perfect. So much for astrology.

We went through Joan's old house, which she hadn't seen since 1932, almost 30 years before. It had become a boarding house with partitions put up to make room for more lodgers. What had been a beautiful house was now ugly and depressing.

We went back to her school. Many of the nuns were still there. One, Sister Bernard, remembered Joan very well and remembered her father who had been pro bono doctor to the school. We were given tea in the best parlor and Sister Bernard kept holding Joan's hand tightly and telling about the students she remembered and the nuns. "Sister Angela, who taught you Religion, has been confined to hospital for the last two years. And you remember Sister Marie-Clare, she's teaching in India. Sister Theresa has gone to God." Joan told her of her father's death. "He had a good life," the old nun said. "A saintly man. We'll be seeing more of him, God willing." Watching them, the nun so full of love and Joan recapturing a small piece of the past, was strangely moving.

14

Finding Focus

Elizabeth and Victoria went to school near our home in Wahroonga—the Bush School. They had gray woolen uniforms with white shirts, green ties and heavy black shoes, which later they hated. The shoes were, however, useful, as the Bush School was set in three acres of the Kuringai Chase reserve and snakes were a fairly common sight. The schoolchildren learned to ignore them. Leave them alone and they'll leave you alone. But the thick shoes helped in cases where the snake was unclear about the local rules. Elizabeth and Victoria instantly made friends with the local children and, within a week, had acquired the Australian accent.

On one side of our house lived Dr. Percy, who had his "surgery," a sort of treatment room, downstairs. On the other side was the Victorian brick mass of Reverend Walker's Anglican church. The belfry was just outside our bedroom window and Sunday mornings, after a night of celebration, the bell could be agonizing.

We spent a full year in Australia and came to love it. It was the United States 25 years earlier. The Aussies are hardy people, with rough exteriors but, as friends, exceptional.

The crime rate was very low. The first child kidnapping in Australian history took place while we were there. The boy's name was Graeme Thorne. For a country settled by convicts, they were incredibly law-abiding.

Part of the arrangement for our Australian stay was transportation. Joan wanted a station wagon for herself, Paula and the children. We were given a Holden, actually a GM car assembled in Australia with, of course, a left-hand drive.

The arrangement, however, was for only one car so I bought myself an MG Herald, a small two-seater with a tiny backbench on which the children could fit. They still speak of the night I brought it home, crammed all of us in and made endless circles in the street. The car had a turning radius that seemed shorter than the car itself.

From that point on it became a contest as to who got the MG for the day and who drove the huge American-like Holden. I would love to have brought the MG home. It was a car not sold in the States and the shipping and subsequent duty made it absurd. So, when we left, I sold it to Bob Lord for a fraction of what I paid for it.

Robert Lord was the manager of Artransa studios. When we first arrived, he showed us through the studio, explained its facilities and showed us our offices. After the tour I had occasion to use the toilet—WC. There was a sign above the urinals that read DO NOT PUT ANY FOREIGN MATERIAL INTO THE URINALS. I went to Bob's office and indignantly announced that, as a foreigner, I took exception to the sign and asked how I was expected to manage my elimination. There was a brief stunned second before he realized I was joking. We were fast friends thereafter.

Bob, like most Australians we dealt with, was very open, democratic and liked Americans. The Australian term for the English was "pom"— a term probably derived from pompous. That is why we were all so delighted when he showed us a letter he received. As studio manager for Artransa he had sent a cable to an English company requesting some equipment and signed the cable, "Robert Lord, Artransa."

He received a prompt reply from the dealer in the Motherland:

> Dear Lord Artransa, We appreciate your choosing our firm and are shipping your Lordship's order forthwith.

That was posted on the studio bulletin board.

We had a domestic problem that had concerned me for some time. Michael was nearly two years old and had never talked. He seemed well in all other ways but with Joan's connection with SHARE, making money for retarded children, the possibility of retardation was a constant source of worry to me.

One day while I was shooting at the studio and the girls were in school, Joan found Michael with a copy of *Time* magazine, flipping through the pages at a rate certain to tear them. "Michael," she said, "what are you doing?"

"Look for picture."

Joan was stunned at this sudden burst of speech. "What picture?"

"Picture Mrs. Khrushchev."

"You mean Mr. Khrushchev," Joan said unsteadily. "Here, I'll find—"

"I saw picture Mr. Khrushchev," he told her. "Want picture of *Mrs.* Khrushchev."

I got a call on the set. "Don't worry about your son any more," Joan told me. "He may become an orator."

Early in our stay we acquired Roonga, a small wriggly puppy, a Labrador-Kelpie cross. Kelpie is the Australian sheep dog. The Kelpie is part dingo—the wild coyote-like native dog. The puppy was named after the village we lived in, Wahroonga."

Since the series I was doing involved a stagecoach line, the kids made poor Roonga pull a wagon with Elizabeth and Victoria riding in it. Michael occasionally rode but otherwise had to help the girls in force-feeding Roonga grass, which was their substitute for hay. I am not sure how Roonga felt about playing the role of a completely different mammal but he took everything in stride, including being repeatedly dumped down the upstairs laundry chute.

He did, however have a role model for the horse he played. Bread was delivered to our house by a horse-drawn cart. All the neighborhood kids knew the horse, Possum, and came out to feed him sugar and carrots. Mr. Bates, the bread man, delivered to the front door. To ask Mr. Bates to go to the back door would have been demeaning and one might risk getting the loaf that had fallen to the ground. The Australians are a determinedly democratic people.

The American elections were taking place at that time and Michael, although not altogether steady on his feet, would get his sisters to lift him atop the low stone wall in front of our house where, having found his voice, he would march up and down calling, "Vote for Kennedy." Had that been possible, many Australians might have heeded him. Australia had been settled largely by Irish Catholics.

The film crew was excellent once you realized that there was no real motion picture industry and many of the things we took for granted were unavailable—even unheard-of. That caused a near tragedy on one location. An actor, playing an outlaw, had a scene in which he is finally caught and, in a shoot-out, killed. The actor had an intense bout of intestinal flu and I sent him home early. I wanted him to get all the rest possible before the next day's shooting. He came back, really in agony and against his doctor's orders, to get the final part of the scene, as we had to leave the location that day.

I had told the prop man to give me quarter loads—that is blank charges for the guns with a quarter of the normal charge held in place by a thin paper membrane.

14—Finding Focus

In Australia (l. to r.) John (and friend), Joan, Michael, Elizabeth and Victoria Lucas, with Paula Gonzalez leading the family dog Roonga (1960).

I thought the instructions were clear but, when we shot the scene and the actor was to be killed, his killer, with his last breath, raised his gun and fired at close range. I was delighted by the actor's performance. He jerked back with the impact and then fell in a crumpled heap. It was perfect. "Cut," I yelled. "That was beautiful."

I told the assistant to have the sick actor driven home immediately and went over to congratulate him on his performance and thank him for coming in. He rolled over, clutching his stomach and I saw blood on his fingers.

We quickly examined him. There was a hole nearly an inch deep in the actor's stomach. While the first aid man was working on him I called the prop man over. "It was a blank," he insisted. "It wasn't a real bullet."

I went to the prop truck and he showed me the blanks. Full loads.

"I told you quarter charge," I said.

He shrugged. These were the only ones he had. "But they're just blanks."

I pointed out that, at point blank range, the large cardboard wad that holds the gunpowder in the shell acts as a bullet.

The prop man genuinely had not understood. A blank was a blank and he'd used the only kind he had. "My word," he said. "I'd no idea they'd do that."

Having almost killed an actor, who was already in jeopardy for doing us a favor in coming from his sick bed, I delivered a long lecture about safety to the crew.

Today, over 40 years later, there is an excellent motion picture industry in Australia and to my knowledge, they haven't lost an actor yet.

Years later, back in the States, in another picture, with a helicopter covering the escape of refugees across a river, the chopper crashed. Vic Morrow and two children were killed. There was a protracted court trial. The necessity of caution was stressed to all picture companies. It is all too easy for a director, anxious to get a good scene, to take risks.

At the end of a year, it finally came time to go home. Our girls, who had been to school there for three full terms, were now Australians. The accent stuck with them through several school grades after they returned.

While still in Australia I learned that, shortly after we left, Mike signed a deal to make *Francis of Assisi* in Italy. On the morning he left, he called Ethel into the dining room and told her he would not be coming back. He asked her not to tell Mother as he would explain it himself. For months he wrote her regularly from location, as usual signing, "Allaise, Mike.

Finally one of his letters to her contained the news. He did not want a divorce but he could no longer live at home. It was a shock when I heard it but not a surprise. Despite all the help she gave him with his scripts, her wonderful sense of humor and his repeated infidelity, he had remained married to a voluntarily bed ridden woman for 30 years.

The Encino property by then amounted to nearly 120 acres. Mother wrote us that much of the land was sold off. Finally she sold the house itself and moved to another part of Encino, to a house that was smaller. The intent was to save money. But Mother instantly enlarged her new bedroom and made other changes that rendered the move more costly than remaining in the original house—which was much nicer.

Before flying home, we let Paula go back to Mexico to visit her family and meet us at our house. We had a shipping crate built for Roonga and had him flown home. The handler at the airport had written a tag for his cage. "Take good care of this dog. He's a nice little chap."

Mother actually got out of bed and was driven to the airport to claim him. He fell instantly in love with her and would hardly leave her bed.

Madeline Page, a distant cousin of Joan's, told her that the Oriana, a new luxury cruise ship, was making its maiden voyage from Sydney to San Francisco about the time we were scheduled to go home. We discussed it at dinner. The flight was long and exhausting and the idea of a sea voyage home sounded good. Joan called the line and learned that the ship was completely booked. She told Madeline that there was no room.

Madeline picked her up, took her to the head office of the ship's line and asked to speak to the president. There was a great deal of "Yes, Miss Page. It will just be a moment, Miss Page." Then they were ushered into the president's office and Madeline was greeted with something akin to reverence. She explained the problem. The president made a phone call. It was arranged. We were to have an outside cabin, and Madeline insisted that we were to sit at the Captain's table. That, too, was granted. Joan had had no idea of the weight Madeline pulled. Her brother was a barrister, who controlled the largest law firm in Australia. Sir Brian Page's sister could have anything she wanted, when she wanted it. The Sydney Opera House was being built and tall buildings were starting to rise along the waterfront. Madeline had a small but elegant house that developers were trying desperately to buy. Madeline liked where she was and so the house remained, a tiny one-story protest against progress.

When all was set for our leisurely return, bags packed and ready, we got a call from London asking for a few changes in three episodes we had shipped them. Changes mean recutting. Recutting takes time. We would not be able to make the sailing date.

So we were back to the long air flight. We left Australia in a flurry of farewell parties and some regret on our part. On our return flight, we hit a massive tropical storm out of Fiji. The pilot tried to climb above it and could not. We were bounced all over the sky for over half an hour— an incredible time for a jet penetration. The stewardess brought the booze cart, locked it down beside us and asked us to help ourselves. For the second time in a plane, I thought I had bought it. As we talked between dizzying drops and out-of-control elevator rises, Joan told me that, at the airport, she had bought a $1,000,000 life insurance policy. The same one I had. Hers was made out to me, mine to her. The three children were with us as we had let Paula go ahead to her home for a visit. Here we were with $2,000,000 and all together. Nobody profits. We started laughing. I don't know whether it also amused God but the storm abated and we flew on.

We had promised the children a couple of weeks in Honolulu and had made reservations at the Royal Hawaiian. We had barely gotten unpacked before I got a call from my agent in Hollywood. He told me there was a new show that was in desperate need of fixing. I was tired and we had promised the children Hawaii. The agent kept insisting. I had been away for a whole year. People forget. This was a chance for me to save the show and be a hero.

I talked to Joan. She only sighed, knowing show business. Finally I agreed. We took the kids out in an outrigger, saw all the sights we could possibly cram into the rest of the day and were on a plane the next morning.

When we returned, we found Mother at her new home with Ethel, round-the-clock nurses, a cook, maid and houseman-driver—for her trips to the doctor in Beverly Hills.

The new show I was to save was called *Acapulco*. It starred Telly Savalas, James Coburn and a young man whose name I have forgotten but who kept asking for close-ups. Presumably someone had told him that only thus could he assure his stardom.

The show might have worked if there had been more time to develop scripts and find a definite approach but there were airdates to meet and no time. Some six shows were made and then the whole thing was forgotten. I did not become a hero.

After that I did many scripts at various studios and directed most of them.

Roonga, when we got him away from Mother, spent the time at his new home escaping the fence that surrounded the property. In Wahroonga he had run freely, as did all the local dogs there. He saw no sense in this strange metal invention that confined him. He treated it as a challenge and was always several steps ahead of our plans to keep him in. We finally got a low-voltage electric wire to surround the place. He shocked his nose on it a few times until he learned that a tree branch or other wooden object, laid across the wire, would short it out, leaving Roonga free once more.

We brought home a puppy to distract him, a local lady Labrador we named Cina, after Encino were we lived. I am truly sorry for the cuteness of the dog's names but the children suggested and loved them.

Cina, in the fullness of time bore Roonga, in three litters, 19 children. That valiant Australian established a dynasty in his adopted country. Even today, driving though the old neighborhood, we can recognize descendants of Roonga by the arrogant lift of the tail, the jaunty angle of the head.

Sunday was always spent at Mother's for dinner. She still had a good deal of money but she was going through it at a prodigious rate and my occasional attempts to suggest that there was no reason to live on such a scale were met with a marked lack of appreciation.

In her new house she had a servant's wing, her own vastly enlarged bedroom, and a bedroom suite for Ethel, and she also maintained a bedroom for Mike with his desk, his Oscar and many mementos. He visited it, and her, frequently but never stayed. There is no indication that she expected him to come back. She was friendly, interested in his career and, when possible, helpful. But she never made the slightest effort to change her lifestyle, to get out of bed. I will not say that nothing was wrong with her; age makes inroads on everyone but there was nothing serious enough to support her interminable invalid phase. To this day, I do not truly understand Mother's motives but they had so hardened over 30-odd years as to be unchangeable.

Mike also visited us at our house, dropping in unexpectedly to see his grandchildren.

Then, in November of 1963, came the assassination of Kennedy. I got a call from Harry Kronman who gasped out, "They've shot the president." Harry used to call me several times a day to tell me any new joke he had heard and I thought, at first, this was another and I was waiting for the tag line. Then I caught the sob in his voice. He couldn't talk. I ran to the television and our entire family remained glued there all through the deathwatch, the swearing in of Johnson on Air Force One and, finally, the funeral procession, the heads of state of a large part of the world marching behind the caisson bearing his body to the Funeral Mass.

Somewhere, in the midst of those terrible days, the love-hate relationship I had always had with Catholicism subtly changed. Now the balance swung, if not toward love, toward interest. The ritual was what got me, the theatricality of it.

The Paulists had an evening class in Westwood. With my tongue still in my cheek, I attended. I learned theory and ritual and, while not belief, a greater fascination with the satisfying theatrics. Jim Moser (creator of *Dragnet* and *Medic*) was an ardent Catholic. He persuaded me to go with him to Manresa, a Jesuit retreat house. While we were there, the Watts riots occurred. At the retreat house we had no television and did not realize the horror of what went on until we got back. Although one part of me sardonically resented the guided tour brand of religion this Retreat represented, I was impressed. I began to surround myself with the symbols though not the faith. I did not—still cannot make that leap of faith that is said to be necessary but I was baptized and received into the Catholic Church by Father Ellwood Kieser. Joan came back into the church at the same time I entered.

I have, ever since, attended Mass regularly, finding a kind of comfort I had never known before. But I do this with a sort of schizophrenia. Emotionally I am enveloped in the warmth of the ritual but intellectually I cannot accept it. I keep thinking that, if I cannot make the leap of faith, I should leap away. It is a problem that I shall probably never resolve.

Mother's self-imposed bedrest continued but one day she developed a cold that Dr. MacDonald was afraid would go into pneumonia. She was checked into St John's hospital in Santa Monica and was making a fine recovery. Then one day I got a call from the hospital asking me to come down. I panicked, thinking she was sinking or dead but they assured me that they were simply having a little trouble with her.

I drove down and found Mother sitting in the middle of the floor in front of the elevator banks, the inevitable cigarette in her hand, staring blankly at the floor. The nurse told me they had been unable to get Mother to return to her suite and could not reach Dr. MacDonald. I thought for a moment, then sat on the floor beside her and discussed what I was doing, asking advice on the line of a story I was writing. She lost the stony look her face had held and shortly I was able to lead her back to her room. I never discovered what the problem had been, whether the result of a medication—God knows she took enough medications—or perhaps a shower stroke. At any rate, when I left, she was fine and went home the next day. Home to bed and her own nurses, that is.

On one of Mike's visits to our house he told me that, from the contacts he had made in Italy during the filming of St. Francis, he was asked to do the story of Abraham. Would I like to write the script?

This was the ideal Biblical enterprise for Mike, a spectacle. We also tried to give it a story. We worked out a very exciting opening and were well into the story before the financing fell apart. Foreign deals were—and still are—never secure until the money is safely in the bank.

Mike went on to make his final picture, *The Comancheros* with John Wayne. On location he suffered a fall, then was X-rayed at the local hospital where his bones were found to resemble lacework. The studio was told but nothing said to Mike.

When, almost five years before, he had had his appendix removed, they also found a prostate tumor and biopsied it. The biopsy was positive and the disease had already spread beyond the confines of the original site so surgery was not an option.

Mother had talked to John MacDonald, the family's lifelong doctor and friend. They made a decision, right or wrong, not to tell Mike since there was nothing that could be done. I did not know. It remained a secret for years until Mike's estranged daughter blurted it out to him. He rushed to Dr. MacDonald and asked, "Why hell you don't told me?"

"How many pictures have you made since then, Mike?" MacDonald asked.

Mike couldn't be sure of the actual count.

"How many would you have made if you'd known?"

Mike thought a moment, shook his head. "Goddamn, Mac, you right. Is better not know."

He continued to live with the girl he had been with since Italy and the girl's mother. I last saw Mike at the hospital two days before he died in 1962. It was a sad and frustrating meeting. I tried to be cheerful without the false smiles that are too often given to the sick. "Well, Jick," he said, his voice low, "I think so this is last time we see." Despite the closeness of growing up with him, of working with him, we had always been slightly at arm's length. I tried desperately that day but could not find a way to put into words the gratitude I felt for all he had been to me.

Mike had expressed a wish to be buried at Forest Lawn where his mother's grave was. Though never an observant Jew, he generally went to Temple on the High Holydays. The rabbi at his synagogue would not go to Forest Lawn and was not very cooperative so I called Rabbi Magnin's Temple on Wilshire Boulevard. Magnin was out of town. I got a Rabbi Maxwell Dugan who knew of Mike and reluctantly agreed to go to Forest Lawn but, as Mike was not of his congregation, agreed to present only a very perfunctory service. There would be no eulogy and no singing. I was not happy with his attitude but felt I had no choice.

I mentioned this to Harry Kronman, who had been the best man at our wedding. His wife, Rosella, had been Joan's close friend since Warner days. Harry had studied for the Rabbinate and had briefly had a congregation on Long Island before starting to write for radio and becoming a producer. When I explained the problems and the strictures placed on the service by the rabbi, no eulogy, no music, he asked if I had spoken to Magnin himself. I said no. The rabbi was Maxwell Dugan.

"Dugan!" Harry started laughing. "Jesus," he said, "Max Dubinsky! We went to seminary together." He picked up the phone and called the temple.

The funeral was arranged per our wishes and Harry even suggested the topic for the rabbi—the meaning of Death to Jews.

Mike's pallbearers were Cary Grant, Danny Thomas, Jack Warner (in panchromatic makeup for the photographers), Gordon Maynard (Maggie's son and my friend from Laguna days) and Alan Ladd. Alan had been driven up from Palm Springs where he had had one of his usual drunken brawls with his wife Sue. He had cuts and bruises on his face and needed almost as much support as Mike.

Mike had left Mother a prime piece of property, several hundred acres in Las Virgines Canyon, on the way to Malibu. Its sale brought her a great deal of money, which she continued to throw away in her usual manner. She seemed determined not to "let down her standards."

I had been doing a large number of assignments, writing and directing for many series. At a cocktail party I ran into Wilton Schiller, my first agent in the Hal Wallis days. He had left the agency business to produce a series

Michael Curtiz's funeral, April 13, 1962, at Forest Lawn Cemetery in Glendale, California. Pallbearers include actor Cary Grant, producer Jack L. Warner at left and actor Alan Ladd fourth from right.

with Teddy Sherman, whose father owned the old Sherman Studios. But with no track record, Wilton could not get the proper financing. He started writing and had just taken over as producer of the *Ben Casey* show. The show had been created by Jim Moser, producer of the *Medic* show, where I had started directing. "Why," Wilton asked, "don't you do a script for us?"

It was not a hard decision, given my interest in medicine. I did several scripts and then began to direct some. When the executive producer, Matt Rapf, left to take over another show Moser had created, Wilton became executive and asked me to step in as producer. I did. I also managed to still do some writing and directing.

The star was Vince Edwards, who had come to the part after they had tested almost every actor in town. Vince had played some small roles, usually as a gangster. He was the last person anyone would have thought of for the surgeon but, with airdates coming up, they were desperate. He was tested. It worked. A gangster with street manners and moist Latin eyes in a doctor's suit was magic. Women loved him.

The downside was that Vince was addicted to gambling. The track took all his concentration, and his money. Our schedules had to be made around the running of the horses at various Southland tracks. When I joined, the show had had several very successful years and its title was *Ben Casey*. If it had been called *The Doctors*, a difficult star could be replaced but how could the face of Ben Casey in a show called *Ben Casey* be changed?

John discusses a scene with Vince Edwards on the set of *Ben Casey*. Looking on are actors Jack Carter and Murray Matheson (1962).

That would have been an affront to the audience that even daytime soaps viewers would not have stood for.

I got a call from Ben Fox, the producer I had worked with in Australia. He was without a current show and, though not a writer, wanted to do a *Ben Casey* episode. "Got a great idea," he said. He had done me favors and was now calling for one. I asked him to come in. His idea was not new but had the possibility of working for us. Ben, however, had no real idea how to develop it. I discussed structure, gave him a few ideas and sent him home to write it.

In a week he was back with a script. It was terrible. I took him into Howard Dimsdale's office. Howard was our story editor for *Ben Casey*. He had produced features, got caught in the McCarthy mania and blacklisted. He had managed to survive by writing secretly under another name. He had the most fantastic ability to lay out the bones of a story—a step outline—of anyone I have ever met. God, how I envied it. I always stumbled along, letting my characters tell me what the story was about. Howard cut straight to the heart of the matter. In an hour, we had laid out, step by step, a story for my friend. All he had to do was fill in the blanks, almost like painting by the numbers.

Two weeks later he was back and turned in his script. It was worse than the first version. It had no relation to the outline he had been given. But I felt I owed him. He was thanked and paid.

I took the script and did a complete rewrite. It followed the line we had had given Ben but had almost no relationship to what Ben had written. I then directed it.

The day after it aired, Ben called me. He quibbled about the casting of minor parts but told me, "I thought you did a good job of directing."

I don't think he was being snide. He really thought what he'd seen was his script. Writers do not see well in certain areas. I did not offer him more assignments. The show went on.

As with *Medic*, we had medical advisors on *Ben Casey*. Since this was a series about a neurosurgeon, we used several of those specialists and found none quite satisfactory. They knew their field, knew if something was wrong, when a certain procedure was improper, but it was all essentially negative feedback. Finally I called my friend Harry Lusk, who had delivered all our children. He was an Ob/Gyn but had a wide range of interests. He had considered neurosurgery when he was young but had finally settled for his specialty.

During the war he had been a flight surgeon with the 8th Air Force in England. He had done much of the early research in the treatment of burns. He noticed that pilots shot down in the North Sea with severe burns, if they survived the cold, survived their burns whereas men shot down in the warm Pacific waters, with even less burn damage, usually died. The standard treatment for burns at that time was grease. The modern treatment to come out of the war research was cold—ice.

One night Joan, taking a roast out of the oven, slipped and spilled the pan of boiling fat over both hands and forearms. I instantly called Harry. He had us hold her arms in a pail of ice water for hours. Then he came over and spread some kind of green ointment over them, then topped that with bread—explaining that penicillin mold had been discovered on bread. He put on huge bandages and told her the bandages were not to be touched for a week. I was not very happy with this, or, rather, I was uneasy. It sounded like a remedy from last century's country doctor. But, when the bandages came off, the only scar was one high up, near her shoulder. In the agonizing general pain she had not noticed that single splash. Harry was Joan's doctor all her life, whatever the complaint.

I was once doing research at March Air Force Base, a Strategic Air Command Center and a week later came down with what felt like the flu. We were having Harry and his wife, Peg, over for dinner. It was clear I was feeling lousy. He asked what I'd been doing. I told him. "I think what you have is Asian equine encephalitis," he said. Strategic Air Force

14—Finding Focus

pilots carry many diseases back from bases around the world. He suggested that, as there was no treatment, I take Joan and go to the beach somewhere and rest for a week or so. "The disease is self limiting."

I was busy with several scripts I had promised and kept trying to work until I was a hopeless mess. Then I called John MacDonald, my internist. He was out of the country at a medical conference but an internist who was covering for him saw me and rushed me into the hospital with a diagnosis of "fever of unknown etiology."

I was put into isolation. Joan was the only one allowed in and then only with mask and gown.

A spinal tap was taken and sent to the Center for Disease Control in Atlanta. I vowed never again to write of a spinal tap as a simple painless procedure.

By the time the report from Atlanta came back, I was feeling much better. The report diagnosed Asian equine encephalitis. I went home, having run up fantastic hospital bills and wasted two weeks I could have spent in some lovely place.

So I got Harry Lusk as our consultant on *Ben Casey*. He had the kind of mind that, when I called him and told him what I wanted to accomplish in a particular story, would instantly tell me what disease would accomplish it, outline the proper procedures and sometimes even suggest story ideas. Thus it was that an Obstetric Gynecologist handled neurosurgical problems on the air.

Vince Edwards and Jerry Lewis were great friends and he brought Jerry in to talk about a two-part show they wanted to do. Jerry would play one of the doctors and also direct. I knew Jerry from our Hal Wallis days. It would be a great coup for ratings. Jerry's name was very hot then. We warned him that television was different from the features he was doing. He had an unlimited budget and time. We had tight schedules—tied also to air delivery dates. TV shows had to be done on time and on budget.

Jerry dismissed all arguments. He would personally pay for any cost overruns. This was what he and Vince had long wanted to do. Reluctantly, Wilton agreed.

All went well the first day. They were a little behind schedule but it could easily be made up. Jerry was working very hard to guarantee success.

In the middle of the second day came a frantic call from the assistant director. We rushed to the set. Jerry was fuming. He had made the master shot and set up for Vince's close-up. When it was ready and Vince sent for, the assistant came back from the dressing room to tell Jerry that Vince had left the lot. It was race time.

"To me," Jerry kept repeating unbelievingly. "He does this to *me*."

He was reminded that we had stressed Vince's habits when he wanted to do the shows. Jerry turned to me. "John, you really put up with this shit all the time? Man, you're crazy."

The two shows were finished at considerable overrun and Jerry was willing to pay. The Bing Crosby Company, which owned *Ben Casey*, generously refused.

I am not sure what happened to the deep friendship between Vince and Jerry but the races continued and Vince was always there.

Despite such problems, I found the show a delight to do. Wilton and I had an excellent working relationship and an active personal friendship.

But we also had Vince. There was always confusion, endless problems. Unlike most series stars, however, Vince's problems were seldom about anything to do with the filming. Personal matters were what concerned him. The girl who should have turned up last night didn't come. Or the woman who had to be carried on the company payroll to give him fresh fruit juices when he was on one of his diets didn't have the kind of juice he suddenly wanted.

Diet was a continuing problem. Once when we had been on hiatus, we had gotten rid of our cameraman and made the camera operator first cameraman. He was delighted at the promotion and was working with all his might to do sensational work. Vince returned from vacation noticeably heavier. We looked at the first day's rushes and his close-up resembled a pizza. We went to his dressing room at lunch and told him about it, phrasing it more diplomatically. "I know I'm fat," he said. He admitted he'd overeaten the whole of the hiatus but was on a strict diet now and we would see improvement in a week.

We returned to the office and went into a story conference with a writer. A call from the set interrupted it. I went down to find nobody working. "What's the matter?" I asked the assistant.

"The cameraman." He pointed toward the rear wall of the stage.

Our new first cameraman was sitting against the wall, clutching his stomach. It was known that he had an ulcer but it had never caused any work interruption when he was operating the camera. He looked up at me reproachfully. "Why didn't you tell me, yourself?" he asked.

"Tell you what?"

What I finally got out of him was that Vince had come back to the set and chewed him out for the way he was being lit. "You made me look fat. The producers were so upset they came to my dressing room to tell me about it."

After some reassurance, I got him back to the camera. Vince came from his dressing room, smiling; the scene went well. And the cameraman began a long and successful career.

14—Finding Focus

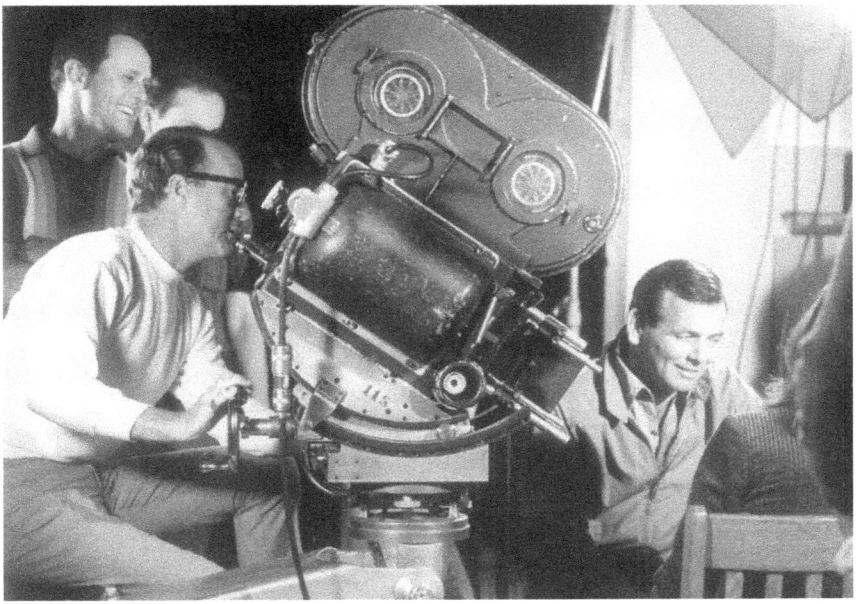

John directs David Janssen in the TV series *The Fugitive* (1963).

A producer spends part of his time as a nanny.

When *Ben Casey* went off the air, Wilton took over as producer of the long running *The Fugitive* series with David Janssen. I came in as co-producer. After a while of that, I started directing the episodes. I enjoy writing, love directing, am less enthusiastic about producing. I am not, as a matter of fact, very good at it. The business side of the industry does not appeal to me.

David Janssen was a very nice man and a pleasure to work with until noon. After lunch, speeches were often slurred. Fortunately the character he played was shy, with downcast eyes and a desire not to be noticed. He was a man on the run and was expected to make himself as invisible as possible. So the drinking sometimes worked for the scene. But when it got out of control, we would sometimes have to reshoot a half day's work.

We did a lot of location shooting and I had David in some dangerous places—rooftops, highway crossings, etc. These we always tried to schedule in the mornings.

I liked the show and enjoyed working on it. The network liked it too. *The Fugitive* could have run several more seasons but Quinn Martin, who owned the show, had had enough of the problems, of which David's drinking made up a large part. He pulled the plug.

15

Gains and Losses

When *The Fugitive* went off the air, Wilton took over as producer of *Mannix*, which starred Mike Connors, one of the nicest actors I have ever worked with. I came in to write some scripts, then Wilton convinced the executive producer, Bruce Geller, to have me direct.

Bruce and his favorite director had spent a lot of time, money and love on the pilot for the series. It was excellent and filled with the flashy camera work Bruce loved at the expense of the story. He was understandably upset when the network wanted to open with the first show I did. It may have been a better story, better casting or some obscure matter known only to the network but it caused Bruce much anguish. He treated it as a sort of rejection. On my third or fourth show, I shot an unforgettable episode in Sherwood Forest, which got its name when Mike Curtiz had shot *Robin Hood* there. Lake Sherwood is essentially man-made, not very deep but it covers a considerable area.

We were shooting a boat chase, with gunplay between Mannix and the dirty guys. Our cameras were mounted on a large barge out in the lake so that boats could circle us. The raft held three cameras and camera crews, grips with huge reflectors, a few electricians and lights, Mike Connors and assorted personnel, 20-odd people.

A jet boat was to run at us, turn sharply and fire back at us. For the first take I lay on the front side of the raft, under the A Camera. The boat came across the lake, moving too slowly, turned almost 70 feet away. I yelled "Cut" and radioed the driver to start again and come as close as he thought safe.

To protect the shot in case he again turned too far from us, I went back to B Camera, which was at the rear of the barge and had the operator

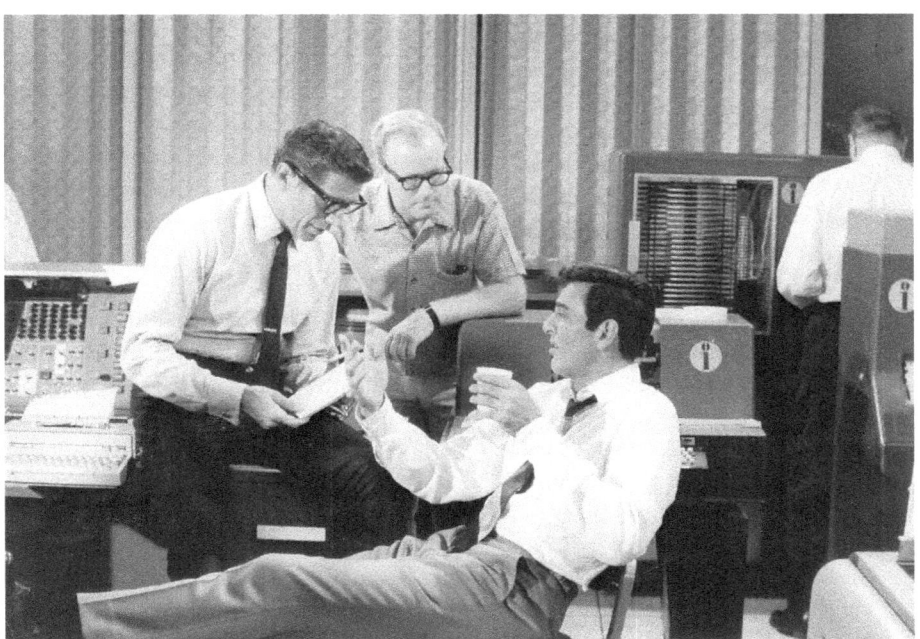

John directs Joseph Campanella and Mike Connors on the set of *Mannix* (1968).

change to a long lens so that the boat would appear closer. When we were ready and the boat back in position, by some freak of luck I stayed back by the B Camera.

The boat made its second run at full throttle. It came closer and closer, its bow wave spraying out in an incandescent V. Then, less than 15 feet from it us, made its turn much too late. The boat slid sideways into our raft, tearing a large hole in its bow. Cameras, men, reflectors, lights went flying overboard. The raft was swept clean, overturned. If I had stayed in my original position, I would have been killed.

When I surfaced, all I could think of was that Mike Connors had been on that raft. If my star was injured, the show was over. I spotted him, dived and got his arm. I am sure Mike is a good swimmer and could have taken care of himself but I did not relax my grip until we got our feet on the bottom.

We lost a lot of equipment, had to cannibalize two of the cameras to get one that worked, sent the film rolls the lab with the lake water still in the cases so that the lab could figure out how to treat them.

I still had one boat left so the rest of the day I spent making it double for both boats, carrying on the gun battle. We were able to make up most of the work for that day but we sent five men to the hospital. No one was seriously hurt but it was a potentially more dangerous version of our mishap with the blanks in Australia. All things considered, I was damned lucky.

Wilton was having a big party at his house that night. I was able to get home, get out of my soggy clothes, dress and arrive at the party that also included Bruce Geller, the executive producer. I was received with mixed emotion.

Despite that, however, Bruce signed me to a multiple directing deal.

My parking space on the Desilu lot, soon to be absorbed into Paramount, was just outside the windows of the *Star Trek* offices. One night, when I had left the set, Gene Coon, who was producing *Star Trek*, leaned out the window and asked if I would write a script for him.

It was my Disney days with Willy Ley all over again, another chance to do sci-fi. I said yes instantly.

The first script I did was "The Ultimate Computer," about Nomad, a probe from Earth which has wandered for years in space but sustains an accident that scrambles its instructions and increases its power a thousand fold. Built in a Clean Room, with every precaution taken to protect it from dirt and bacterial life forms, it has, in its damaged wanderings, translated that into a directive to destroy all organic life forms. It comes back to threaten the *Enterprise* and the entire Federation, stopped only by Kirk, whom it mistakes for its creator. The story was later used as the premise of the first *Star Trek* movie.

While I was still directing for *Mannix*, I wrote another script for *Star Trek*, finding time at night and between takes. Then Gene Coon called me on the set and asked me to stop by his office when I was finished. He told me his health was bad, he was going to leave the show and asked if I would like to take over as producer?

I said I would like to very much but I had a problem—my contract with *Mannix*. Coon asked me to talk with Roddenberry.

On a Sunday I met with Gene Roddenberry, creator and executive producer of *Star Trek*, at his house. I met his wife Eileen and his children. We got on well, exchanged our mutual love of science fiction. I left.

Gene Roddenberry stopped me the next day on the lot and said, "My wife says she bets you're the one." That was flattering but hardly a firm offer. The following day I got a telegram from Gene officially offering me the job.

I talked to Wilton, who saw the advantage to me and knew where my heart was. He was willing to release me but his boss, Bruce Geller, was not forgiving. I got my release but years later, when Wilton had left the show, Ivan Goff and Ben Roberts took over as producers of *Mannix*. They screened all the episodes that had been shot and told me they liked the style of the ones I had directed best and asked me to write and direct again for the series. I wrote a script, then many others but they were always silent on the issue of directing. Finally I asked outright and they had to tell me that Geller did not like my work. Hell hath no fury like a producer scorned.

I was in heaven with *Star Trek*. This was the sixties with the Civil Rights movement and the Vietnam War. Our stories could tackle any subject, touch current political issues such as race relations which networks considered dangerous and untouchable. But we were fiction and far in the future. We were not discussing present-day problems. So we got away with things no other show could do.

I felt I was finally where I wanted to be. But there were two shocks. The first one came at once when the company was shooting on location in caves in the Hollywood Hills. Roddenberry drove me up to introduce me as the new producer. When I got out of his car, many of the crew, people I had worked with on other films, came up to speak to me. It was reunion time. Roddenberry was impressed. Then William Shatner (Captain Kirk) came around the corner of a camera truck, took one look in our direction, turned on his heels and left. I was stunned. I had never met the guy, what the hell could he have against me?

Gene said nothing but, next day I found that it was Gene that Shatner was mad at. As a matter of fact, none of the principals were speaking to each other. There were feuds everywhere. I cannot say I came in with heroic measures and solved the problem. I simply decided to avoid confrontations. I went on the set, never bringing up the problem, listened to complaints the actors had about their parts and each other and acted as though there was nothing wrong. Gradually the tension eased and we had a happy company again—save for the inevitable occasional friction encountered when dealing with any actors.

The second shock came when I, and all other producers on the lot, were called into the executive offices of the studio and informed that, due to a high level corporate takeover, we were now part of the Leisure Time Division of Gulf and Western Industries.

I suddenly felt like Charlie Chaplin on the production line in *Modern Times*. From a command position on the sort of show I had always wanted, in which I felt pride, I was reduced to a cog in the wheel of a vast industrial machine.

On the positive side was Bob Justman, the associate producer who had been with the show from its inception. I also inherited Gene Coon's secretary, Andy. She was a tall black girl, very efficient, who, before I actually took over from Gene Coon, had introduced herself to me as Coon's Coon. She said she hoped I'd buy her. One day, as I came out for lunch, she had a diminutive and very attractive black girl at her desk. "This," Andy announced, "is my sister. See, we don't all look alike."

During his tenure as producer, Gene Coon had functioned mainly as a writer. The show (as is unfortunately common in television) was in constant trouble for scripts and lead time to prepare and make air dates. Networks did little to contribute to the welfare of their series. They would wait until the last second to announce pickups for the following season. If it was yes, money was released, writers hired and stories could be put in work but by then it was almost too late to make delivery dates. There was a constant frantic race to get the problems attendant to *Star Trek*—the involved special effects, which by today's computerized standards look primitive but were then state of the art—done in time. Coon had been so snowed under writing and helping Roddenberry rewrite scripts that he had time for little else. Bob Justman, the associate producer, managed all the hands-on aspects of production and post-production.

I was not used to working that way. I insisted on handling casting, working with the writers and directors on and off the set, getting involved in editing and scoring. I was, however, delighted not to have the budgetary problems, which I loathe, as part of my agony.

When I arrived, everybody had a dictating machine and would write long communications, critiques and suggestions on the scripts in work. These were sometimes helpful but the time consumed in the practice of gathering everybody's opinion was considerable. Everybody dictated, secretaries were tied up in the typing of these memos and everyone read everyone else's comments, using up still more time. I would have preferred a call to say, "This isn't good." Or "We can't afford this." I discontinued the use of my machine and, of course, so did everyone else.

The NBC representative on the show was Stanley Robertson, a tall, well-spoken, very nice black man. The only African-American, as far as I know, to be so employed by a network at that time. He was diligent but, from what I could gather, sometimes a bit stubborn in his views.

In preparing scripts and shooting them there was (1) Roddenberry (that included all of us), (2) the Desilu-Paramount Management and then (3) NBC to please. Such committee agreement did not come easy. NBC had approval on all stories before they went to script and I once, in the frantic rush to keep production flowing, violated this agreement.

We got a submission from a scientist at the Jet Propulsion Laboratory, a mathematician who had written a script with a very good premise

William Shatner and John on the set of *Star Trek* (1966).

involving a new generation of computer, impressed with engrams of the mind of its builder, which gives it the ability to think for itself. On its first test it takes over the *Enterprise* and destroys several starships. Starfleet's only recourse is to try to destroy the *Enterprise* unless Captain Kirk can come up with a solution. Readers will be surprised to learn that he does. It was undeveloped as a script but I liked the idea and we bought it. In the rush to get it before the cameras, I neglected to inform NBC and get official approval. Stan Robertson took exception. He had previously written me about a script Roddenberry had tried to revive without his approval and threatened to take "an arbitrary position" should it happen again. It had happened.

I did a complete rewrite with Dorothy Fontana, our story editor, adding the needed story and tension and when the hubbub about the violation of protocol died down, directed it, using a black actor as the inventor of the computer.

We were able to use a number of black actors in important parts at a time when the television screens were glaringly white. Roddenberry had already started this and was completely in favor of the practice. The Starship *Enterprise* was crewed by people of all races. Gene and NBC both urged minority involvement in the show and this, after all, was the future where such racial acceptance was natural. At the height of the Civil Rights movement, we were implicitly saying that, if any kind of civilization is to survive, this is the way it will have to be.

Meanwhile Mother continued living in her new house, rarely leaving her bed, never leaving the house, surrounded by Ethel, servants and nurses—a fortune in upkeep. I wondered how long it had been since there was anything she really enjoyed. We had talks—all one-sided—about her cutting back but she was not about to change her lifestyle. Her hair and nails were done weekly, the beauticians making the house calls gladly for the 50 or 100 dollar tips.

When Ethel died quite suddenly, we were finally able to persuade Mother to live with us. We had a wonderful Mexican couple, the brother and sister-in-law of Paula, who had accompanied us to Australia and was now—to make room for her relatives to come to us—working for Edward G. Robinson.

Mother's business manager had told me that her cash was getting low and she was running though it at an alarming pace. We told Mother we could make an upstairs addition, large enough for her—far larger, as it turned out, than she ever used. She could get rid of all her servants and the house expenses. Her nurses would, of course, stay. She was never voluntarily going to give them up.

The addition, when we suggested it, seemed simple. It turned into a monstrous operation, as it entailed putting a second story on a one-story house. To give Mother a very large bedroom, dressing room and bath, vast closets, a room and bath for a servant, an upper entry hall with stairs and elevator, a bar-kitchenette and a living-dining room large enough to hold

15 — Gains and Losses

her piano, pool table and library shelves that covered two walls floor to ceiling, all completely separate from the downstairs, required that steel beams be run down through the walls to support the extra weight. In effect, the lower part of the house had to be nearly destroyed to build the upstairs.

Joan was President and then Chairman of the Board of SHARE, the group of movie wives and stars which raised money for retarded children. They had a huge yearly show, a Hollywood event with an all-star cast no picture could afford. The core of the show was always Sammy Davis, Dean Martin and Frank Sinatra, with many other star volunteers. The women of SHARE made up the chorus, rehearsing under top choreographers at various studios. During one very heavy downpour, Janet Leigh complained of having to park and run through the pelting rain. Joan said, "Hell, it's raining in my living room."

Janet was up for an Academy Award for *Psycho* in 1961. There was a lot of betting that she would win but the Oscar went to Shirley Jones for *Elmer Gantry*. Again Joan caught Janet at a SHARE rehearsal, walked up and said "Shit!" Janet jumped up, threw her arms around her and said "I love you. Everybody has been offering condolences and saying, 'There'll be another time.' You said exactly what I feel."

My first meeting with Father Elwood Kieser, who would later baptize me, was less than pleasant. Jim Moser, from my *Medic* and *Ben Casey* days, had created a program for Father Kieser of the Paulists, called *Insight*. It started as a sort of taped lecture and, by the time I got involved, had become a half-hour dramatic series.

John Furia, a writer friend who was later to become president of the Writers Guild, was producing the shows and either he or Moser suggested me as a writer. I talked to him and he suggested a story topic. I wrote it, sent it in and got a call from Father Kieser to discuss a few small changes. We met at his office. He was a good-looking man with an open face, athletic and at least six foot six. He was obviously in a hurry. He gave me the changes quickly. The changes were good. I liked them and suggested I direct the show.

"We tape at CBS," he said. "Ever done that?"

I admitted I hadn't worked with tape and multiple cameras "But I have—"

"Well," he broke in, "We don't do on the job training."

I was about to tell him what he could do with his show when he got a phone call. Clearly it was a serious problem that would take some time. I simply left, made the changes and sent them back. I had promised the script and had now done my duty.

John on location for the series *Insight* (1975).

He called to say how much he liked it and had obviously found out my background in producing and directing. He asked if I could shoot the script in two weeks time. "We do a reading with the cast, a day of camera rehearsal and a day of shooting. Could we get together about casting tomorrow?"

He did not apologize about our first meeting but his enthusiasm carried me along. I agreed and then went on to write and direct many episodes. When Furia left, I took over as producer for the next five years.

The job took a couple of months' bite out of each year. We used top Hollywood writers, directors and stars to do a series that explored every conceivable subject. It did not stress any specific religious message. The shows spoke for themselves. Some were very far-out and were excellent fun. Father Kieser had only a brief summation at the end.

All this was done by volunteers. The writers, directors, stars—all the actors—worked for minimum pay and most gave the money back as a donation. If one happened to be in real need—God knows it can happen in Hollywood—they kept the check. No one got rich. I worked several times with Jack Albertson, with whom I would later shoot a series in Canada. Also with Sam Groom, the co-star of that series. Casting was always a problem, as it had been in the Laguna Playhouse. No matter how good the cause, stars hesitated to commit to a non-paying show that might block some high-paying part. There was often last minute casting changes. We used Ron Howard, now one of the industry's top producer-directors. Martin Sheen always made himself available. One show I did with Ida Lupino and her husband Howard Duff was a beautiful illustration of dealing with actors. The last commercial television show I had done with Howard was several years previously. We finished on a night exterior location and the shoot ran very late. Howard insisted we have a drink at a nearby bar and I went with him. The drink extended to many and I finally said I had to go home. I did. In the morning, I got a call to say Howard was in the hospital. On his way home he had met a telephone pole that wouldn't get out of the way. Ida knew her husband too well to blame me. She was an excellent actress and a very talented director. All had gone beautifully through rehearsals for *Insight* but she stopped me the morning of our shoot and said, "John, darling, I look so awful, please don't get the camera in too close." I told her she looked great and we began taping, using multiple cameras to shoot the entire scene with me cutting from camera to camera in the booth. When I had okayed the first take, Howard came to me and asked if I would speak to Ida as she was very depressed. I said I would. She was still sitting at the card table used in the last scene, looking dejected. "John," she said. "I don't blame you for not using close-ups. I look so horrible."

How, I wondered, did she know what shots I was taking? Then I spotted a monitor on the very edge of the set. She had got one of the crew to put it there and, while playing the scene, was watching the way I was cutting it. As I said, she was a very talented director. I reminded her that she had specifically asked not to be photographed close but I agreed to reshoot the scene. I did, with all her proper closes-ups.

In another episode, a very far-out script called for a worn-out actress. This is a delicate situation. Few actresses know when to admit they are no longer young and lovely. We finally managed to get Ann Sothern to read the script and were surprised when she agreed. She came for the first day of rehearsal with no makeup and showing all her years. I was delighted. She was ideal. My elation continued until shooting day. She brought her own makeup man and arrived on the set looking like a slightly overdone ingénue. My stomach hit the floor. The whole concept was out the window. After much discussion and anguish it was resolved. She played the part and played it brilliantly. It was different from what we envisioned but it worked. She was willing to play an old, worn-out woman but refused to let the public see her looking anything but perfect.

Insight was a wonderful experience.

Having got Mother to agree to move in with us, the reconstruction took nearly a year. I had hoped that living in new surroundings would alter her lifestyle, at least bring her downstairs to dinner occasionally. She came a few times but never with company. We hoped that Joan and the kids would provide companionship and interest her in something beyond the confines of her bedroom. I got a new idea. I hired a maid to sleep beside her room and get her anything she needed, thus eliminating the expense of her round-the clock nurses. The idea did not take. She found constant reasons to complain about the maid. The nurses were too firmly entrenched.

There were rare times when she would invite some friends over—still maintaining a firm hold on the bed. Virginia Zanuck came to see her and they talked for hours. Their friendship had gone back many years when Virginia was a Mack Sennett bathing beauty when she married Darryl, a struggling writer at Warners. Both she and Mother had husbands who found other female attractions. Darryl was known for the multitude of starlets who had tested on his casting couch. But the friendship of the foursome remained despite domestic problems. They traveled together, partied together, worked together.

Virginia had given up her acting career to become the perfect wife and mother, giving Darryl three children, Darrylin, Susan and Richard, called Dickie.

Darryl's first really serious extra-marital relationship was Bella Darvi, which rocked the home relationship and destroyed the very expensive *The Egyptian*, which under Mike's direction should have been a real blockbuster.

There had been a good deal of gossip about the strange relationship in the Zanuck household. Darvi lived with Darryl and Virginia and the screen name she was given was a combination of DARyl and VIrginia. This was not a new concept. The name used to designate their Palm Springs house: Ric-Su-Dar was an amalgam of the names of their three children.

Mother refused to listen to the whispers that the Zanucks had a *ménage à trois* with Virginia as a willing participant.

Whatever qualities Darvi possessed, star quality was not one of them. She faded fast. Darryl, in the midst of his mid life crisis, appointed his son Richard studio head and left home for Europe and a succession of mistresses, each of whom he tried to make into a star. Predictably he made a series of flops. Virginia had to watch from the distant sidelines as his extravagant losses caused trouble at the studio. The Board of Directors begged him to stop. Virginia's one flash of anger was when, without seeing or calling her, he returned briefly to the studio and fired his son. But then she went on to become the peacemaker in the internecine warfare of her children.

Richard never really forgave his father for the abandonment and the firing but went on to become a producer in his own right and is said to have made more money than his father ever did. With Darryl in Europe and Mike moved out, Virginia and Mother had their loneliness in common.

Shortly after that visit, Darryl, old now and sick, asked to come back. He arrived with his current mistress, who was quickly eased out of the house. Virginia wrote Mother a long and very happy letter. "Romeo has come home."

Maggie Ettinger, dying of cancer and far sicker than Mother, came. But she had to come upstairs in the elevator to Mother's bedroom. That was where she held court for visitors. She never lost her wry sense of humor. The few people who saw her, laughed and loved her but her lifestyle did not change.

She had a succession of nurses and loved to play practical jokes on them. With one she went to the bathroom and the nurse, after a suitable wait, knocked then opened the door to find Mother lying on the floor with a bottle of sleeping pills scattered around her. The nurse worked hysterically to get her back to bed and was phoning the doctor when Mother grinned and replaced the receiver on the phone. "Got you!" she said.

Another nurse wore a hearing aid. Mother would very slowly, by very minute increments, lower the sound of the television, which ran night and day. When the nurse had finally turned her hearing aid up as far as it would go, Mother would crank up the TV sound full volume, blasting the poor woman's ears. The nurse would frantically fiddle with the controls of her hearing aid and check the batteries. It took her some time to realize what was happening.

Mike had left Mother a considerable sum of money but she was running through it at her customary supersonic rate. I talked to her business manager. He talked to her, trying to find ways to cut back but Mother had reached what she considered her level of comfort and refused to change. I could never understand what comfort she could derive from being surrounded by nurses around the clock and never moving from her bed. The nurses were merely there as companions.

When we moved her into the house, I hoped that Joan and the kids could take up some of that slack—keep her occupied. The nurses continued. The cost of 24 hour nursing care, three shifts a day, is astronomical and she had no insurance, nothing but the money Mike had left her and that was almost gone. She sold a few of the paintings she had amassed and some jewelry. It was a meaningless stopgap. Her business manager finally told her that her money had run out. I begged her to allow me to get a maid back who would get her whatever she needed or wanted and still have a nurse come in part of the day to administer any shots or medications necessary. That was not acceptable. Her business manager threw up his hands. He suggested the Motion Picture Country House and Hospital. A hospital had always been acceptable to Mother and we could come up with no other solution. I wanted no part of it but now, to make matters worse, just before her seventy-ninth birthday, Mother finally became really sick and needed constant medical attention. What she had been fearing all her life finally caught up with her.

In the 1920s, Mother had been a founder of the Academy of Motion Picture Arts and Sciences, which gives out the Oscars. It also funds the Motion Picture Country House and Hospital. Over 40 years after the founding, she and the other surviving founders had been sent gold life membership cards.

I felt awful as I drove her out to the Woodland Hills complex although it is beautiful and had a very well-staffed hospital. Joan and I had sat up night after night and exhausted every possible way to keep her home but that did not stop my feeling of guilt. She settled in sooner and with less fuss than I would have believed.

I was able to bring her home with a nurse for her birthday, her seventy-ninth. We had tables, a party catered and her friends over for the celebration. She did come downstairs for that. She stayed overnight. With a nurse, of course.

At the hospital she had many visitors, Fran Marion among them. Virginia Zanuck came out and, fearing that I had simply turned Mother out to pasture, offered to take her to her beach house and get the nurses when she needed them. We discussed it with Margaret Herrick, executive director of the Academy and a family friend and she advised against it. Virginia remembered Mother from the old days and had no idea what the present was like. Still, that caused me more guilt. Why the hell wasn't I able to afford what Virginia offered? Margaret Herrick assured me Mother required a hospital and was where she ought to be at this stage of her life.

One Sunday I was able to drive her over to Auntie Vi's who, 12 years older than Mother, was still climbing trees to prune branches.

Once or twice we watched pictures with Mother. We would wheel her into the excellent theater on the grounds of the Motion Picture Country House. I saw, for the first time, *Wings*. It had been shot as a silent picture and had had a talking sequence added when sound came in. The same thing that had happened with her *Don Juan* with Barrymore.

I didn't notice much change in Mother though I visited her in the hospital every day I wasn't shooting. Probably because I was so used to her being an invalid she seemed the same. It came as a terrible shock when the hospital called one Sunday morning in July and asked what funeral arrangements I wanted to make. She was not expected to live out the day.

I drove out furiously and found her awake and quite rational. I told the head nurse there must be some mistake. She said the doctor had seen her that morning. She had renal shutdown and toxins were building in her blood.

I got the doctor and asked why the hell he hadn't used dialysis. He said that there were so many things wrong that it would only stretch her life a few days and cause her needless pain. After 50 years, she had become as sick as she always claimed.

It was still frightening to face. And she had a fear of death. All the unaccustomed volume of activity and examinations had alerted her that something was wrong. She asked the date. It was July thirteenth. "My God," she said. "I'm going to die on the thirteenth." As long as I could remember, she insisted she was going to die in October. She could, however, move the date at will, sometimes just before Christmas or other holidays but it was always October that she came back to. I reminded her of that. "This is July," I assured her, "not October."

The nurse the hospital supplied was a typecast cheerful caregiver. She fluffed up the pillows and arranged the sheets and earned my eternal enmity by saying to me, "They get so little when they get old," as though Mother couldn't hear.

But hear she did and told the nurse to shut up. "It's the thirteenth and I'm going to die on the thirteenth."

"Now, we mustn't talk like that, Miss Meredyth," the nurse said. "You won't be dying today."

"Bullshit," Mother replied. The nurse looked shocked.

But the nurse had been right—by exactly two hours. Mother died at two o'clock the next morning, the fourteenth of July, Bastille Day—six days before Neil Armstrong set foot on the Moon. She died so peacefully in her sleep that I was not aware of the transition and had to get a nurse's confirmation that she was gone. True to the family traditions of marking public holidays, she was born on Lincoln's birthday, died on Bastille Day.

I had to drive over early the next morning to tell Auntie Vi, then 92, to put down the hoe she was wielding and tell her that her baby sister had died.

Father Kieser was celebrant at the funeral. The church was packed with her friends, those in the industry who still survived. There were also a great many people who had worked for her and loved her. I got a telegram of condolence from New York signed FROM THE GRANDCHILDREN OF NELLIE SEAGRAVES. Nellie had been our laundress who got me out of trees in my childhood. She hadn't worked for Mother in over 50 years but her memory had passed down through three generations. This I considered the greatest single tribute to Mother.

She is buried in the family plot at Forest Lawn with Auntie Vi, Uncle Bill, her father and mother and Ethel. I gave up the grave they had long ago bought for me to accommodate Ethel.

For her tombstone, I debated a long time. She had two husbands. At her death she was still legally Mrs. Michael Curtiz but I finally chose Bess Meredyth, the name she had made for herself.

I had spent a lot of time at the Motion Picture Hospital and, some time later got a call asking me to stage and act as Emcee of the Wheelchair Chorus. This is a yearly entertainment of patients who are, obviously, chair-bound but who do various songs, recitations—whatever their specialty had been in the business. With the wheelchairs they also did a sort of dance routine. The performances were given for the long-term care patients and those who could survive the trip to the theater on the grounds. It sounds like a downer but they had great fun and it gave them a sense of renewed identity, of still being in Show Business. These people who had strokes or any number of problems still wanted to perform.

I got my kids to help and recruited people like Cesar Romero and our neighbor, the composer John Williams. (His wife, Barbara Ruick, shortly afterward died so tragically of a cerebral hemorrhage while shooting on location.) I did the show for two years. It was strange working in proximity to the place where Mother died but I think she would have enjoyed it.

One of the wheelchair chorus was Blossom Rock, sister of Jeanette MacDonald and "Grandmama" on TV's *The Addams Family* series. Gene Raymond, widower of Jeanette, came to visit Blossom often although the aphasia her stroke had caused would allow her only two words: "shit" and "cute." She used them interchangeably. Gene would sit holding her hand and talking about the old days while she nodded happily and responded with either word of her total vocabulary.

I continued writing and directing, episodes of *Harry O* with David

Janssen again, working with *Insight*, keeping busy. The children were growing and I had managed to use them in a few episodes of *Insight*—constantly stressing that they should not think of acting as anything more than fun. It is a terrible life and achieving success had roughly the same chance as wining the lottery. For every spectacular winner, there are countless thousands of equally talented people who were simply not in the right place at the right time. These people try to sell real estate, wait tables, park cars while waiting for the Big Break.

The 1971 Sylmar earthquake hit very early in the morning, shaking our Encino house like a terrier with a rat, creating a tidal wave in our swimming pool that splashed the water over the yard and reduced the level down to the halfway mark. We were lucky. Across the Valley, nearer the epicenter, it was collapsing freeways and hospitals. I got Joan in one doorway, myself in another. As soon as I could use the stairs, I made sure the kids were all right. They were more excited than scared. Angelino and Virginia helped examine the house for structural damage. We lost a few possessions but the house stood and all humans were safe and well.

Later that day I got a call from Toronto from Wilton Schiller. He had just been given the okay for the pilot of a series in Canada and wanted me to direct it. They had an air date and casting and preparation had to start right away.

I had never been to Canada, my father's birthplace. Joan urged me to go. The house was secure. The kids were all right. I had been through many earthquakes before and knew there would be aftershocks. As a matter of fact there were several, diminishing in intensity soon after the main one. Joan insisted there was nothing to worry about. I was on Air Canada the next morning.

When I arrived in Toronto, headlines indicated that Los Angeles was wiped off the map. They quoted massive aftershocks with terrible damage and loss of life. I spent over an hour trying to phone, sweating more with each passing moment, until I finally got through. The family was well. Yes, there had been terrible damage across the Valley but the house stood safe and as sound as I left it.

It was deep winter in Canada. Snow everywhere. I, born in California, had to drive to the mountains to find snow. "Look," I'd tell the kids, "see that white stuff at the side of the road? That's snow."

Wilton and Chester Krumholtz, a writer who had done many *Ben Casey* scripts and was Wilton's partner in this enterprise, had gone through the whole long process of putting a company together. When I arrived, we started casting and location spotting.

When we began shooting in the snow, I was like a kid in a candy store. I wanted to photograph each individual flake. The rest of the crew, who had been born in the East, hated it. Our hairdresser wailed, "Who do I have to screw to get off this picture?"

The pilot was called *Dr. Simon Locke*. It was the old doc-young doc formula with Jack Albertson as the grumpy country doctor with a heart of gold and Sam Groom as the eager young eager Dr. Simon Locke. It had schmaltz and lovely backgrounds. We used the Massey mansion as both office and background. It was a beautiful old place. The Masseys were a rich and famous Canadian family. Vincent Massey was the first Canadian to serve as governor general of Canada. Americans will better recognize the name of his younger brother, Raymond Massey, the actor, famous for, among many other roles, his portrayal of Lincoln.

When the pilot show was finished, I went back to California and resumed shooting various episodes of various series. I did several for *Night Gallery* and many of the Rod Serling introductions to the series when Wilton called me again. The pilot had sold and he asked if I would come up and direct every other episode of *Dr. Simon Locke*. "Canadian content" was required in the show as had been "Australian content" in *Whiplash*. The Canadian content supplier and alternating director was Gerald Mayer, nephew of Louis B. Mayer, a friend from Hollywood who had directed several episodes of *Ben Casey*. The Mayers had been born in Canada and Gerry had retained his Canadian citizenship.

When the *Night Gallery* season was ending I was signed for the next season after their hiatus. I asked Jack Laird, the producer, if I could start shooting next season's show after the date that *Dr. Simon Locke* would finish—leaving myself a few extra days for safety in case we ran over. I assumed that since Jack was a very good friend of Wilton's and, though under contract to Universal, had moonlighted several scripts for us when we were shooting *Ben Casey*, that he would be cooperative. He was not. He said he would have to check the matter out. Every time I asked for a decision, I got an evasive answer. Finally I sat down with the production manager and worked out when the first *Night Gallery* episode I was scheduled to begin would start. We discovered there would be no conflict. Laird was out of the office so I wrote him a note explaining that all would be well, thanked him, left and flew to Toronto.

I got a large apartment as Joan was driving the kids up to spend the season. For the next four years I was in Canada three or four months a year. It took me out of the Hollywood mainstream and was a terrible career move but a lot of fun.

We did the season in a different mansion, which had belonged to the man who invented Roman Meal Bread and other healthy things. The

15—Gains and Losses

mansion and its grounds functioned as both our set and production offices. The gentleman who built it had been so committed to health that he had health mottoes carved into the lintels above the windows and doors. Over the fireplace in the main hall was carved SUNLIGHT IS HEALTH LIGHT. Every morning, he ran nude through his estate, winter and summer. We were told that one very cold winter morning he found that he had locked himself out of the house. Not wishing to call and display his nudity before the maids, he decided to wait for the butler. He waited too long in the snow, got pneumonia and died. We, in due time, got his house.

Joan, after the grueling drive, arrived with the children. Her trip did not start well. As they turned out of the driveway, Michael, the youngest had asked, "How much longer will it be?" For the next four years, we spent three to four months a year in Toronto while the series was shooting. Again I was out of the mainstream of Hollywood but the terrible career move was worth it to us.

Like the start of the movies that my parents were involved in, there were no rules. You made them up as you went along. There was room for a lot of experimenting. Since this was a police story, it involved a lot of car chases. Remembering, from my script clerk days, how difficult it was to match action from one shot to another, I used three cameras in car scenes, one, with a wide-angle lens, on the driver's side, holding both people in the front seat. Two other cameras were mounted on the hood and shot thorough the windshield, which gave individual closeups of the actors. Since the three angles were shot simultaneously, there was no possibility of the action and the background of the shot not matching. The camera truck was hooked directly behind the car being filmed. It held the sound man (the actors wore radio mikes), the lighting man the cinematographer and me. We imported many actors from Hollywood, including my *Star Trek* star William Shatner.

In any film crew, there is a lot of togetherness. Actually, during shooting, one sees more of the cast and crew than one's own family. I have always found it sad to finish a picture and break those ties.

Albertson and Groom were wonderful to work with but the show lasted only one season. When I was shooting the final episode of the season and was ready to go back to *Night Gallery*, the phone rang. It was my agent to say that he got a call from Jack Laird announcing that he would pay my contract in full and get another director. He said Laird sounded angry and would not give a reason for his decision. He subsequently directed the first episode himself and it was terrible.

There was no question of my not getting back in time and I still do not know why it bothered him so that I directed in Canada. He had not

Sam Groom, John and Jack Albertson on location in Toronto for the series *Simon Locke, MD* (1971).

been asked to alter his schedule or sacrifice anything. He was helping his friend Wilton. I guess it was because I *wanted* to do it. Another case of a producer with wounded pride.

The last episode of our first-year Toronto season concerned an overturned tanker truck with the injured driver trapped inside. Dr. Locke must get him out before he bleeds to death. But he must do it in a way that will not explode the tanker, killing himself, the driver and the police he has summoned to the rescue. The slightest spark could set off the conflagration. Unfortunately almost the entire episode took place outside on the lakefront. After a full day's shooting, the weather deserted our side. It rained incessantly. We were working in deep mud. There was a delay while cars were sent back to town to buy dozens of raincoats and rubber boots — the heaviest boots to protect the electricians who were managing their cables in gooey mud and water with the constant threat of electrocution.

Audiences will be surprised to learn that our hero did succeed. The driver was removed, treated and sent to a hospital by helicopter.

Because of the inevitable delays, the last shot, where the helicopter takes off with the patient, was not ready until the sun was setting. The cameraman announced he hadn't enough light to make the shot. I told him I had to have it. He refused. I told him his objection was noted. I would have the lab force develop the film two stops and take full responsibility. The blame would fall on my head. Grumbling, the cameraman rushed to the set up.

My original plan was to have the actor carried to the helicopter and strapped to the outside basket. I would them cut and put a stunt man in the basket for the takeoff but it was getting darker by the second. Without informing anyone, I let the actor be strapped into the basket, signaled the helicopter to take off. It did with the startled actor taking an unexpected trip into the setting sun. By the time I called "cut" it was so dark another shot would have been impossible.

As soon as the chopper landed, I explained the problem to the still ashen actor and got his forgiveness. He admitted it was his first helicopter ride and had been quite a thrill.

I said goodbye to the crew and cast, got into the waiting car with Joan and the three kids and started a tour of eastern Canada.

At every stop on our trip, I sent post cards to Jack Laird, thanking him for giving us this vacation by peevishly paying off my contract on *Night Gallery*. It amused me but did nothing to increase my popularity with him.

I recently got a call from a writer who was doing a book on *Night Gallery*. This sort of thing happens to me often—calls from people doing books on *Star Trek*, *The Fugitive*, *Ben Casey*, *Mannix* and many others. I had to honestly tell the writer the questions he asked happened 30 years before and I remembered very little of *Night Gallery*. He had taped four episodes I had directed and sent them to me to refresh my memory. But, after watching them, I had to tell him that so many pictures came in the intervening years that I could still remember very little. He wanted incidents and, regrettably, the only thing I could clearly remember was one that episode that I did with Larry Hagman, later the star of the incredibly successful series *Dallas*. Larry's mother was Mary Martin. We were both show biz kids and talked a lot about that. Though not an alcoholic then, Larry kept bottles of Le Domain champagne in his dressing room and insisted on introducing me to it. It was a repeat of my Kellino experience of years before.

My friend Roy Kellino, a film director, had been Pamela Mason's first husband. When she divorced him and married James Mason, Roy continued their unusual relationship—which drew the usual speculation from

Hollywood gossips. For quite some time Roy lived in the guest house on the Mason property. We used to visit Kellino frequently when he moved and married. I had worked several times with his new wife, Barbara Billingsley. Kellino introduced me to his favorite brand of scotch, Cluney, to which Mason had introduced him. One night he insisted I take home a case. It was excellent and also very cheap. Later, as its popularity increased, its price rose but, at the time, in was an incredible value. I drank it exclusively until, much later, on *Night Gallery*, Larry Hagman converted me to Le Domain champagne. It was incredibly cheap and amazingly good. Thereafter I drank it constantly. At the sound of the popping cork, my children would shout, "Daddy's home."

16

Letters of Transit

After the Toronto season, I returned to Hollywood to do a lot of television, excluding *Night Gallery*, of course. I was also producing *Insight* and was constantly amazed by Father Kieser's ability to get stars to work free and negotiate with CBS Network executives for incredibly low rates on studio time, crews and equipment. Bud explained: "Irish and Jews have a strong sense of guilt, and I have the Teutonic ability to use it."

I loved working with the three-camera system and the speed of taping an entire episode in one day—often a long one.

When not in our CBS offices, we worked out of Paulist Productions, Thelma Todd's elegant three-story beach house on the Coast Highway, which had been somehow acquired by the church. Thelma Todd was a glamorous blonde star of the '20s who was found dead in a car in the garage of the home, apparently of carbon monoxide poisoning. It was ruled a suicide but rumor persisted that it was murder. Mother had known Thelma very well and always subscribed to the murder theory.

While producing *Insight*, I found time to write scripts for other series and then it was time to go back to Toronto for the second season.

The series was no longer *Simon Locke, M.D.* so we needed new main titles. The sponsor, the Colgate Company, had decided they did not want a gentle dramatic show. They wanted something faster and more "important." They wanted a melodrama. So Wilton kept Sam Groom and created a melodrama called *Police Surgeon*. I had never heard of a police surgeon nor, I am sure, had Wilton but it had a good sound. For the second season we worked out of Lakeside studios where we had a standing set for the police station but still used many exteriors and locations. For an entirely different show, we obviously needed new Main Titles.

For the opening of the show I made a montage, shooting all over Toronto to get a really exciting look for the main credits. In one fragment I had the ambulance—lights flashing, siren going—with Sam Groom at the wheel, drive up to the camera. As Sam opened the door and looked back, I panned with him to show a large hotel, then zoomed in to a jumper on the outside of a window on the top floor. It was a difficult shot and took several tries to get the camera movement right. I had just finished when two police cars screamed up. Officers leapt out.

For any location shooting, permits are required and it is customary to advise the local police. This had been done but somehow the notification fell between the cracks and suddenly the police switchboard was flooded by calls reporting a man about to jump from a hotel room. Not being aware of our permit, the police had made a frantic dash to avert the suicide and were understandably furious to find it was staged for television.

The lieutenant demanded to know who was in charge. I was clearly the one to take the heat but I just happened to see Chester Krumholtz walking casually up on one of his rare visits to a location. "There's the producer," I said.

The police grabbed Chester and braced him up against a wall, while he sputtered incoherently, having no idea what was wrong. It was finally settled and the police departed but Chester's face remained ashen.

I continued working between Hollywood and Toronto. One night, during our third season, we were having dinner at our apartment with Sam Groom, our star, and Wilton and his soon-to-be second wife, Patricia Payne, who was doing our casting. Bob Crone, who owned Film House, where our film was processed, was there. We talked about Toronto, a wonderful, clean and crimeless city. Joan mentioned that as she drove up from Los Angeles, she was tempted to go to Niagara Falls, a short distance off her route but had been too tired.

"You've never seen the Falls?" Bob Crone asked. She hadn't. He set down his drink untasted and asked if we'd like to see the Falls at night. We would. He finished dinner quickly and left. We met him at the airport, climbed into his plane and he flew us over the Falls—a fantastic sight at night, floodlit and magnificent.

Joan later repaid him when his friend, Budge Crawley, bought a Japanese film called *The Man Who Skied Down Everest*. He did some minor recutting and scoring and finally got a release. It was an excellent film but it was getting very little play. Joan, when we got home, began a campaign among all her friends in the Academy and ended by getting an Oscar for the picture.

Shooting each season of *Police Surgeon* took about four months. As my agent once said, "Don't stay away too long. Hollywood has a short memory." But I had a lot of fun.

When, after four years, *Police Surgeon* finally ended, I took Joan on an extended trip to Europe, England, France and then to Italy where her cousin Charles and his Italian wife lived. They had the very elegant Villa Parioli near the Borghese Gardens in Rome. They also had a "farm," of God knows how many hectares of vineyards, wheat, stables and a house that was, itself, almost a palace. It was near Anzio, where the American invasion took place in the Second World War. Forty years after the fighting, they were still finding unexploded shells on the property.

Eloise was Charlie's second wife, he her second husband. Her first had been to the grandson of Benjamin Harrison, twenty-third president of the United States. Her father, an architect and builder, had left her many important properties in Rome. That, and Charlie's millions, gave them a very comfortable life.

When we were about to leave, they gave a dinner for us at the Cacciao Club, probably Rome's most exclusive. I was seated between two princesses, one quite attractive. Charles had told them I was a director and they wanted to talk about movies and how they could get into them. Royalty isn't what it used to be.

We explored Florence and Venice and would have gone on but, as had happened before in Hawaii, my agent reached me in Rome. Howard Dimsdale, who had been our story editor on *Ben Casey*, was now at Fox with the TV series of *Planet of the Apes*. He had convinced the producer that I was the right one to do a script, direct it and then go into a multiple-show contract. I had been out of the country for quite a while—out of sight is out of mind. It was a welcome call.

To accept the job would mean cutting our vacation short but after some discussion Joan, knowing how I loved science fiction, suggested I do it.

We flew home. I had several meetings with Howard and came up with a story about the making of a primitive hang glider.

Planet of the Apes was a difficult but interesting assignment. Roddy McDowall and Joanna Barnes were playing the lead apes. I loved Joanna and had worked with her many times. Roddy was a friend whom I had yet to work with.

The series was a killer, more for the actors than for me. Roddy was picked up at four o'clock in the morning in a Winnebago carrying a makeup man. He would start makeup on the way to the studio, gulp down coffee and what breakfast he could. He would go over his lines while furry parts were being attached to his face. The makeup was finished at the studio. The entire procedure took four hours to put on, almost an hour to remove. Joanna had almost as terrible a schedule.

I shot a lot of the show at a beach hang gliding spot and at the Fox ranch in the Valley where an ape village had been built. The rest was done on sets at the studio.

On the final day of shooting, it was announced that the show had been canceled—almost a replay of my experience with Jack Webb on *Noah's Ark*. I had lost a lot of time we could have enjoyed in Europe. Perils of network television policy.

However, the show had brought us back from Europe early and Joan and I were home to celebrate our twenty-fifth anniversary with all our Hollywood friends in a huge tent set up in the yard. It was an impressive gathering.

I settled down and wrote a pilot for a series Universal was interested in. The producer was Stan Robertson, who had been the NBC representative on *Star Trek*. He loved it and was trying to get it okayed for production but it was sci-fi and would require a very large budget. Aside from the special effects, the main set would be more costly than had ever been approved for a television show. Of course, since more than three-quarters of every show would be played there, it could be amortized quickly once the show was in production. Still, it needed a very large outlay and it is always a gamble whether a show will ever go beyond the pilot stage.

While waiting for Universal to deliberate, I got a call from World Vision. They wanted me to do a world tour, directing a documentary showing hunger in Third World countries. The film was to raise money for the needs of these peoples and had, for me, the added advantage of going to places I had never been and would never be likely to go—four African countries, India, Pakistan, Thailand, Hong Kong, Manila, Guatemala and Brazil. I talked it over with Joan. The kids were all in school and we had Virginia and Angelino to drive, feed and care for them, so I made it part of my acceptance of the job that I take Joan.

As the date for leaving approached, Joan was not feeling well—the doctors said there was no specific problem, but we were going into some very unhealthy places. Over a period of days I had to get shots for diseases I had forgotten existed, including Bubonic Plague. I talked to Harry Lusk and we decided Joan should stay home.

We had a very tight schedule. Reservations and arrangements had been made in advance and, mostly, they worked out. My crew was comprised of a cameraman, an assistant, a sound man and a production manager. We used a 16mm Arriflex. This was not like the dozens of people on a Hollywood location but it was a challenge. The bare bones of moviemaking. Probably, with the exception of sound, it was what my mother's early movies were like.

Our first stop was Dakar, Senegal—magnificent swimming beaches. Then on to the Gambia (an enclave in Senegal, a narrow strip on both sides of the Gambia River) whose Capital, Banjul, was formerly called Bathhurst. It was one of the main slave markets in the eighteenth century. Among the human cargo Arab slave traders delivered here was Alex Haley's ancestor, the hero of *Roots*. Its control passed back and forth between European powers after the Portuguese discovered it. When Briton abolished slavery in 1807, they built Bathhurst fort on the waterfront to keep foreign ships from collecting the slaves that the Arabs still continued to smuggle in. Ancient iron cannons still stand on the grass of the fort, which has a park-like look.

I have my old passport covered with visas. All other countries used a simple stamp to grant visas. The Gambia used a heavy white paper with a multicolored national crest at the top and elaborate gold lettering. It had to be glued into the passport. The Gambia, one of the smallest countries in the world and also one of the poorest, thought big.

In Banjul we photographed hospitals, packed with patients getting what pitiful medical care was available. Children died on the treatment tables as our cameras rolled.

The first village location we chose was far upriver on what turned out to be Election Day.

Our first opposition came when we asked the villagers to move their market stalls out from under the shade of the huge banyan tree, which is the town's center. We wanted them in sunlight to better photograph them. They thought we were insane. Who tries to sell anything in the midday heat? They finally allowed themselves to be persuaded but with a good deal of head-shaking and laughter. That morning there had been a child's funeral, a not uncommon occurrence. Child mortality is not due solely to the lack of sanitary and medical facilities. Babies are breast-fed for two or three years. After that, there is no middle ground, no transition from milk to pureed foods. One day they are refused the breast and given the normal adult diet, very rough, very spicy. The strong ones are able, after a while, to make the transition. This day they buried one who didn't.

The shooting had taken longer than anticipated and we were late starting back downriver to the coast. Night fell. Each village we passed through was filled with people celebrating the election and celebrating with a good deal of drink.

In one large village, the festivities had spilled over onto the highway and our small VW van was suddenly in the middle of hundreds of happy and extremely drunk villagers. We could not move forward. The driver tried reverse but the people had already swarmed around behind us. There was nowhere to go. The driver made the mistake of honking his horn. I shouted for him to stop.

We had now attracted the attention of the revelers and they stared in at our foreign white faces. One laughing drunk started to rock the van. Others took it up. They were still in a playful mood but the van was rocking at an alarming rate and one false move from us could have turned the crowd angry. We smiled, and waved, trying, despite panic, to put up a show of enjoyment but never have I see seven white faces turn quite so pale. At last, the fun growing stale, they let us pass.

The Gambians are a friendly people. Going from Jambul back to our hotel, my sound man and I were in a taxi when the driver suddenly pulled to the side of the road. We got out. Another taxi, its driver, probably drunk, had run off the road and was down the embankment in the middle of a salt marsh. "My cousin," the driver explained and went down to help. It took the four of us to push the second taxi out of the swamp and get it back on the road. The cousin wanted to buy us all a drink but we had no time. Our driver refused to accept the agreed fare when we got to the hotel. He waved away the money and thanked us "in the name of my cousin."

The next day, shooting inside a mission hospital, I was shown the first tapeworm I'd ever seen. This was from the gut of a seven-year-old boy and must have been almost five feet long, a hideous white worm coiled upon itself in a glass jar. The hospital also handled cases of malnutrition. Again a child died under treatment as our cameras were rolling.

We left from the Gambia International Airport, which turned out to be a metal mesh strip that U.S. Seabees laid down in World War II as a temporary airfield.

From there we went to Monrovia in Liberia. The country was settled by freed slaves from America. Then we flew east across the continent to Nairobi, Kenya. In Nairobi, we stayed at the Norfolk hotel, a lovely old place that had been the pride of British rule. Kenya was then under the government of president Jomo Kenyatta, who had been the leader of the dreaded Mau Mau uprising, which slaughtered so many British settlers.

In Nairobi, at the same time we were doing our documentary on world hunger, UNESCO was having a meeting in Nairobi to discuss methods of eliminating that hunger. Delegates from a dozen nations were staying at the Norfolk. When we went into the large dining room, the UNESCO banquet tables were literally groaning with a selection of salads, breads, meat and fish courses, desserts heaped high with whipped cream. This for the delegates while they discussed how to keep starvation from the Third World.

Nairobi is not a very lovely city but there are impressive sections, glass and steel world-style high rises, contrasting with some awful slums. There is also the University of Nairobi, surrounded by a riot of bougainvillea used as a ground cover. I had never seen bougainvillea used that way and I examined it closely. Wooden stakes, only a few inches off the ground, supported a mesh of barbed wire on which the bougainvillea grew. This served the double function of making a magnificent setting for the buildings while the underlying barbed wire kept people away from areas where they were not wanted. That, for me, became a symbol of Africa—incredible beauty with cruel barbs beneath the surface.

From Nairobi, we went to photograph Masai villages. The Masai are the tall, beautiful people you see tending their cattle, standing on one leg and leaning on a spear. It was a time of a great drought and the Masai had lost 80 percent of their cattle, their source of wealth and nutrition. They rarely eat their cattle. They bleed them. Each warrior has a gourd in which cattle blood is mixed with milk. There is even a special tiny bow and sharp arrow used to pierce the jugular and catch the blood in their bowls. When enough blood had been drawn, the vein is plugged with mud. It is a high protein diet and they are a healthy and beautiful people. But now their cattle were dead of the drought. Their bloated corpses littered the landscape.

The typical Masai village is built inside a fence of nettles, forming a huge corral into which the cattle are driven each night. The nettles keep out lions. The Masai houses are square, made of branches covered with a mixture of mud and cattle dung, which makes an effective cement—and a horrible stench.

Masai hair is also coiffured with cattle dung and I have an unforgettable memory of giving a sub-chief a ride to a neighboring village. We had all the van's windows cranked wide open and were still gasping.

Next we flew up into Turkana country. Because of the inexplicable twists of mapmakers, the north end of Lake Turkana, near Uganda, juts up into Ethiopia. The Turkana people are warriors, not as well-known as the Masai, nor as photogenic, more stocky. We went in three planes, two single-engined Cessnas with cargo pods and one Beech Baron, twin-engined with navigation equipment. North of Nairobi there are no navigation aids—you turn left at the giraffe.

We flew over agonizingly beautiful country, the lake where *Born Free*, the series featuring Elsa the lioness, was shot. We flew over elephant country, then into dense clouds.

The navigation technique fascinated me. The two Cessnas spread out on either side of the Beech Baron, covering a distance of perhaps ten miles. When one pilot saw an opening in the clouds, he would signal and the others would peel off and follow. These were ex–RAF pilots. It was instructive and thrilling.

There is a lodge at the southern end of Lake Turkana, a peninsula, almost a true island, where European royalty and the common rich from all over the world have come for generations, lured by the Nile Carp, really a kind of giant goldfish that grows to 200 pounds. The lobby is full of pictures of fishermen, from the eighteenth century to the present day, proudly photographed beside their catches.

Landing at Lake Turkana involved coming in on a short dirt strip, barely possible for the twin Baron. Once we set down we were met by Land Rovers, which took us to the shore of the lake. Two natives were waiting to wade out and put our luggage into an oversized rowboat with an outboard motor. Shoes removed and pants rolled up, we followed them to the boat and got in. The slimy bottom was so shallow that the natives had to then push the boat some hundreds of feet out into the lake before they could put the outboard down. Once the propeller spun, it kicked up mud and dark green, oily slime. It was the filthiest water I have ever seen. Lake Turkana, like the Dead Sea, has no outlet and, over time, evaporation has thickened it into an unattractive pea soup.

We tied up at the Lodge's dock, a pier jutting far out into the lake, went ashore and unpacked in our separate bungalows, comfortable but Spartan. The toilets were outside.

In the Lodge, the main room was full of trophies and skeletal heads of various animals protruding from the wall. We admired the photographs, some quite ancient, showing sportsmen from all over the world and in varied dress and uniforms, smiling in triumph as they held aloft their catches. Then we went in to dinner.

The main course was fish, the best I had ever tasted. From the filthy water of this dead sea came an exquisite dinner. It was like the Buddhist symbol of the lotus, perfection growing up from the mud. We ate the Nile carp that generations of fishermen had prized—justly.

Our cameraman had mentioned to the pilots that I had produced *Star Trek* and the rest of dinner was taken up with answering questions about it. I would have much preferred to discuss their fascinating form of bush flying but all three of them were Trekkies.

It had been a long day and we went to bed early. There was little choice. The generator was turned off at ten.

By our beds were flashlights (electric torches is the British term) and signs advising us to use them if we had to leave the cabins, and to be careful where we stepped. To avoid falling into the lake, I assumed.

In the morning, after breakfast, I looked again at the photographs and trophies, among then several large skeletal heads. I recognized a rhinoceros but asked what one huge set of jaws was. Crocodiles, I was told, and shown others. They were gigantic monsters. The lake was full of them. The management routinely lost several servants to them each year. I blessed my bladder that I had not had to leave the cabin in the night.

We had to load our equipment into the boat and it was with an anxious eye peeled that I crossed the water to shore.

We used a schoolteacher to interpret for us as we went into the Turkana village. He went first because a New Zealand documentary crew had been there earlier in the year and, not understanding the protocol, walked in unannounced. A cameraman was speared.

We waited by our Land Rovers as he went into the village and arrangements were made. From the corner of the huts, a couple of children peeked at us. We kept quiet. Soon more children appeared. Gradually, since we made no hostile move, they approached the Land Rovers, circled us. Some of the crew had candy, which the children timidly accepted. When our gestures told them it was to eat, they tasted it. That won them over, they swarmed about us, staring, sniffing.

I am very sun-sensitive and always wear gloves on location. These fascinated the children. They sniffed my hands, felt the texture of the leather, then cautiously bit at it. The mothers were now watching from just outside the circled huts of the village. Seeing the children climb over us in the Land Rovers, they were satisfied we meant no harm.

The teacher returned and we were ushered to the chief's hut where he sat on his elaborately carved stool supported by a single pole. It resembled a truncated English shooting stick. We were given the run of the village. The Turkanas are fascinating people. They used a weapon I have never seen anywhere else in the world, a wrist knife. It is a bracelet holding erect a flat iron blade, honed to razor sharpness and protected by a hard leather cover, which could be quickly pulled off for combat. They fought with slashing movements of the arm and the effects could be terrible. One such knife was among the souvenirs I brought home.

As in most villages, flies were everywhere and many of the children had the white sightless eyes of trachoma, the fly-borne disease that Egyptians call River Blindness.

The next day we were scheduled to fly to a village on the border of Uganda but we had a problem. A conference of all teachers in the Northern Territory was called for that day. Our teacher-interpreter had to attend and could not, therefore, escort us into the village. To reach the conference would take him six hours each way over roads that were mere suggestions in the landscape.

We solved the problem by sending him in the Beech Baron, which would take only minutes. The Baron would wait until the conference was over, then fly him to the village to meet us. He took off at first light. We had a leisurely breakfast and traversed the, to me, terrifying crocodile-infested water to our small planes. We flew to the village, which had a fairly clear spot of land that would be our airstrip. The Baron with our teacher was expected momentarily.

We had just touched down and could see the villagers waiting near their circle of huts when we got a radio from the Baron pilot. "Do not land," the pilot said. "Or, if you have already landed, stay beside the planes. Do not approach the villagers." He would be there in ten minutes to explain.

We got out of the cramped planes but had to wave some of the more venturesome children back toward the village. Finally the Baron circled, landed. The pilot told us he had intercepted a message from the Flying Doctor Service—the same type of service that operates in the Australian Outback to bring medical aid to far-flung villages.

There had been an outbreak of Green Monkey fever and the Flying Doctor Service was calling for a quarantine of the entire Northern Territory. We had our cameras and all our equipment. We had our teacher-interpreter. The villagers were waiting, puzzled and annoyed at our delay.

We held a conference in the shade of the plane's wings. "What in the hell," I asked, "is Green Monkey fever?" It sounded like a joke. It wasn't to the people who lived in Kenya. The doctors quoted a mortality of 98 percent. I digested this and weighed the odds. I could get all the film of the village I needed in an hour and leave. I wanted that film. I am no hero and certainly had no desire to risk catching a vicious disease but since this village was far to the east of where the outbreak had been reported, our chances seemed better than fair that the disease was not here. Then it was pointed out that, even if we escaped the disease, to be trapped in a quarantined area would knock out the rest of our worldwide trip. That was too much to risk. We got back into the planes while the schoolteacher yelled across to the unhappy villagers that we had an emergency and had to leave at once.

We returned to the lodge as quickly as possible, broke all records for packing and getting back into the planes.

Following the Baron, our two small planes sped south, down the Ugandan border, avoiding all civilized places. The whole project had taken on an exciting cloak-and-dagger aspect. When we were well south of Nairobi, it was getting dark. The pilot of the Baron called Nairobi and filed false flight plans, saying we had been in the south, flying over Lake Victoria and the Serengeti. Then, in the dark, following the Baron's lights and feeling very James Bond–ish, we approached Nairobi from the south and landed with no questions asked.

After returning home, I had no reason to think of the incident for over five years until a group of friends went up to Mammoth to ski. I brought along reading material, among it my monthly issue of *Science* where I read an article on an outbreak of Marburg fever, so called because the research was done in Marburg, Germany, on African Green Monkeys. The virus had probably been around Africa for centuries but affected only green monkeys. A mutation had made it interspecific, transferring it to humans. I had been a witness to the birth of AIDS.

In my hotel room at the Norfolk, a telegram awaited. Stan Robertson, the producer at Universal, wanted a couple of minor changes that would get our series pilot moving. Due to the time difference, the studio was closed then. I couldn't call him and we were leaving that night for Rome. Our destination was New Delhi but, because of political problems, some now sovereign African countries prohibited overflight by other countries. The only way to India was through Rome, far to the northwest. From there we would catch the Pan Am flight to Teheran and New Delhi.

We arrived in Rome and, at three in the morning, went in taxis to the Hilton where reservations had been booked but the records had been lost. Every room was full. The desk clerk made a few calls to other hotels and was able to accomplish nothing. They would allow us to sleep in the lobby. Finally, our taxi driver said he had a cousin who worked at the Flora. He called and they could take us. Piling back into cabs, we went off with considerable misgivings toward a hotel I had never heard of and one that would take us in the middle of the night. It was like Groucho's gag that he refused to join any club that would accept him.

I was startled to find the Flora on Via Venato, right next to the entrance to the Borghese Gardens and almost across the street from where Mother's apartment had been during the shooting of *Ben Hur*. The hotel was small but charming. We were to leave that night for New Delhi. After a few hours' sleep I called Charlie, Joan's cousin, to say hello and goodbye. He insisted I come to lunch. I protested that I had to make a call to the studio in Hollywood. "Use my phone." He picked me up and drove me to the Villa. His chef was one of the top in Rome and I looked forward to eating with Charlie and Eloise. Unfortunately I missed the promised lunch because I spent an hour and a half on his phone with Stan discussing changes in the pilot script. I was able to grab a sandwich, thank my cousin, repack at the hotel and catch my plane.

I reviewed my notes from Stan on the flight. As they always do, minor changes turn out to be major rewrites.

We photographed in New Delhi, then went to Agra. The Taj Mahal was every bit as impressive as advertised, shimmering white and lovely in its long reflecting pool. Inside, we saw the magnificent jewel-like tombs at the mosque level—built for the public view and beneath them, at ground level, the simpler tombs which actually held the bodies of the Shah and Mumtaz Mahal.

Looming above it, across the river, was the Red Fort where the Shah was imprisoned by his son, who had snatched the throne and allowed his father to spend his last days in his prison room, looking down on the Taj which had taken him 22 years to build as a last resting place to hold the body of his beloved wife.

We flew to Bombay, Poona and Hyderabad with many stops in between. All the time, in cars, in the hotel rooms at night, I worked on the pilot script for Universal.

At one location we stayed at a large private home in the interior of the country. I slept beneath mosquito netting—a first for me. In the morning, our host introduced me to the spacious tiled bathroom. It reminded me of the Alice Springs bath although it was the exact opposite in terms of water use. It contained a small tiled enclosure perhaps one foot high and five feet square. There was a drain but no other indication that it was for bathing. Beside the enclosure stood a galvanized pail full of water and a small electric heating element. I was to plug in the heater, put it into the pail until the water warmed, then step into the enclosure and pour the contents of the pail over my head. Washing hair under these conditions was a feat I never successfully mastered. The facilities, however, were hi-tech in that part of the world.

Perhaps the most memorable impression was one location we shot— a fairly large mission hospital with a galvanized iron roof, onto which sacred monkeys jumped and threw stones and coconuts, making a sound in the wards like a city under bombardment. In India, of course, nothing could be done to sacred monkeys and the patients did not seem to mind or notice. We spent the day there, shooting the hospital inside and out. We had a two-hour drive back to our hotel and a plane to catch the next morning but the administrator of the hospital insisted we take tea with his family. It was getting dark but we reluctantly accepted. He had been very accommodating. We got away as quickly as possible without insulting our hosts and, as we started through the tall grass for our cars, the

John in front of the Taj Mahal during the filming of a documentary on world hunger (1978).

doctor warned us to use our torches and watch where we stepped. The place was full of cobras. We had been walking in that grass all day long, setting up cameras and completely exposed to whatever venom the snakes might have in store for us. Now, as we were leaving, he told us. Our feet barely touched the ground as we made it to the safety of the cars.

Of the entire time in India, Calcutta was, for me, the most unforgettable place. We had been hoping to photograph Mother Teresa but she was called to Rome by the Pope and we missed her by two days. We did, however, interview Sister Luke, her second-in-command at the Mother House. We shot there and I was permitted to attend Mass with the sisters. Then we photographed the shoe factory that Mother Teresa's order ran, giving employment to lepers, most of them horribly disfigured, some with no fingers, some missing feet, some without noses. Everything that could go wrong with a body had gone wrong with theirs but each found the task he was capable of doing and took pride in it.

The House of the Dying was even more terrible and beautiful. The

House of the Dying was an unused corner of the Temple of Kali—Hindu goddess of death—that had been given to Mother's order. Here we photographed the dying, brought in from the streets and given a blanket, a place to lie in relative comfort and eat, if they could still eat. Some of the unlucky ones recovered to go back on the streets. Calcutta's streets are full of poor, sick and dying people; the sidewalks, at night, are impassable with them. Each morning the dead carts come around to pick up the bodies of those who did not make it through the night.

The brothers and sisters of Mother Teresa's order tend them, make no attempt to convert them, only to make them comfortable, to let them die in dignity. They ask, "Are you Hindu? Are you Muslim?" Then they would be addressed in their own language and treated according to their own customs, told, "You are a good man. Your family respects you. Your children are proud of you." A bit of kindness at the end of lives so devoid of kindness.

In the hotel in Calcutta I decided to mail a copy of my script changes to Joan to type up and have ready when I came home. She was the only one who could decipher my scrawl. As insurance, I kept my original in case there was a problem with mail. I asked at the desk where the Xerox machine was. It took several clerks to understand what I meant. Oh, yes, there was a copying machine, not in the hotel but only a short distance down the street. I went.

The short distance turned out to be miles. Fending off hordes of beggars, I almost missed the small sign high above the sidewalk. The store was on the fourth floor, up very rickety stairs. I was ushered grandly into a back room where a Rube Goldberg device waited. It was a German machine, God knows how old but it looked like something out of Jules Verne. It was a thermal process. Each sheet took almost five minutes to register. I had an afternoon off to rest from the frantic pace of our shooting. I spent that afternoon and well into the night getting my handwritten pages copied.

Back at the hotel, the clerks were undecided about the best way to mail the package. One thought I would have to take it to the post office myself, the other insisted it would be handled by the hotel and said the words I came to dread most in a foreign country, "No problem." As we were leaving for Bangladesh in the morning, I had no choice. I trusted; miraculously, the package arrived.

We went on to Bangladesh. Here was poverty, almost worse than Calcutta. Then to Thailand, and after shooting the footage we needed in Bangkok, we had a chance to visit its magnificent temples. The Jade Buddha, the Reclining Buddha, the Royal Palace. We covered most of the tourist stops. After India and Bangladesh, Thailand was Eden.

From there we flew to Hong Kong. The poverty there is not so evident. In this city of gleaming skyscrapers, the poor pay exorbitant rent to sleep in the open on the roofs of the high-rise buildings. American cities have not yet discovered this ingenious method of keeping the homeless out of sight. Finally we came to Manila.

All these countries were beautiful. All had rich cities and abject, grinding poverty. In Manila whole streets, whole districts had no electricity, the only water the filthy canals that ran, stinking, by the makeshift shacks. A family of 14, all ages, sizes and sexes, jammed into one tiny room which was dining room, living room, bedroom and toilet. The Neanderthals in their caves had better lives.

From Manila we flew to Tokyo, narrowly skirting and outrunning a typhoon.

In Tokyo there was a layover of some hours and I took a "sleeping accommodation" at the airport. This consisted of a closet-like room where I could crawl into what resembled a train's upper berth and doze until our flight to the States was called. I got little sleep because I had put in a call to Joan. She was out to dinner with Peggy Knudson, our friend from the old Warner days. Despite my telling them not to bother, the kids insisted Joan would want to talk and would call me as soon as she came in. The "sleeping accommodation" was not only tiny but had thin walls. I answered many calls meant for other sleepers before Joan's came through. I finally got up, hoping to sleep on the plane. A vain hope. I did, however, learn from the captain that, on the flight from Tokyo to Los Angeles, the plane burned 26,000 pounds of fuel, one hell of a lot of pollution. A great convenience for the traveler, not so good for the ozone layer.

17
Fade Out, Fade In

I had only two weeks at home before the final leg of our tour, Guatemala and Brazil. I cleaned up the rewrite Joan had typed and got it into Universal. Stan, the producer, was sure this would meet production demands.

Joan was still not feeling well. I took her to Harry Lusk, who thought she might be suffering a mild infection and gave her a course of antibiotics. Then I left.

The first stop on the final leg of our tour was Guatemala City. We shot the shantytowns on the outskirts, where squatters attempted to establish some semblance of village life. They washed, not at a well but at a dirty pool whose water they then carried, in scavenged tins or whatever they could find, back to their families for drinking.

We drove south into the mountain villages. Guatemala had just suffered a catastrophic earthquake. Along our drive were the ruins of dozens of ancient cities and the homeless people who had lived in them.

In some mountain villages only the church bells had been salvaged and hung on makeshift poles near the rubble of their belfries. People worshipped there.

Then we flew down to Brazil. The beauty of Rio's location is unsurpassed. Above the rows of magnificent hotels lining the beaches of Copacabana and Ipaneama, higher up in the mountains, above the mansions of the rich, and having the best view of all, is the squalor of Favela. All slums in Brazil take their names from this place and are called favelas. Narrow streets wind, nearly vertical in places, nearly impassable even on foot, between huts made of discarded sections of tin, scraps of wood or cardboard. Here is a city of the dispossessed, the hungry and forgotten, a breeding ground of disease and crime. Turning your back on the horror that surrounds you, you look down on the gorgeous coastline, the gaily patterned mosaics of wide avenues fronting the sea, the other world—a Heaven that these people will have to die to achieve.

We flew up the coast to Recife, on the easternmost tip of South America. It is a large city, not as beautiful as Rio and without the vast urban sprawl of Sao Paulo. A lot of business is done there, however, and it has many wealthy people.

It also, of course, has its favela, which keeps moving farther inland as the city grows. The poor are pushed farther and farther back. This favela now is on marshland and is fairly new because a developer took the land the old favela was on, brought in bulldozers and landfill and built homes and apartments. The poor were pushed deeper into the marsh, which is tidal. In the afternoons and early mornings, the middle of the dirt streets are salt streams. These streams are also their sewers. Children play in those streets, looking like feral animals.

The really ironic part is that these favela dwellers, the few lucky ones, work in the homes of those who dispossessed them. The laundry of the rich is brought back here to be washed and ironed, washed in the foul water of the swamp.

God pays back.

We also went to an old colonial Town called Olinda, which translates as Oh, beautiful. The name is deserved. The ancient churches and buildings of the Portuguese empire still stand in their baroque splendor. It was humid and hot and before the Municipal Palace were scattered markets. One man had a large tub filled with ice water in which coconuts floated. He punched holes in one and I drank the most delicious coconut milk I have ever tasted. It was unforgettable. But here, too, there is hunger if you go only a little way back into the country. We did.

In a tiny village called La Gloria we were shooting in a huge open pit, which had been dug to quarry building stone and where a well had subsequently been dug for drinking water. I noticed bees buzzing around the well-head. This was the late '70s and African killer bees had just made the news. They were thought to have been brought into Brazil on a cargo ship from Africa. Joking, I told the cameraman, "Get a close-up of the killer bees." The joke lost humor when the locals told us that two people had been killed at this well the week before, each stung hundreds of times.

We flew back to Rio to catch the flight home. It was Carnival time and all planes were solidly booked. It was lucky for us because it allowed us to see the Mardi Gras parade. I would have fought to stay and see it anyhow. The Carnival was fantastic, an unforgettable spectacle, the songs, the bands, the floats. Each district of the city has its own bands, its songwriters. They plan and practice the entire year. The sound and color were dazzling and continued far, far into the night.

I looked out my hotel window the morning after. The broad swirling mosaic sidewalks in front of the hotels, and the beaches themselves, were littered with bodies. It looked like the aftermath of a terrible battle. By noon, the burning sun had wakened many of the celebrants and they began to drag themselves away, nursing headaches they had saved up all year to achieve.

The entire trip had been an incredible education to me. I had never seen real poverty before. Oh, during the Depression of the '30s, there had been breadlines that people talked about but most of the unemployed seemed to have some sort of housing available. They suffered hunger but not the awful daily grinding agony that formed the existence of much of the Third World.

Also the riot of customs and viewpoints had been stunning. It is not the kind of education I could have found in school, books or films. It is necessary to have lived it—to have seen babies die in mission hospitals and the elderly achieve final peace in the House of the Dying while our cameras were rolling.

Our takeoff from Brazil was delayed because we had to change planes due to some undisclosed mechanical problem and, instead of the 747 we had embarked on, were given a smaller 707. We then waited on the runway for a good hour, late at night while they checked a faulty landing gear on that alternate transportation. The tropical night was sweltering and the plane was closed. Since the engines were not running, there was no air conditioning. I could hardly breathe as I watched mechanics swarming outside the windows, working under the ship. Finally we were cleared for takeoff, the engines started. The air conditioning came on.

As we lifted into the night, I turned the vent above my seat on full and held my face up to suck in great lungs full of cool air. At the very moment I was beginning to break the sweaty grip of the tropics, the native Brazilians on the flight were getting up for blankets to wrap themselves in, fighting the unfamiliar chill.

The 707 was a plane I knew well from trips I had made and the picture I had shot with the Strategic Air Command. I chatted with the co-pilot when he came back and he invited me into the cockpit where I stayed until our landing. It was interesting to look down on Cuba, where, but for the advent of Castro, I could have made my ballet feature with Alicia Alonzo.

We had two more stops on the tour, one in Jackson, Mississippi, and one at home in Los Angeles—in Watts.

The Jackson slum we photographed had poverty and some of the despair I had seen on the tour. Certainly it was the closest to Third World I have ever seen in America. But it had something else, a rage, blind, senseless. A man chased his woman down the street with a knife while we were shooting something else. Our cameras simply happened to be rolling and caught it. She had a slash on her shoulder that was probably aimed for her neck. A neighbor and one of our crew grabbed him and stopped what would have been a filmed murder. Neighbors told us this was the second time that week he had been after her. She always went back to him.

"He gonna kill that girl, sure," the neighbor said.

We were housed in a Holiday Inn, in rooms a little below their usual standard but the beds were clean and the sheets fresh.

My habit when traveling had been—and generally still is—to drink only bottled water, and only fizzy water at that. Still water can be refilled from a tap. I had, as a result, never had a problem, even in the worst pestilential places. But we were back now in the United States and, in the shower, I tilted back my head and drank in the cold water, thanking God I was back in the States. In the middle of the night I awoke and barely made it to the bathroom. Never in my life have I been so sick.

We took off for home in a terrible rainstorm. It was still daytime but, since morning, the sky had been almost black. The takeoff was frightening. We climbed with lightning flashing all around and the plane dropping sickeningly, then rising as the storm tossed us upward. At 20,000 feet we broke into the clear, or at least got above the rainstorm. But we got into something else, something I had only read about in Steinbeck—a dust storm. It covered Mississippi, Louisiana, Arkansas, Texas and was almost as terrible as the Dust Bowl that had brought the Joads to California. The plane made frequent stops and, at each landing, the choking dust was blowing. I was puzzled as to how the jet engines could function but they did and finally we were clear of it. I was home again.

Joan had a bad cold, a cough. I asked if she had seen Harry. She hadn't. I noticed she was drinking a lot but I didn't pursue the problems. I had only two days of shooting in Watts to complete the film.

When I got to Watts, I was stunned. We were shooting world hunger and poverty and here I found it difficult to get camera angles that would make these homes look bad. Many of the houses had trees and lawns, with cars parked on them, a couple even had trailers with boats. This was a condition of life that the people I had been among could never even dream of. Imagine a man dying of starvation on the sidewalks of Calcutta being offered the chance to live in a house, surrounded by a lawn and trees. Yet it was an unfair comparison. This was after the Civil Rights marches, the time of Dr. King, and, having learned that things did not have to be the way they had been, these people thought themselves as depressed in our society as the Third World's dispossessed were in theirs.

We had tons of footage and long weeks of editing ahead—but I was home.

Joan's cold persisted and she was clearly in pain. I insisted that she see the doctor. She did not want to. The antibiotics had not helped. I learned from the kids how sick she had felt. I took her back to Harry for x-rays. Something turned up in the chest plate. Harry suggested she go to the hospital for further tests.

We got old x-rays for comparison. There was clearly something in the lung.

We grew up in a time when it was smart to smoke; everybody did. Look at the old pictures on television—someone always has a cigarette going. I smoked five packs a day when I was in my early twenties. That doesn't mean that I was actually inhaling that much but there was always a cigarette lit. I had a history of asthma and all sorts of allergies. I awoke every morning with an irritated throat which took a lot of coffee—and a cigarette—to relieve. No one told me to stop or I would get cancer. I was simply sick of the constant irritation, the worrying at night whether I had enough cigarettes to get me through or should I try to find a store on the way home. I stopped with sheer will power—meaning that I swore off repeatedly. Sometimes I would go until way after breakfast without smoking. But I finally did kick the habit. I was going with Joan at the time. She made an effort, too, but it had too firm a hold. After the first month, it was easier for me. Joan could never make it.

In retrospect I think that she knew, or at least suspected, what was wrong. Her father, a physician, had died of cancer.

The hospital tests caused concern and an "exploratory" operation was needed. A tumor was found that involved the left lobe of the lung and two ribs. The tumor and the two ribs were removed.

We knew we had not got the primary, that it had spread. Many meetings were held, many doctors consulted. Should there be a chemotherapy follow-up? Pros and cons. The enemy was invisible until it showed itself again. Chemotherapy and radiation might give a better chance but at the cost of much agony. Nobody could come up with a firm answer. The course we choose was to wait, hope, watch.

Joan led a fairly normal life after she got out of the hospital but I was doing less and less work, trying to spend time with her, time that could never be made up. Every month I took Joan back for x-rays and the treatment seemed to be holding. Then, just under a year after the surgery, something showed again on the chest plate. It was back.

The second surgery was more destructive and invasive. She never fully recovered. Like my mother, Joan now had nurses around the clock. Then a CAT scan revealed a metastasis in the brain. Almost daily radiation slowed that down but at a terrible cost. Joan loved to drive, was proud of her skill. One day after her treatment, she wanted to drive home. I let her, then had to take the wheel away from her when we began veering all over the street. She moved over to the passenger side, saying nothing. It seems a small thing but it was devastating, more so because she did not protest or speak of it.

The great mistake and my greatest regret was that neither of us spoke of what was obvious—that she was dying. I was trying to protect her from the knowledge and she trying not to depress me. We both kept up a brave front and never got a chance to express feelings, to confront the situation, discuss it.

I was back to my childhood, crouching outside Mother's door, praying that she wouldn't die. The disease was doubly terrible because it so stripped Joan of dignity. In addition to the radiation, which left her bald, she was taking heavy doses of chemotherapy.

For 20 years Joan had been part of the SHARE Show, which was now rehearsing on a sound stage of Fox Studio. I took her there. She was wearing a wig and, by now, pushed in a wheelchair, to receive an award from SHARE as past president and chairman of the Board.

On the night of the show at the Santa Monica Auditorium, I got our table together as we always had and I took her, with nurse and wheelchair, to see her final show.

She developed increasing pain over the next few weeks. The doctors tried everything. Nothing would alleviate it. And they couldn't find any immediate cause. She went back to the hospital. That night they had her in intensive care and weren't sure she would make it to morning. I sat there braced for it to end at any minute. It wasn't until the next day that they discovered the intense pain was coming from an ulcer, probably caused by the chemotherapy.

The irony is that the radiation had shrunk the brain tumor to almost nothing but the disease was too widespread and the drain on her strength too great for that to help. Yet, irrationally, I did hope.

She survived that first night, by a thread. She improved but was in and out of consciousness. I started calling every research project I, or any of my medical friends, had ever heard of. One group in Philadelphia was willing to take her—until they got her latest EKG. They were using a technique of raising the body temperature to 107 degrees and holding it there for several hours. As weakened as she was, her heart could never have survived that and they refused. There were other plans, equally foolish, but I was reacting in a way I would never have otherwise considered. At one point a friend suggested Christian Science. I had given up on that in early childhood but now I grasped at it. I talked to a Practitioner. He told me everything would be well but he was very busy and could not come to the hospital because he had many papers to correct for a class he was teaching. He carefully explained what I should tell her to stimulate the healing process. I barely stopped myself from screaming that she was unconscious and couldn't understand what I was telling her. I only slammed down the phone.

I had authorized a Code Blue for her. I would never have done it for myself, certainly not for anyone else I knew in her condition. They revived her twice. The surgeon and his assistants made it clear there was no point in putting her through any more.

I was finally able to locate the doctor who had managed her chemotherapy. He was in Honolulu, giving a paper on oncology. He flew back and, that night, reviewed her case. We sat together in the nurse's station until just before dawn going over her chart. On its cover was typed, "Terminal Cancer." Despite all the medicine I'd been exposed to in one way or another, I was stunned. At last I was forced to face the truth. He tried his best to comfort me but the story was there in the records.

Night after night I spent at the hospital. At first Harry Lusk had gotten me doctor's rooms to catch some sleep. I tried it but preferred to sit in the ICU waiting room, dozing a bit but close at hand in case there was any change. I was drinking heavily. The bottle never left my side. The days blurred together. I went home only to shower and change. Our children and Joan's sister put in a lot of time there, too.

After the last Code Blue, they had worked almost half an hour to revive her. I had to admit that it was cruel and pointless. I gave permission not to try again and sank into a kind of dazed hopelessness. It had become a deathwatch.

Our three children and Joan's sister came and insisted on taking me to dinner. I don't know how long it had been since I'd had a real meal. I didn't want to leave. But they insisted. There was a Sizzler two blocks away. The hospital had the number and would call at the first sign of change. I gave in and went. We were away less than an hour.

When I got back, the cardiologist who had been working with Joan—there were whole teams of doctors by then—met me in the hall. It had happened suddenly and without pain, he told me. She was dead.

17—Fade Out, Fade In

By the time I went in, the nurses had cleaned her up and, for the first time in months, she looked peaceful. After great pain, Death comes as a friend.

But I never forgave myself for not being with her at the end. I had held Mother's hand at the last but I was away at the critical moment when Joan died. It took me a long time to deal with that.

The funeral, the choosing of a casket, the burial plot is a kind of blur but the funeral went well. Father Kieser, for whom I had produced the five years of *Insight*, conducted the funeral mass as he had some years earlier for Mother. The house, as we like to say in show business, was packed.

I was not interested in work. I was not really interested in anything. My heavy drinking continued. One day my son came into the study, and, despite his 20 years, seemed nervous. "You busy?" he asked. I shook my head. "Pop, we're all worried about you," he said.

I muttered something as inane as "So, stop worrying. I'm fine."

"You've been drinking a lot," he said. "Can we talk?"

It suddenly struck me that this was going to be a reverse of Andy Hardy being lectured by his father. I knew the glass on my desk didn't reassure him and I expected a plea that I go to an AA meeting.

What he said was, "Pop, we're worried. Your friends are worried." He was right, of course and I was about to tell him that I would cut back and try to make some sort of life again but before I could speak, he slid several crudely wrapped cigarettes across the desk. "Try these instead."

I stared and then started to laugh at this odd reversal of generations. Suddenly I felt better—even without the marijuana.

A friend of Joan's from SHARE had called repeatedly, asking me to dinner. I kept to my home, doing nothing, refused to see old friends. But Joan's SHARE friend kept calling. She was divorced from a mutual friend and kept asking me to come to dinner with her. One night I gave in and went for dinner at her house. She gave me the address. It was a condo and there was something familiar about the street. I drove around the block several times and at last realized what was troubling me. The condo was built on the same spot in Beverly Hills where Jani's apartment had stood so many years before.

She had prepared an excellent dinner but as was my habit then, I over-drank, actually passing out.

She continued to call and see me. She was a recovering alcoholic and although the AA cure calls for total abstinence, she drank a little wine. She got me to try it and gradually converted me to a more temperate lifestyle. She helped me through a very rough time. I am forever grateful to her. If more than gratitude was expected, I am sorry.

A lot of friends kept calling and I finally took an assignment that I thought might get my mind back on a more rational track. It helped. I did quite a few scripts for various series.

I got a call from Lou Shaw, a producer I had known at Universal. He was at MGM and had a series he was about to put together. He wanted to ask me to produce the pilot when it was okayed. I lunched with him in the studio commissary where I'd spent a good deal of my early youth. We discussed the project. It verged on sci-fi and I said it sounded interesting that, when he was ready to go, I'd love to see the script. He walked me back to my car. It had been six or seven months since Joan's death and he said, "I don't know how you feel but if you're ready to date again I'd like you to meet my wife's aunt from Pasadena."

I considered that Lou must have been close to my age so the aunt must be—God knows how old. My mind's eye saw a little old lady from Pasadena rocking on her veranda in a pair of sneakers. It was funny enough that I had to turn away, cough and say that I wasn't ready yet.

"Well, when you are, let me know."

I promised I would, thanked him for lunch and drove away without thinking of it again.

Wilton called me from Universal. He was now connected with *The Six Million Dollar Man*. I did a couple of scripts and was getting back into the spirit of work. After writing several segments, I came up with a premise of an underwater breathing device with an atomic module that breaks water down to its constituent hydrogen and oxygen. The hydrogen is bubbled away but the oxygen is a constant source of air. The wearer could stay under indefinitely. The switch was, of course, that the whole thing was a scam, which the hero uncovers. But it required a lot of underwater shooting and I was going to direct it. I had never been in scuba gear. My old research fascination rushed back and I got an instructor to give me lessons in my pool. All the time I wasn't writing, I spent at the scuba stores, checking out equipment. I had finally gotten my mind back in a useful channel.

My check-out dive was at Santa Monica Beach. We went down 25 feet, which didn't seem deep until the mouthpiece was jerked from my mouth and I was motioned to surface. In my eagerness to get back to an air supply, I momentarily forgot my training and the instructor, rising with me, had to pound my chest to force me to exhale all the air in my lungs. To have held it at 25-foot pressure would have burst my lungs.

The graduation dive was at Catalina Island where there are huge kelp forests rising 30 or 40 feet from the bottom. To swim through avenues of these waving underwater trees with sunlight filtering down in kaleidoscopic patterns is one of the most beautiful sights I have ever seen.

The whole procedure was, of course, unnecessary. A second unit could easily have shot the underwater sequences. The picture was budgeted for that. But my education had been advanced one more step.

Every year at Christmas, dozens of invitations for parties are sent out, some from friends, most from agents, actors and people wanting something. Most I glance at and throw away. This is not as cavalier as it looks in print. It was the way things were done—like disposing of junk mail.

On the twenty-third of December, I was sitting home, finishing a script when I got a call from Howard Dimsdale. He asked if I was going to Lou's party.

"What party?"

He said Lou Shaw had sent me an invitation some time ago. I couldn't remember any such invitation but then I recalled that my daughter Elizabeth, an actress, had an agent named Glenn Shaw. Despite my warnings and discouragement, the kids still had acting ambitions. "I probably saw Shaw on the envelope, thought it was the agent and simply tossed it out," I explained to Howard. "I'm sorry. Apologize to Lou."

Howard kept bugging me. I had planned to have dinner, wrap up the script I was working on and go to bed. But he insisted his house was only a couple of blocks from Lou's and there would be plenty of food there. "Come over. We'll have a drink and all go together."

I liked his wife, Dorothy, an Englishwoman with a great sense of humor and a Cordon Bleu cook. I agreed, had a drink at Howard's then we all went over to Lou's.

The place was sardine-full of people. I talked to Lou between greetings and was about to tell Howard goodbye and sneak out when an attractive woman was beside me, urging hors d'oeuvres on me. Her long dark hair was pulled straight back in a no-nonsense way which set off a face that had a vaguely Irish look. We talked politely and drifted over to the ledge of the fireplace and sat. She was fascinated by the black suede moccasins I was wearing. For many years I had been wearing moccasins made for me by a Western shop in the Valley used by the studios for authentic Indian and Western costumes. These were not an Indian type. I had modified them and had them made in all colors and types of leather. It was not an affectation—I found them more comfortable than shoes. Also, they required no socks. They were made to my design and came up over the ankles. I wore them even in Africa, ones with thick soles and I had some with sheepskin linings for Canadian snow. We got drinks and spent hours sitting on a narrow ledge by the fire talking, first about the mocs, then just talking. The evening had become fun. Her name was Pat. She was divorced and had four children, three away at college, which would put them about the age of my children. She looked too young but I did not comment on it as it sounded like the obvious approach. Actually she was young. She had a sister 15 years older, a second sister 12 years her senior, a brother 8. She was the baby—much like Mother's place in her family hierarchy.

It was only after a long time when she happened to mention Lou's wife as "my niece" that it hit me. My God, this was the aunt from Pasadena. We talked a while longer. People were leaving. The house was getting empty. It was late. I left, too.

Going down the hill, I became lost and returned to ask directions back to Ventura Boulevard. Pat answered the door and I explained my problem. Pat has always maintained that it was a ploy. But I really was lost. I got my directions, we talked a bit longer but there were no guests left in the house. We kissed. She said, "I'd like to see you again."

I said, "You will."

18

New Horizons

I woke up the next morning and realized I knew only her first name, Pat. I dialed Lou to ask her last name and her phone number. The answering machine picked up. I left a message. The call wasn't returned. I phoned the next day and again the machine picked up. After my third try I phoned Howard. He had no idea of her name or phone number but told me that Lou and Michelle had gone to New York. He had no idea where they were or when they would return. Christmas passed. The New Year arrived. Early in January, the phone rang. It was Lou. He said my message had been the first one he got on his return. He gave me Pat's name and number. I called and got an automobile agency. Thinking I had misdialed I asked if there was a Pat Hightower there. There was. She came on the line and I later found that she owned the agency. I asked her out for the next Friday. That evening I got a call from Dimsdale asking me to dinner on Friday, just a small diner. Wilton and his wife were coming. I said I had a date.

"Bring her," Howard said. Then Dorothy came on and gave me the entire guest list.

Pat lived not in Pasadena but in Flintridge. She gave me elaborate directions but I got lost. I am not usually such a bad navigator but Flintridge was Terra Incognita to me. I found a gas station, phoned and was soon there. Months later, cleaning files, I found a baby book Mother had started, kept for a few months and then apparently lost interest in. One entry read: Baby's first motor trip, to Flintridge and home. On the drive back to civilization, I had to explain to Pat that the guest of honor at the evening's dinner was the hostess' former brother-in-law who was now her sister-in-law. It was Pat's icy plunge into the world of Hollywood. The honored guest was Angela Morley, former RAF fighter pilot, now musician. She got an Oscar for her score of *Watership Down*.

Pat and I started seeing each other exclusively. Lou and Michelle, who had introduced us, lent us their cabin in Arrowhead. It was a beautiful spot and a beautiful time. A few months later, we were married at Bette and Hans Lorenz's house in Newport Beach. A judge we knew and a good friend of Bette's did the honors. Later we had a church wedding. Father Kieser conducted the ceremony in the Priest's Chapel at St. Paul the Apostle Church in Westwood. All four of Pat's children and my three attended. It gave a very *Brady Bunch* feel to the occasion. But even Pat's youngest son, the most adversely affected by her divorce and least in favor of her relationship with me, was impressed. "That was no wedding," he said. "It was a real marriage." There was no honeymoon. That would come soon enough—and from an unexpected source.

I got a call from Arden Albrecht, a Lutheran minister who, for a number of years, had produced a television show called *This Is the Life* for Lutheran Television. He had bought a book called *In the Footsteps of Jesus* and wanted me to do a script for a mini-series. It was to be a co-production of Lutheran Television and an Israeli production company. That unlikely religious combination fascinated me but the subject did not sound like the sort of thing I would be interested in. I stalled, saying I had a pretty full schedule. He asked me to read the book and sent it over. As I had thought, it was a coffee table book, large, with excellent pictures of all the expected holy places, nothing new, nothing novel or interesting. Yet the more I thought about the project, the more ideas came.

What was it I disliked about religious films? Their sameness, their mawkish reverence. People in striped bathrobes with towels around their heads, were evil or incredibly good and Jesus, photographed in a halo, performed miracles that everyone knelt down about.

But if it could be made real, if we could understand the historical background in which Jesus operated, knew the messianic expectations of the Jewish people—their history—it would be, for me, at least, something worth watching.

I talked to Arden about the idea. He liked it. So I was back at research again. I read Josephus' History of the Jewish Wars and all the contemporary history I could find. When we had formed a kind of general approach, Arden and I flew out to Israel for a month to scout locations, to do on the spot research.

The Israeli producer, Arnon Zuckerman, had been Israeli Minister of Television. This impressed me until I watched some Israeli television. I may have been the only one in Israel who did. Most Israelis watched

John sets a shot on the series *This Is the Life* with actress Ketty Lester (1982).

Jordan TV. This, after the endless shots of King Hussein reviewing troops, greeting visitors, opening buildings or just standing around, did provide some entertainment. Whether it was Egyptian belly dancers or old American movies, something was happening.

We started in Jerusalem with tours of the old city, which is fascinating enough but decided we would need a guide who could show up the entire country, stressing, naturally, Bethlehem, Nazareth, Jerusalem and the Galilee.

The guide recommended was the official teacher of all guides in Israel, an American. He was busy for the whole period we would be there but he offered his assistant. We had to settle for that.

The substitute guide showed up. His name was Paul Dunn. He lived in the Arab section of the Old City, was American but he was 22 and seemed much too young to be of any real help. As we talked, it developed that Paul had spent time in China, working with the Bible Society, and had taught Biblical Archeology at Hebrew University in Jerusalem but was not yet old enough to drive a car.

Paul turned out to be invaluable. When we returned to the United States, I wrote the script of the mini-series and Paul shuttled back and forth, carrying whole acts back to Israel so that a production schedule could be set up. However, when, months later, we returned to Israel, ready to shoot, I found the script in the production office, untouched. When I complained to Zuckerman, he assured me they had a schedule. He produced a few sheets of paper listing locations taking scene by scene from the script and giving them consecutive numbers. No attempt to put locations together and arrange a logical order of shooting. No one there had any idea of how to make up a production schedule board.

The contract for the co-production called for the Israeli company to supply cameras, cameramen, lighting equipment, crew, everything.

The entire four months of the shoot was bugged by poor maintenance of the equipment, hairs in the camera gate, dust. I kept asking how the nation that gave us the magnificent planning and precision of the Raid on Entebbe, could not keep a camera clean.

On the other hand, the crew members were wonderful. They would do anything in their power to give us what we wanted. Unfortunately we wanted what was available in Hollywood. Israel's priorities were dictated by their history and geared toward survival. Making a movie was not at the top of the list of necessary things. It is a dangerous country. The crew carried weapons. It probably was, on the average, no more risky than walking in New York or Los Angeles but Israel's normal life was on a wartime footing. Soldiers, male and female, even on leave, carried their weapons at all times. We had a few tense moments during the shoot but no real trouble. Of course we shot all our footage before the time of suicide bombers.

Before we left home, a doctor friend had given us an introduction to the head of the Cardiac surgical team at Hadassah Hospital in Jerusalem. Like their military, Israel's medical practice is flawless. But for picture equipment we had to stumble along with what we could manage.

18—New Horizons

We went to the doctor's home for dinner on a Friday night. His wife was someone you would cast as a chic Parisian hostess, blond hair, blue eyes, beautifully dressed. She was twelfth generation Jewish Palestinian. Their two children, a boy and girl, arrived in uniform, put down their Uzis and took part in the dinner. The candles were lit, welcoming the Sabbath, and the hostess sang with a beautiful voice. It was an evening I will never forget. They invited us back to Seder but we had to refuse since we would be shooting the Samaritan Passover on Mount Gerazim, above Nablus.

The Samaritans are a group with only some 500 members surviving. These are split between Tel Aviv and Mt. Garazim. As Samaritans can only marry Samaritans, they show many of the unfortunate effects of inbreeding. The High Priest at that time was over 90 and his designated successor was his brother, 87. Jews and Samaritans diverged long ago. The Samaritans claim to be keeping the Law as it was handed down by Moses. It is the Jews, they say, who have fallen away.

In pre–Roman times the Passover was celebrated in the temple in Jerusalem with animals sacrificed on the altar. On Mt. Garazim, above Hebron, they still sacrifice but there is no temple there, no altar. They dig a long trench and drive the sheep into it. This becomes a slaughter pit.

We photographed 24 sheep being killed—mothers holding their children down to get the sacred blood on their hands. It is one thing to read of blood sacrifice in the Bible but it does not translate happily to film.

At another location I had a shot that required a crane, a mechanism that raises a camera high in the air and allows it to move in any direction, sideways, up or down. In Hollywood, these are routinely ordered are there next morning ready and manned. There were two cranes in Israel. One was being used by an American company, the other was either broken or promised to someone else; at any rate, not available. So you do what you can. I called for a 20-foot ladder and a tilt head for the camera, so it could shoot nearly straight down. I would have to use the zoom lens for the movement I wanted in the shot.

"No problem." I was told. We would have the ladder on location in the morning.

Morning came, the entire company was assembled on the location at 7:30, the camera out, examined and ready. No ladder. I turned to the associate producer who had promised it. He went to phone. Half an hour passed. Nothing. After nearly an hour, he came back. He was sorry but his cousin, who owned the hardware store, did not open until nine o'clock.

"The hardware store? " I asked.

"Yes," he said. "My cousin has a ladder he's going to loan us."

"You're *borrowing* a ladder?"

He nodded and explained that a man was waiting at the store and would bring it the moment his cousin opened up.

My protest that he should have bought the damned ladder yesterday and had it at the location as promised did not seem reasonable to him. "But my cousin has one. Why spend money on something you would use only once? What would you do with it afterwards?" Excellent reasoning until you consider the cost of the entire crew, sitting and waiting all those hours until that happy moment when the ladder, like a gift from Heaven, came to us.

With few exceptions, our entire shoot went like that.

One morning we left Jerusalem at 5 A.M. and drove up the Jordan valley to the Sea of Galilee to photograph fishing boats. The boats had not changed substantially since Jesus' time. I delivered a long lecture on the necessity of coordinating the boats and the fishermen, as we would stop briefly at a kibbutz on the way. The schedule was tight; we had a lot to fit into that one day.

The kibbutz was no problem. It was a fish farm and we quickly got all the shots of fish coming up in nets we needed. We were on schedule. But, when we arrived at the dock on the Sea of Galilee, I saw no fishing boats, only the associate producer pacing up and down. He explained that he had been trying all morning and hadn't been able to locate any fisherman.

Why had he not made the arrangements last night? It was a long distance call and he thought he'd just arrive early and set things up.

I blistered his ears, did some other shooting and finally, in the afternoon, when the light was wrong, the boats arrived.

On the two-hour drive back to Jerusalem, I was fuming. Arnon, the Israeli producer, should have been there. He should have supervised his assistant. There was no excuse. Also, I wanted a drink. In those days I was drinking vodka and Angostura bitters. But our hotel had no bitters. I had brought a bottle from the States but that ran out. We looked all over Jerusalem and finally, in a liquor shop in the Arab quarter, found one single dusty bottle that had been forgotten on the top shelf. I had been hoarding it, using it sparingly. Tonight I would take an extra dose. It had been that kind of day.

By the time we reached the building that was used for the production office in Jerusalem, I was ready to kill. I literally wanted to do some damage. As we pulled to a stop, Arnon Zuckerman came quickly out of the building and down the steps, turning away down the street. I thought the associate must have called and warned him how I felt and he was running away. I leaped out of the can. "Arnon!" I shouted. "You bastard, I want to—"

He held up his hand in a placating gesture, then turned to his car. As I strode up to him, he turned back, holding out two large bottles of Bitters. "I drove down to Tel Aviv to get them," he said. His smile was beatific.

My rage melted into frustrated gratitude. How could I yell at a man who had made the long search and even longer drive for my Bitters?

That was Israel.

Another aspect of Israel was watching the F16s that flew below us when we were shooting atop Masada. Those supersonic jets skimmed the Dead Sea at the base of the mountain. Masada was Herod's fortress palace and was also the site of the last stand of the Jewish patriots who held the entire Roman Tenth Legion at bay for almost a year in 70 C.E. Today, all Israeli armed forces recruits take their oath of allegiance on Masada. The holocaust will happen "never again!"

Boris Sagal, a friend and colleague, had shot a feature here based on that siege, with Peter Strauss as the Zealot leader and Peter O'Toole as Silva, the Roman commander of the 10th Legion. He had used the same helicopters and pilots we did. The pilots were all Israeli Air Force and fantastic. Some spun their rotor blades so close to cliff tops that I was certain they would touch and smash.

Later, on location for another film, Boris got out of his helicopter and, momentarily confused, turned toward the rear instead of the front. He walked into the tail rotor and was decapitated. He had just married Marge Champion, widow of Gower and a best friend of Joan's. Her children loved Boris. It was a terrible loss, both personal and industry-wide.

Pat flew out for the last two weeks of our shoot. We stayed at the Jerusalem Hilton, on a hill above the Knesset (the Israeli parliament) and the House of the Book. Here we interviewed Yigael Yadin, who had been chief of the general staff of the Israel Defense Force and the archeologist who had done much of the work on the Dead Sea Scrolls. He was one of the most fascinating men I have ever met and Pat fell instantly in love with him, as did the entire company. I was able to show Pat most of Israel, from the Arab markets at Beersheba, to Bedouin tents, to one of which, while we were shooting elsewhere, she was invited in. The tent was filled with goats, chickens, a grandmother with a festering leg and flies feeding on the pus.

Pat was offered food and tea out of foul-looking utensils and was saved only by my entrance and our need to move on to the next location.

John and Patricia Kay Lucas in Israel during the filming of *Yeshua* on the Mount of Olives, Jerusalem (1983).

She saw the Dead Sea and Masada, the ruins of Jericho, the world's oldest city, the Sea of Galilee, the fabulous harbor of Haifa with the city high above it and the ancient Roman port city of Caesarea.

Pat was able to see the wonders of the Old City of Jerusalem, the Arab suks with everything from food to furniture, jewelry, religious items for all religions. We walked the newly excavated Roman road that bisects the city.

Ben Dov, the archeologist who did most of the excavation on the South Wall, took us on a guided tour past the huge stone blocks, weighing tons, that formed the support base of Herod's temple. That wall continued all around the base of the temple mount. The West Wall is where Jews pray at the base of the mount which held the first and second temples of the Jews.

It is now Moslem ground holding their El Aqsa mosque and the Dome of the Rock. After Mecca, this is the holiest place in all Islam.

We were escorted down through the innumerable layers of civilization which had occupied this place, Arab, Byzantine, Roman, Jewish and, through the Bronze age, to prehistory. Thousands and thousands of years of cities built one atop the other.

The tomb of Jesus is claimed to be in the Church of the Holy Sepulcher, itself a mass of competing Christian sects, with separate chapels for Roman Catholic, Greek Orthodox, Coptic, Armenian, etc. Below ground level is the gold- and marble-lined space venerated as the tomb of Jesus.

For Protestants that sepulcher competes with Gordon's Garden tomb outside the north wall of the Old City. The British general Gordon, who had distinguished himself in the Crimean War, in China, in Egypt and who was ultimately to die in Khartoum, his troops slaughtered by the Moslem forces of the Mahdi, lived in Jerusalem for a time and developed a vision of mystic Christianity which made the city of Jerusalem the body of Christ. His legs were the Kidron and Hinon valleys. The pool of Bethesda was the wound in His side. His head was in what is now the Arab quarter. Therefore, Gordon reasoned, the tomb must have been outside the north wall. He found a tomb—which does not seem to be of quite the right period, near what is now the bus station. The cliff, below which the tomb lies, has a formation, which, with a little faith, resembling a face. This, Gordon declared, was the true sepulcher. It seems to be for many Protestants. Catholics favor the Holy Sepulcher. In Jesus' time, no executions were permitted inside the city walls but the Holy Sepulcher's advocates maintain that the wall was in a different place 2,000 years ago. Archeologists, too, differ among themselves.

We, of course, included all this "information" in our mini-series.

Although a great many Israelis are not religious Jews, a short distance from the Old City is Mia Sharim, the ultra Orthodox Jewish community. There they speak only Yiddish, a low–German dialect developed in the ghettos of Eastern Europe, instead of Hebrew. Hebrew, their rabbis claim, is too holy a language to be used for everyday. Only when the Messiah comes will they speak Hebrew. In the meantime, they defiantly speak Yiddish, do not pay taxes, do not serve time in the military, do not vote, will have nothing to do with what they consider the Godless Zionist government. They scream at any tourists they consider to be immodestly dressed and, sometimes, stone them. Women in shorts are special targets. From Mia Sharim, on Saturdays, they stone cars that travel on the main highway north. Driving, among many other things, is breaking the Sabbath.

On the Sabbath, the Israeli Army puts up roadblocks, not to restrain the inhabitants, but to keep tourists out. Israel has many problems other than the Palestinian one. But it is fascinating.

The various factions within the country, super-right Orthodox, Conservative, Reformed, Atheistic or at least agnostic Jews, are bitterly opposed to each other. I asked everyone whose view I respected if they thought, should a miracle occur and the Arab threat be suddenly removed, whether the state of Israel could hold together. Generally they shrugged.

The Hilton, as do all Israeli hotels, has an elevator that stops at every even floor, another that stops on the odd floors on the Sabbath so that Jews may go from floor to floor without doing any work. Pressing the button would technically break the Sabbath. All food for the Sabbath must be cooked beforehand. Non-religious Israelis often go to Arab restaurants on this day to get hot food.

It took Pat a little time to get the kosher laws straight. There are separate restaurants, or special section in the restaurants for meat or dairy. Milk and meat cannot be eaten together and she tended to want butter for the potato with her steak.

The only thing that disturbed me is that I drank a great deal of club soda. That was my way of avoiding "tourist" complaints in all countries. During Passover I could not get any, not because club soda water broke any dietary law but because the bottling plant had no rabbi employed who could certify it "Approved for Passover."

19

Full Circle

In Bethany we shot scenes in what is advertised as the Tomb of Lazarus and had a real challenge getting our equipment into the tomb of the man raised from the dead by Jesus. The tomb is at the bottom of a tunnel descended by a steep stone stairway, deep underground. As was usual in tombs of the era, it comprised an outer chamber where the family could come to mourn and pray and a smaller inner chamber for the body. This chamber had a rectangular hole cut into the stone floor. I had a sudden whim to lie in the grave of the man Christian tradition asserts was resurrected. I did, feeling, I confess, a little anxious. It worked out well, however. Like Lazarus, I rose again. But I do not delude myself that I will get a second chance.

We had been waiting for weeks for decent weather and availability of helicopters to finish the shots I needed in the north, to photograph Nazareth, Mt. Tabor and the Galilee from the air. On my final day in Israel, although the weather was bad, it was the last opportunity I'd have, so we went out to the airfield near Tel Aviv.

The whole area was socked in, the end of the runway barely visible. We drank coffee for an hour before the fog lifted enough for take off. Through a few breaks in the clouds we were able to get a couple of shots. Nazareth was completely covered. The top of Mt. Tabor stood out like an island from the sea of fog. The Galilee was also under cloud cover but we thought it might be worth a try since we were so far north.

We hit solid overcast. Then, over the sound of our own rotors, we heard what sounded like hundreds of jets heading north. We could see nothing and the sound was a little unnerving. The farther we flew, the thicker the weather got. Near noon I threw in the towel and we dropped low and headed for home. I would have to trust my cameraman to get the shots by himself another day. Just before landing we again heard the thunderous sound of jets, now heading south in the opposite direction.

It was not until I got back to the States that I found out what the jets were about. Israel was bombing the missile sites in Lebanon that had been causing such havoc in the northern kibbutzim. There was an expectation that the raid might bring Syria into war. Had it not been such a lousy day, we might have been up there in the middle of Armageddon.

We made one stop in Rome for a few shots. We stayed at the Villa Parioli and Pat had a chance to meet cousin Charlie and Eloise. Pat and Eloise had much the same no-nonsense attitude toward life. Both loved gardening so they got on well. Eloise, however, resembled Joan in that a cigarette was never out of her hands. Since we visited them, Eloise, after many cancer surgeries, died.

Returning to Hollywood, I did a series of *Harry O* scripts, working again with David Janssen. I did *Rafferty* with Patrick McGoohan, another medical show, and *Matthew Starr*. But a lot of the joy was going out of the work. It was, if not hackwork, at least routine.

Between shows, Pat and I traveled.

We've been back to Israel on pleasure trips twice since shooting *Jesua* once with our friends from Newport, Sheron and Mike Mersch. Mike was Chief Financial Officer for Purex and its many acquisitions. We have traveled much of the world together. In Israel there are new things to discover each time. Beside the overwhelming sense of history, the country with its contradictions is fascinating—its constant struggle for peace, both within and without. In Roman times, there were two routes north through Palestine. The inland route ran up through the Jordan Valley to the Sea of Galilee. The Via Maris, the way of the sea, ran along the coast.

In the process of writing I had always had trouble in two ways. I could not spell and I could not type. I had been brought up in studios where I was given a secretary to whom I dictated. She would give me typed pages to correct and then retype them. But when the studio system broke down, it was more difficult. Joan bought a Teach Yourself Typing book and would transcribe my scrawl into readable form. She became very proficient.

Then, with the advent of small recording machines, I would dictate and Joan would transcribe for me when I was working at home.

I had a series of secretaries after Joan's death until, when Pat and I were at the beach, I finally did what many of my contemporaries were doing, used a computer. I shopped around and found one that had a spell check—not common in those days. It was an Exxon, costing almost

$14,000 but came with a great deal of help. The woman who sold it would come to the house and teach me. Exxon was interested in getting writers to use the product—writers influence other writers and make for good business. Now, with this computer, I had to stop thinking with my mouth as I had when dictating and learn to think with my fingers—double jeopardy. I was able to master the word processing part of it. I did not, nor have I with all my subsequent computers learned anything beyond that. I cannot do any of the fantastic things my present computer is capable of. That first Exxon, however remarkable it seemed at the time, began to bug me because it had serial access. That is, if I wanted to go from the beginning of a script to page 150, it scrolled through, page by page. I could go out and make a cup of coffee and come back and still wait until it gave me the desired page. New ones, of course, accomplish this instantly. In the early 1980s we had our friend David Scott and his wife, Lurten, to dinner. David was an astronaut, three times in space. He drove the lunar buggy on Apollo XV. Among his other accomplishments, he was a fan of *Star Trek*. When I happened to mention my frustration with my serial access computer, he wanted to look at it. I showed him this dinosaur I was working with, and asked what replacement he thought I should get. It was then three years old. He studied it carefully, grinned and said. "You know, this is much more complex than the computers that got us to the Moon." That is the rate of progress in electronics.

Paul Dunn, when we came back from Israel and gotten an apartment in Newport, was always at our house and almost adopted us. He married Jeannie Schuller, daughter of Robert Schuller, who had built his Crystal Cathedral from a drive-in church to an international institution. His stepfather had made him producer of the world-famous yearly pageant *The Glory of Easter* and Paul asked me to help him stage the script he had written.

It is an elaborate spectacle for which the Cathedral is famous. The stage is crammed with people, all volunteers from the congregation and all manner of exotic animals. It and their other show, *The Glory of Christmas*, pack in people from around the country and many from abroad.

Dr. Schuller traveled a lot. Through Paul, we became friends with the Schullers and went with them on a cruise to Tahiti where, among other things, I tried to teach Schuller to snorkel—without success. But the doctor swims in other very exalted waters, dealing with politicians and business leaders, with heads of foreign governments and with presidents in Washington. Pat still had her Toyota dealership and once, when we were going to Washington for a foreign car dealer meeting, we mentioned to Paul that we wanted to hear Michael Feinstein, who was playing at the

Ritz Carlton. Paul, who had just had dinner there with Dr. Schuller and Senator Robert Dole, said we should also try the food—it was the best in Washington. "Call the maitre, his name is Michel, and say you're a friend of the Doles. You'll get a good table." We called Michel and tossed out Dole's name. It worked. We were promised a good table. At the close of the Dealer meeting, we grabbed a taxi and rushed to the Ritz Carlton. Michel beamed and led us to a table, second from the door. "Your friends, the Doles, are here," he told us as he seated us at a banquette. Next to our table was the one always reserved for Dole, beside the door where he could see everyone who entered. At the table sat the Doles. "Oh, shit!" was the first thought that occurred to me. How in hell could we explain this away? Pat, however, was quick to realize that the Doles must meet hundreds of people every week. She turned to Elizabeth Dole and started talking about our mutual friends, the Schullers. They probably assumed we had met them with Bob and carried on a wonderful conversation. What started as a threatened disaster turned into a great evening.

Back home I got a call from Lou Shaw at MGM. The CBS network had finally given his pilot the go-ahead. Would I come aboard as producer? I would. It was, however, the last show I would ever produce. Fittingly it was done for Lou, who had introduced me to my wife and, fittingly at MGM, where my mother had worked so long. I remembered the lot very well from my childhood when I would drive in with Collins to pick Mother up. Sometimes she would still be working or in conference. Then I would wander over to the commissary where Slickum's shoeshine stand had stood just outside the door. Slickum provided, beside a gleaming spit shine, grain alcohol for sale during Prohibition. He and Collins would joke and talk about things I couldn't understand. At such times I would wander on the back lot.

Some afternoons I used to ride my horse from Pacific Military Academy, my nearby school, tie up at a cafe across the street and go through the impressive front gate, where the guards knew me, to see Mother. Her office was a two-story wooden building over the Publicity Department and was done in bright chintzes over comfortable sofas and chairs. Now the cozy wooden building that had been Mother's office was gone. A blank-faced building now stood in its place. The commissary was rebuilt but the look of the lot hadn't changed beyond recognition. To produce Lou's pilot, called *Beyond Westworld*, I was assigned Louis B. Mayer's original office. It was at the front of the studio, near that impressive old auto gate which was locked now, no longer used. The executive offices had moved to the grander and more modern Thalberg Building. For me, it was a real trip sitting in the place that had once been the seat of supreme power. Lou had already signed a director, Ted Post, with whom I had worked on *Medic*, my first directing job. From the beginning there were problems. It was a CBS show in conjunction with MGM. So there were two groups of executives to please. When I called casting directors, they were eager to work with me again until they heard it was a network pilot, then they passed, asking to be called again if it became a series. I quickly found why pilots were not desirable. *Beyond Westworld* was a spin-off of a MGM feature from Michael Crichton's novel. I had worked with Michael on scripts he had written for *Insight*. The script had elements of sci-fi. The adversary was an android whom nobody realized was not human. Lou had a unique technique of writing. He called in his six-year-old daughter and told her the story. If she could understand it, that's how it was written. This is not to denigrate Lou's writing or the intelligence of audiences but it does address the audiences' attention span. The system had worked well for Lou. Casting was a huge problem, worse for a series than for a feature. In a feature, a star must commit for a limited period of time. In a pilot, he must commit the time it takes to shoot the pilot, wait until the network decides to pick it up and air it and then be committed for however long the show runs. It is clearly not easy to get name stars for such a questionable venture. Then our casting had to please not only the producers but also the executives of both CBS and MGM. A camel is said to be a horse designed by a committee. Doing anything by committee produces a camel. We ended with one. Then there was the nature of television itself. At that time there were still only three networks, each at war with the others and using their shows as weapons in the fight for ratings. They would willingly risk killing a show that was building a good audience by changing its time slot to pit it against another network's show in the hope of killing the competition. *Beyond Westworld*, one of the highest budgeted pilots ever made, was fourth in line for the new CBS lineup. That is, they put a series on the air. If it does not get instant ratings, they pull it and put another on in its place. There would have had to be three failures before our show even got on the air. The waste is appalling. In former times a network would support a show it believed in, let it run and gradually gather an audience. Now there is such nervousness that, unless a show hits the top the first night, it is tossed out in panic. The script had extensive submarine sequences. Shooting the exteriors would have added immeasurably to the budget but I found that MGM owned a feature called *Ice Station Zebra*, which had footage of a helicopter landing a man on a submarine. There were also various shots of the sub submerging and surfacing. I ran the picture, selected the shots we could use and integrated them with footage we would shoot. It was a big saving. Otherwise, the show was hell. Everything was a compromise and compromise produces more camels. Because the various groups could not agree on casting, we ended with no "names" in the show. That, if not a guarantee of failure, certainly tipped the balance in that direction. After we had shot for a full week, I got a phone call early Sunday morning from the leading actress. She had just been diagnosed with German measles. I informed Lou and then spent the whole of Sunday on the phone with the assistant director, rescheduling all the scenes we would have to reshoot with whatever new actress we could get. Monday, we frantically recast. After much effort and great cost, the show went on the air for a few weeks and then was pulled. I do not know what replaced it but the experience convinced me that I wanted no more of network television.

I regret *Beyond Westworld*. I regret it for Lou's sake. It was a premise that should have worked. I also regret that it was my farewell to network shows but after that experience, I had had enough. Despite my dismal academic record, I managed to learn one thing—when to quit. I kept thinking back to Joe May, the German director with whom I started my career, a man trying in vain to recapture his past. That mistake I will not make.

When we got our first small house in Newport Beach, I bought a tiny ten-foot boat that required no slip. It was pulled up on the beach. That got tiresome very quickly. Then I bought and shared a 19-foot Erickson with Mike Mersch. That was fully seaworthy and we sailed often to Catalina. Mike's wife hated the water and Pat lost interest after we got into a major squall one day with white water breaking over the cabin. It is amazing how quickly the sea can change from calm and peaceful to vicious and deadly. So Mike and I formed a relaxing friendship of weekend sailing, trips to Catalina Island interspersed with the land trips we took with our wives. With Sheron and Pat we went to Ireland, Switzerland, Germany and the Middle East. Paul Dunn had come sailing with us quite a few times, became fascinated and wanted a boat. We moved up to a three-way ownership of a still larger boat, the *Via Maris* (The Way Of the Sea), after that highway in Israel that has carried traffic between Africa and Europe for millennia. Mike, Paul and I celebrated our seagoing partnership by flying to Tahiti and renting a 48-foot catamaran that could make an easy 18 knots sailing between islands. French Polynesia is exquisite but unbearably hot. The cabin of the catamaran was a sauna. We slept on the lowered sail on the boat's trapeze and almost nightly awoke drenched by tropical rain. The entrance to the various Tahitian islands is through small breaks in their surrounding coral reefs. These are difficult enough to manage but the hazard is increased by the natives' habit of stealing the markers to use as floats for their fishing nets. Paul and I had been in Tahiti before but sleeping in the luxurious berth of a large, air-conditioned cruise ship was quite different from lying under the incredibly brilliant stars on the folded sail of a gently swaying boat. The night sky, however, more than made up for any discomfort.

I sold my house in Encino, loaned Angelino and Virginia money to buy a house for themselves and their three children, ending a long chapter of my life, a relationship of almost 18 years. We moved everything we could to the beach. I gave some 4,000 volumes to public libraries when I sold the Encino house and still had three storerooms of furniture.

John and Patricia Kay Lucas, on vacation in Rome, 1982.

With that move I had physically cut myself off from Hollywood. Pat sold her small beach house and we moved to Corona Del Mar, a couple of miles south of Newport and only a few miles from our slip that held the *Via Maris*. As soon as we had settled in the Corona house, we immediately, of course, began reconstruction, adding rooms, redoing others, putting in a swimming pool that looked out on the ocean. Between us, Pat and I have seven children. The house got a lot of visitors. It is only 60 miles to Los Angeles but it made it more difficult to see old friends. One night I got a call from Wilton to tell me that Howard and Dorothy Dimsdale were dead. For years Dorothy had suffered from a mysterious disease of the lungs, which became more debilitating with the passage of time. No one could diagnose it. No antibiotics could touch it. She was an avid bird watcher and I wondered if she could have caught some rare avian disease. But specialist after specialist had failed to come up with an explanation or a cure. Howard was considerably older than Dorothy and not in very good health himself. When it became clear that the end was not far off for Dorothy, Howard, as methodically as he did everything, researched the most painless way to die, laid in the necessary supplies. He wrote letters to everyone who had a need to know, explaining why they were taking this course. He provided for his family, a son by a previous marriage, and arranged a fund to care for his dog. He gave explicit instructions for the disposal of their bodies and mailed the letters on a Friday afternoon so they would not be received before Monday. Then he and Dorothy lay down, took the potion he had prepared and painlessly made their exit. It was sad but, when I think of the agony Joan went through, it made sense.

Pat still had her Toyota agency to run and it was a very long drive there and back daily but it brought us many benefits. There were Toyota dealer trips to Japan, to St. Kitts in the Caribbean, Las Vegas, Washington and Beijing. To keep my hand in, I did a few directing jobs, usually staying over in hotels in town. Scripts, I wrote at home. In 1987 we had a directors' strike, the first in the history of the Guild. I had marched on the picket line in several Writers Guild strikes, but the Directors Guild had always managed to maintain steady progress without resorting to strikes. When, at the last moment, negotiations with the producers broke down, the Guild moved. Like the preparation of a picture, Guild committees were formed, which with military precision prepared for conflict. A strike requires picket lines drawn around all major studios and members to man the lines. Lists were drawn and dates arranged for the members to march. I, living in Newport Beach, some 60 miles south of Hollywood, was made responsible for recruiting all members in this area, arranging dates when they should show up for picket duty. From that distance it was difficult to manage the logistics. I went carefully through the list of members who lived in the South Bay area and called them. Many were retired and, in some cases, transportation had to be arranged. Some had had strokes or were otherwise incapacitated and unable to participate. A few enthusiastically agreed. Then I came to the number of a member I shall call Mike Prost. A woman answered the phone. "Mike Prost, please," I said.

"Who is this?" The voice was instantly suspicious.

I gave my name and said I was calling about the Guild strike.

"Where did you get this number?" She sounded like a Most Wanted talking to a member of the FBI.

"From the Directors' Guild." I explained about the strike and the need for pickets. "Now," I asked, feeling we had danced around long enough, "is this still Mike's number and, if so, when will he be back?"

There was a long pause. I thought she might have hung up on me. "Hello," I said, "Are you still there?"

"Since the surgery," she told me, "my name is Michelle. I haven't worked in the business for six years."

Now the pause was mine as I digested this information. "Well, then," I said at last, "why don't I just keep you informed of the progress of the strike?"

"You do that, dear," the former Mike Prost said.

After all the preparation or, perhaps, because of it, the strike lasted exactly five minutes. We were all on the picket lines and just starting to move when the producers came back to the table.

I have always wondered how Michelle would have made out on the picket line.

In the last few years I have a flood of calls, letters and visits from people who are writing books about the various series I have been part of and books about Mike, about *Casablanca*, Fran Marion, Mother's *Ben Hur* and the various series I have done. I had Bill Shatner down for long talks about the two books he wrote on *Star Trek*. Bob Justman, who was associate producer when I did the show, came down with Herb Solow, who had been Head of Production at the studio. They put together an excellent book called *Inside Star Trek*.

During my *Star Trek* period, I was producing but also directing one of the episodes, using some of the office buildings on the Paramount lot as backgrounds. Between set-ups I ran up to say hello to Hal Wallis, with whom I started as a feature writer and with whom I probably should have stayed. As I rushed back to the set, I was intercepted by a man who introduced himself, wondering if we might be relatives—his name was Lucas. He was very friendly and obviously wanted to talk but I had spent more time than I had planned with Hal. My assistant told me the crew was ready for the next shot and I was skirting the outer edge of my schedule. I quickly brushed the visitor off and shot the scene. When I looked up again, he was gone. George Lucas went on to do his unforgettable *Star Wars* trilogies and now has an empire north of San Francisco doing most of the elaborate special effects for all companies. My timing has never been very good.

Despite my late and fitful start, I have, between movies and television written, in my lifetime, well over 1,200 scripts, directed more than 800 and produced 4 series. I tell myself that should be a satisfying amount but at times, I still miss it. I wonder if my mother missed her work in all the empty time she had. She never said.

Mother started off like a rocket, doing everything and doing it well, directing, acting and writing. Then, like a rocket with its fuel suddenly cut off, she stayed in orbit for 30 unproductive and mostly unhappy years.

Mike, besides the work he did in Europe before 1926, directed 99 films in America. A good many of them will never be forgotten. In my front room sits his Oscar for *Casablanca*, a constant reminder of what I had to live up to.

I have done my share of contemplating "what might have been" and "if I'd only." If I had gone through the proper schooling, if I'd been responsible in my early work, I might have "done better," whatever that means.

If I'd stayed with Hal Wallis I might have had a good life in feature pictures, made much more money, perhaps even have had a shot at an Oscar of my own. But there is much that I would have missed. There are no free rides—everything costs. I might have missed many of the experiences I have had, the people I've known and loved.

Some 15 years ago, I was diagnosed with Atrial fibrillation—the heart runs out of control. Medication helped for a while. Then John MacDonald, my friend and internist for many years, retired with his pacemaker. I went to my friend Gene Farber at Stanford and he arranged for the head of Cardiology to do a Cardioversion—the heart is stopped with the paddles you see on the present-day TV shows, then started again, this time in proper running order—called sinus rhythm. That lasted only a few weeks. I was referred to a cardiologist in Newport near my then home and had another done. That one held for almost eight years. Then I went back on medication alone with chemicals to keep my blood thin and lessen the possibility of a stroke. That went well for a while. Then, as I was going through a routine physical exam, a suspicious mass appeared in the prostate. Biopsied, this proved to be malignant but a slow-growing cancer. Various strategies were considered—surgery, chemotherapy, etc. It was finally decided to simply wait and watch my PSA, a test that is specific for prostate cancer. It remained low for a year and in 1998 it began to inch upward. Now we had again to decide whether to pursue more aggressive strategies or take what time I have to enjoy myself and see some of the things I have yet to see.

Pat had now sold her Toyota agency. We began to travel in earnest, Alaska, The Caribbean, Russia, Ireland. Pat has relatives, Bonnie and George Heigold, who live in Costa Rica. We go there once a year. They have a large motor sailor and the Gulf of Nicoya, on the Pacific side, is almost an inland sea, dotted with islands. Among the best of things George and Bonnie had was a miniature poodle called Spunky. She sailed with us, went ashore when we did. We fell in love with her. When she had puppies, Bonnie sent us one. We went to the airport to pick her up. At the age of two months she had been in a cage for probably 12 hours during the long flight from Costa Rica and the delay of customs. We let her out of the cage and she clung to Pat's neck on the long ride back from the airport. Having prepared for her arrival by carefully reading a book on dog training, we took one look at the cage in which the author recommended she sleep and promptly broke every rule. She had slept in our bed ever since. I named her Julia, after my grandmother. The following year we went to Costa Rica again and bought Julia's half sister. She is named Bess, after Mother. Ultimately a third dog joined our family—a half sister of the other two. We five were inseparable, except on the occasions when our travels would not permit it. Then we get Pat's sister to come and house/dog sit.

Paul Dunn has a home and also a condominium on Maui and we visit there frequently. I have been on six continents (all except Antarctica), visited Buffalo, where Mother was born, Montreal, home of my father, but only in the fall of 1998 got to Budapest, Mike's birthplace. There are still many parts of the world I have not seen. Pat and I have started to fill in the blanks.

Although I hated to leave the water, we moved closer to town, closer to the children and less than a mile from Southwestern Military Academy, which I had attended as a child. It is now a co-ed school.

In 1997 we bought a house built by a famous architect. It was a beautiful location but had no room for a pool. Three years later we bought a house in Altadena, even nearer our children. Although San Marino was beautiful, our present house is in the hills with a fantastic view across the pool we put in. If the Los Angeles smog permits, we can see the ocean and Catalina Island.

Recently I was approached to do an animated interactive version of *Star Trek*, using a new computer technique, which unlike most computer animation, is extremely realistic and looks very close to the old series I did. The computer generated characters of Kirk, Spock, Uhura, Scotty and Bones look exactly as they did in the '60s. I was impressed and interested. I talked to the producer. The company he worked for had made a fortune on interactive game shows, arcade stuff, which needs only primitive technique. This was nearly real. I was interested but how do you direct a computer? I told the producer I would need a storyboard man. He asked what that was. I explained. But neither he nor the kids who so magically manage the computers had experience with a dramatic show. He agreed to my demand, signed a contract and hired a storyboard man who would work at my home.

A few days later I called the producer with a question. I was told he was no longer with the company. I then talked to his assistant who was to take his place. The producer I had dealt with had had the project for over a year and had run up fantastic costs, all with no definite plan. Sets were computer-designed, characters created and realistic movement worked out but with no real idea of how to make a picture out of it. Despite the very young age of the computer artists, this new technique was extremely labor intensive, which didn't bother them but the costs ran out of control. The idea was to create a six-part story, which would be issued on six CDs.

Dorothy Fontana, who had been our story editor on *Star Trek*, did a script but no one had any idea of how to create camera angles. So I began with the technique I learned at Disney. Then it was simply to show Walt how the picture would look and get his approval. This time I selected the camera angles exactly as I would in a film, had them rendered as sketches, almost like the cells in a Disney feature. The sketches were then given to the strange young people who sit at computers and make all the magic happen. Film techniques I know very well. This computer magic I do not understand at all. I use my own computer as a sort of super typewriter. The one I have has almost unlimited capabilities which, for the most part, I cannot comprehend or use.

I was amazed as the *Star Trek* characters came out looking as they did in the '60s. We then had to consider voices. The actors from the original series were now considerably older and voices, too, age. I recorded the original cast, recording all the dialogue in advance so the computer operators could arrange the lips to match the sound. The only actor's voice we had to replace was DeForest Kelley, the ship's doctor, who was very ill and unfortunately died a short time later.

When I had done perhaps a thousand sketches with the storyboard man, sketches that would take months to animate, I decided to go on a European trip with the Mersches. I told the producer I would continue when I returned. That was agreeable to the producer and we left. We drove through Germany, Austria, Czechoslovakia and Hungary.

When I returned, I called to tell the producer I was back and found that the whole project had been shelved. The cost was too much. The company had decided more money could be made with arcade games. Having already sunk so much money and having developed so much footage, I suggested they use it to release a single *Star Trek* episode instead of the six that had been planned. That would thus recoup at least *some* of the money. But from somewhere on high the decision had been made and was final. I walked away from my final connection with—what shall I call it—entertainment?

Recently I attended the funeral of Father Kieser, with whom I had done the *Insight* series. He died suddenly, before I even knew he was so ill. It was the loss of a great friend. But, speaking of fathers, I think a good deal of my life has been, unconsciously, a search for a father. Collins, Mort Werner, Ben Fox, Hal Wallis, Wilton Schiller, Michael Mersch—relative ages have nothing to do with it. Why I never settled on Mike Curtiz I don't know. Perhaps we were just too different. Perhaps, despite all he did for me, he didn't offer himself as a father or, if he did, perhaps I couldn't recognize it. Blame has nothing to do with it, either.

From the high ground of age I find it fascinating to look down on the course of my life, to remember but hardly recognize all the different people who were me climbing blindly toward the place where I now stand.

I see where the strands of my life come together, see this multitude of me following paths not of my making, at least, not with any conscious decision—following the course of least resistance. I have never come near what my parents accomplished. I have been an ineffectual son, an indifferent father—neither willingly. If my life were a script, I see many needed rewrites—but should they be made? Would tampering with the past make things better—or only different? Beside seeing the wonderful work some of my friends accomplished, I have also watched many of the great fall as quickly as they rose. As Mike often remarked, "Goddamn, picture is terrible cruel business."

I was born into and lived through the Golden Age of Movies. They really were golden although, at the time, we didn't know it. It is only in comparison to what the business is today that the gold of the past shines through. The three studios I worked at in my youth were like city states, having their own police and fire forces, shops, construction crews, wardrobe departments that could produce clothes from any period past or present or any period imagined. Symphony orchestras. Prop Departments bulging with furniture from every period of history. All these fiefdoms were ruled by the iron hands of Warner, Zanuck, Mayer. They were true Tsars.

Hollywood had three really great decades, the '20s, '30s and '40s. In the '50s, things began to fall apart. It wasn't noticeable at first—a few big stars formed their own companies. Over the years TV grew, and the studios, producing fewer pictures of their own, had many empty stages. They began to rent space to the enemy. The Golden Age had rusted and we are gradually left, at the beginning of the new millennium, with the frantic mess that making movies has become.

It would never have occurred to people living in the Dark Ages of Europe that their lives were squalid—that they had lost the worldwide unity, the safety and comforts of the Roman Empire and were stuck in the mud, confusion and chaos of constantly warring petty states. To them it was today, it was the way life was. The changes in my own lifetime have been incredible—commercial aviation, the golden age of radio, television, atomic power, the computer revolution, the space age. I have been exposed to so much and only regret that I have contributed so little. I have been Life's voyeur. This is by no means a complaint. I have, all things considered, had a damned good life. At any rate, my life is the way it is and I have seen and done the things I have done and, like it or not, the aggregate makes up me. In my first year on Earth, I was taken to Australia. Forty years later, I went back there to do the *Whiplash* television series. Cameras have taken me around the world and into some very strange places. My life began with travel.

Life is a circle. Where does a circle end?

It ends in watching the disintegration of my body, watching almost as an observer, as though it were someone else's problem. Watching as my skin seemed to grow several sizes too large. Seeing this with a kind of morbid interest but mostly without fear. I hope this attitude continues. But whether or not, my life had been full.

There is a poem by a Mexican poet, Amado Nervo, who died in the year I was born. It is called *En Paz*. Compressed it reads,

> Muy cerca de mi ocaso, yo te bendigo, Vida.
> Ame, fui amado
> El sol acaricio mi faz.
> Vida, nada me debes.
> Vida, estamos en paz.

My very rough translation renders it:

> Very close to my death, I bless you, Life.
> I loved. I have been loved.
> The sun caressed my face.
> Life, you owe me nothing.
> Life, we are at peace.

Not quite the end but ... *enough*.

Epilogue

This book has its origins at dinner tables and gatherings over the years when we would listen enthralled to stories of our family's lives and careers during the Golden Age of Hollywood.

Some time ago, we begged our father to put this unique family history on paper so it could be shared with others. During what proved to be his last illness, we discovered great joy working with him on these memoirs, which brought us closer than ever.

Shortly after completing the revised manuscript, our father passed away peacefully, surrounded by his family.

For John Meredyth Lucas:

Elizabeth MacGillicuddy Lucas

Victoria Michaela Lucas

Michael Meredyth Lucas

Index

Numbers in *italics* represent photographs.

Acapulco 224
Adventures in Iraq 188
The Adventures of Huckleberry Finn *208*, 210
The Adventures of Robin Hood 24, 95–96, *96*, 234
Affairs of Cellini 105
Albertson, Jack 243, 250–251, *252*
Albrecht, Arden 282
Alonzo, Alicia 206–207, *207*
Alvarado, Ann (later Ann Warner) 94
Alvarado, Don (aka Don Page) 94
Angels with Dirty Faces 187
Applegate, Fred 93
Arliss, George 81
Artransa Studios 210
Astor, Mary 35, 95
Atwill, Lionel 62–63
Atwill, Louise 62–63

Bainter, Fay 114
Banner, "Nanny" (Nell Wauchope Banner) 177
Barnes, Joanna 257–258
Barrymore, John 35–36, 106, 247
Bartelmess, Richard 100–101
Beery, Wallace 105, 179

Ben Casey 142, 228–230, *229*, 231–233, 241, 249–250, 257
Ben Hur 5, 27–29, *28*, 167,
Bennett, Constance 157–158, 159
Bennett, Enid 25, 27–28
Bergman, Ingrid 142, *143*, *144*
Bess the Detectress 21, *23*
The Best Things in Life Are Free 203
Beyond Westworld 294, 296
Bickford, Charles 187–188
Biograph Studios 19
Blanke, Henry (Heinz) 128, 147, 148, 149–150
Bogart, Humphrey 142, *143*
Boone, Richard 183, 186
Brackett, Rogers 146, 149–150
Brando, Marlon 203–204
Brent, George 108–109, 128, 187
Brigadoon 189
Brown, Harry Joe 178
Bushman, Francis X. *28*, 29

Cabin in the Cotton 100–101, *100*
Cagney, James 34, 138, *139*, *140*, 142
Campenella, Joseph 235
Captain Blood 34, 62, 69–71, *70*, 95
Captains of the Clouds 138, *140*, 142

308 Index

Carson, Jack 147
Casablanca 34, 142, *143*, 162, 299
The Case of the Curious Bride 69, 116
Cassidy, James B. 181–183
Caufield, Joan 193
Champion, Marge 179, 287
Chaney, Lon, Jr. 157, 166
Chaplin, Charlie 32, 37
The Charge of the Light Brigade 34, 91, 92
Chevalier, Maurice 105
Clark, Dane 157, 166
Clark, Fred *194*
Clooney, Rosemary 189
Cobb, Lee J. 181
Coburn, James 224
Code Three 205
Cohn, Harry 178–179
Collins 6–8, 10–11, 13,1 4–15, 31, 40, 41, 44–45, 48, 49, 52, 56, 59, 62, 65, 71–72, 75, 90, 121–122, 294, 302
Columbia Television 187–189
The Comancheros 226
Confession 94, 95
Connors, Mike 234–235, *235*
Coon, Gene 236–238
Costello, Dolores 35
Costello, Maurice 35
Cotten, Joseph 168
Crawford, Joan 37, 44, 75, 146, *147, 148*, 166
Crawley, Budge 256
Crichton, Michael 295
Crone, Bob 256
Crosby, Bing 189
Curtiz, David (Desider) (MC's brother) 120, 146
Curtiz, Gabriel (Gabor) (MC's brother) 120, 146
Curtiz, Michael (JML's stepfather): appearance 48; "Curtiz-isms" 10, 69, 91, 100–101, 102, 120, 131–132; directing style 56–57, 95–96, 101–102, *104*, 107–108, 118–119, 142; European films 9, 78–80; family 120–121, 146; home life 5–6, 7, 10–11, 71, 82, 143–144, 149–150; Hungarian friends 89–90, 98, 102–105, 189–190; illness and death 226–227, *228*; later films 202–204, *203*, 208, *209, 210*, 222; marriage to Bess Meredyth *51*, 51–52, 72, 73–74, 89–90, 9, 93, 98–99, 131–132, 138–140, 187, 208, 222; Michael Curtiz Productions 160, 193–195, *194;* polo 45, 63, *83;* relationship with A. Korda 78–79, 148–149; relationship with JML 53–54, 93, 110, 130, 144–145, 165, *178*, 226, 227; relationship with Wilfred Lucas 33; relationship with Hal Wallis 83, *83, 162, 162,* 170–171; relationship with Jack Warner 85, 113–115, 162, *162,* 170–171 ; relationship with Darryl Zanuck *38,* 58–59 63, 81; travel 75–78, *77;* Warner Bros, films at 34, 38–38, *38,* 39–40, 62, 69, *70,* 71, 91, 95, *96, 97, 99, 100, 103,* 106–107, 118–119, *139, 140,* 142, *143, 144,* 146–147, *147, 148,* 150–151, 161, 189

Damita, Lily 69
Dance Out of Darkness 206–207
Dark City 163, 191
Darvi, Bella 203–204, 244
Daughters Courageous 114
Davies, Joseph 144–145
Davis, Bette 100–101, *103, 171*
Day, Doris 175, 194–195
Dear Ruth 158–160
De Fore, Don 163
deHavilland, Olivia 92, 95, *96,* 107
De Mille, Cecil B. 21–22, 31, 169
The Desert's Sting 19–21, *20*
Desired Woman 37
The Devil's Disciple 80, 190
Dieterle, William 163–164, 168–169
Dietrich, Marlene 167–168
Dimsdale, Dorothy 279, 281, 297
Dimsdale, Howard 229, 257, 279, 281, 297
Disney, Walt 196–202
Dive Bomber 118, 186
Doctor X 62
A Doll's House 174, 181
Don Juan 34–35, 95, 247
Dragnet 178, 179, 191, 225
Dressler, Marie 87–88
Duff, Howard 243
Dugan, Rabbi Max 227
Dunn, Paul 284, 293, 294, 296–297, 301
Dunne, Irene 161
Dwan, Allan 174

Easy Rider 180
Edwards, Vince 228, *229,* 231–232
The Egyptian 203, *203, 204,* 205, 244
Emerson, Faye *171*
Ettinger, Maggie 11, 68, 71, 153, 157, 158, 161, 196, 206, 227, 245

Fairbanks, Douglas, Jr. 44, 166
Fairbanks, Douglas, Sr. 75
Farrow, John 164
Ferrer, Mel 158–159
Fields, W.C. 8–9, 12, 48
Flamingo Road 148
Flash of Darkness 183
Fleisher, Richard 196, 197
Flynn, Errol 33, 69, *70,* 71, 91, *92,* 95–96, *96,* 116, 118
Folies Bergere 105, 179
Fontana, Dorothy (D.C Fontana) 240, 302
Four Daughters 114
Fowler, Gene 105–106, 142, 179
Fox, Ben 116, 205–206, 207, 210–211, 213, 216, 229–230, 302
Fox, Frank (Francisco Kowalski) 98, 99
Francis, Kay 94
Fraser, Elisabeth *171*
The Fugitive 223–234, *233,* 253
Furia, John 241

Gable, Clark 37, 54, 105, 128
The Gamblers 40
Garbo, Greta 37
Garfield, John 114
Geller, Bruce 234, 236–237
Glad Rag Doll 39
Glover, Rita 155–156
Goff, Ivan 237
Gold Is Where You Find It 106–107, 109, 187
Goldwyn, Sam 80
Goldwyn, Sam, Jr. 186, 208
Gonzalez Ayala, Angelino 61, 240, 249, 258, 297
Gonzalez Ayala, Paula 25, 210, 212, 218, *221,* 223, 240
Good Night Sweet Prince 106
Good Time Charley 37
The Gorilla Man 118

Grant, Cary 69, 86, 227, *228*
Graves, Peter 116, 188, 205, 211, 213, *214,* 215
The Gray Seal 201–202
Griffith, D.W. 19, 21, 38, 184–185
Groom, Sam 243, 250–251, *252,* 256

Hagman, Larry 253–254
Hammerstein, Dorothy 64
Hammerstein, Oscar 64
Hammerstein, William 64
The Hangman 208
Harry O 248, 292
Hasso, Signe 159–160
Hayward, Louis 178
Hearst, William Randolph 193
Hearts in Exile 40
Heigold, Bonnie and George 300
The Helen Morgan Story 203
Herrick, Margaret 246
Hightower, Patricia *see* Lucas, Patricia Kay
Hodges, Eddie *210*
Hopper, Dennis 180
Horse and Buggy Doctor 111
Howe, James Wong *114*
Hunt, Marjori ("Portia") 141, 152, 153, 156
Hunter, Ross 175
Hussey, Ruth 157

In the Footsteps of Jesus 282
Ince, Sandor 89
Inside Star Trek 299
Insight 241–244, *242,* 249, 255, 277, 295, 302
The Iron Duke 81
Irving, Richard 152–153

Janssen, David 233, *233,* 248
The Jazz Singer 95
Jolson, Al 40
Justman, Bob 237, 238, 299

Kane, Candy 94
Kaye, Danny 189
Kelley, DeForest 302
Kelly, Orry 69
Kertesz Kaminar, Mihaly *see* Curtiz, Michael
Kid Galahad 98–99, *99*

Kieser, Father Ellwood "Bud" 225, 241–242, 248, 255, 277, 282, 302
King Creole 208, *209*
King of the Wind 174–175
Koch, Howard 146
Korda, Alexander (Korda Sandor) 72, 78–79, 80–81, 148–149
Kronman, Harry 173, 225, 227
Kronman, Rosella 227
Krumholtz, Chester 249, 256

Ladd, Alan 163–164, 208, 227, *228*
Ladd, David 208
Lady and the Tramp 197
Laemmle, Carl 22, 37
Laguna Playhouse 151–152, 153, 172, 189, 243
Laird, Jack 250, 251–252, 253
Lane, Lola *114*
Lane, Priscilla *114*
Lane, Rosemary *114*
Larkin, George 22
Lederer, Francis 174, 181
Leigh, Janet 241
Lester, Ketty *283*
Lewis, Jerry 170–171, 231–232
Ley, Willy 197–198, 199
Life with Father 161
Lincoln, Elmo 21
Lindfors, Viveca 163
Litvak, Anatole 173
Loos, Anita 37
Lord, Robert 212, 219
Lorenz, Bette 282
Lorenz, Hans 282
The Loretta Young Show 179, 190, 191–192
Lowe, Marcus 27, *28*
Lubitsch, Ernst 147
Lucas, Elizabeth MacGillicuddy (JML's daughter) 61, 106, 116, *178*, 210, 212, 220, *221*, 276, 305
Lucas, George 299
Lucas, Joan MacGillicuddy (JML's first wife): acting career 58, 116, *171*, *172*, *203*, 204–205, *204*; Australia trip 210, 212, 216–217, *221;* charity work 179, 241; early life 171–172; family life *107*, 116, 157, 173–174, 177, 181–182, 186, 219–220, 230, 249, 256, 257; last illness of 270, 274–277

Lucas, John Meredyth (career): actor 140–142; assistant director 130, 133; dialogue director 116–118, 145; documentary (World Vision) 258–274; junior writer 109–112; Laguna Playhouse 151–154, 157–160; miniseries (*In the Footsteps of Jesus*) 282–292; Office of War Information (WWII) 136–138; radio 146, 150; screenwriter 174–177, 177–179, 206–207; script clerk 93–94, 95–98, 109–110; staff writer (Hal Wallis Productions) 162–165, 167–169; staff writer (Michael Curtiz Productions) 193–195, 202–203
Lucas, Mabel "Sylvia"(JML's stepmother) 32–33, 122
Lucas, Michael Meredyth (JML's son) 106–107, 116, 202, 210, 220, *221*, 251, 276–277, 305
Lucas, Patricia Kay (Hightower, Pat) (JML's second wife) 279–280, 281–282, 287–288, *288*, 290, 292, 294, 296–297, *297*, 298, 300
Lucas, Victoria Michaela (JML's daughter) 106, 116, 186, 201, 210, 220, *221*, 276, 305
Lucas, Wilfred (JML's father) *20*, 21, 22, 24, *24*, *25*, 27, 29, 31, 32, 33, 121, 122–123
Luke, Sister 267
Lupino, Ida 243
Lusk, Dr. Harry 177, 230, 258, 270, 273, 274

MacDonald, Dr. John B. 121, 122, 123, 208, 225–226, 231, 300
MacGillicuddy, Joan *see* Lucas, Joan MacGillicuddy
MacGillicuddy, Dr. Maurice 171, 274
MacGillicuddy, Mauricette (Dale Melbourne, "Billie") 106, 171–172, 174, 180, 181, 182, 276
MacGillicuddy, Nell O'Conner 171, 173–174, 216
MacGlashan, Andrew Fuller (JML's grandfather) 15, 17, 18, 19, 24, 248
MacGlashan, Florence Brewer(JML's aunt) 10, 17, 49–50, 56
MacGlashan, Helen Elizabeth *see* Meredyth, Bess

Index **311**

MacGlashan, Julia Ginther (JML's grandmother) *16*, 24, 50, 52–53, 146
MacGlashan, Viola *see* Reynolds, Viola
MacGlashan, William Frederick (JML's uncle) 10, 17–18, 49, 146
MacGlashan, William Frederick, Jr. (Sandy) (JML's cousin) 17, 146
MacMurray, Fred 118, *119*
Macpherson, Jeanie *20*, 21–22
Madame Sul-Te-Wan 184–185
Madison, Cleo 22
Madison, Guy *207*
Madonna of Avenue A 40
Mammy 40
The Man from Kangaroo 24
The Man in the Net 208
The Man Who Skied Down Everest 256
Mannix 234–236, *235*, 253
Manon Lescaut 35
March, Frederic 105
Marion, Frances 37, 160–161, 173, 178, 246, 299
The Mark of Zorro 124, 200
Martin, Dean 169–170, 241
Martin, Quinn 233
Mathis, June 27, *28*, 37
Matthew Starr 292
Mature, Victor *203*, 204
Maxwell, Kathleen 211, 213
Maxwell, Peter 116, 211, 213
May, Joe 94, 159, 296
Mayer, Louis B. 25, *26*, 29, 37, 39, 46–47, 303
Maynard, Gordon 71, 227–*228*
Mazurka 94
McCarey, Ray 109–110
McDowell, Roddy 257–258
McEvoy, Mae 27
Medic 179–180, 183–186, 187–189, 295
Melbourne, Dale *see* MacGillicuddy, Mauricette
Meredyth, Bess (JML's mother): acting career 19–21, *20*, *23*; *Ben Hur* 25–31, *28*; death of 247–248; early life & family 15–19, *16*, 49–50, 81; extravagances of 127–128, 222, 227, 245–246; friendship with John Barrymore 35–36; friendship with Ramon Novarro 29–30; home life 61, 81–82, 83–84, 121–122, 142–143, 222, 240–241;

illnesses of 58, 62, 72–74, 124, 224–225, 225–226, 244, 246–247; marriage to Michael Curtiz 5, 48, 51, *51*, 72, 89–90, 91–93, 119–120, 131–132, 138–140, 142, 152, 160, 187, 222, 224–225; marriage to Wilfred Lucas 21, 22, 24, *25*, 27, 31; relationship with JML 8, 13, 14, 15, *42*, 44, 52–53, 123–124, 163, *164*; relationship with LB Mayer 25–27, *26*, 37, 44–45, 105; relationship with JL Warner 94–95; relationship with D. Zanuck 39, 91, 105, 124, 244–245; screenplay collaborations 105–106, 142, 160; silent films 19, *20*, 21, 22, *23*, 34–36; travel 75–77, *77*, 98–100
Mersch, Michael 292, 296, 302
Mersch, Sheron 292, 296
Metro Goldwyn Mayer 25, 27, 31, 37, 44, 54, 105
The Mighty Barnum 105, 179
Mildred Pierce 146–147, *147*, 174
Miller, Marvin 168
A Million Dollar Bid 37
Minter, Mary Miles 154
Mission to Moscow 144–146
Moon of Israel 79
Moore, Archie *210*
Moran, Polly 87–88
Morgan, Dennis 94
Moser, James 178, 179, 183, 225, 228
Murphy, Father Edward *107*, 173

Navy Blues 171
Niblo, Fred 25, 27, *28*
Night Gallery 249, 250, 251, 253–254
Niven, David 91
Noah's Ark 37, 38, *39*
Noah's Ark (TV series) 191–192, 258
Novarro, Ramon 25, 27, *28*, 29–30

Oberon, Merle 78, 80–81, 105
Of Mice and Men 166
The Old Mill at Midnight 23
Olympia 208
One Clear Call 26
The Other Woman 195

Page, Sir Brian 223
Page, Gail *114*
Page, Madeline 222–223

Palmer, Ernest G. 26
Parker, Dorothy 193
Parsons, Harriet 206–207
Parsons, Louella 5, 11, 68, 106, *107*, 128, 193, 206–207
Pasadena Playhouse School of the Theatre 140–142, 152, 155
Pascal, Gabriel (Lehol Gabor) 78, 79, 80, 98, 189–190
Payne, Patricia 256, 281
Pek, Desider 102–103, 105
Peking Express 167–169
Pickford, Mary 19
Planet of the Apes (TV series) 257, 258
Police Surgeon 255, 257
Powell, William 161
Power, Tyrone 124, 200
Presley, Elvis 208, *209*
The Private Lives of Elizabeth and Essex 103
The Proud Rebel 208
Purdom, Edmund *203*, 204

Rafferty 292
Rains, Claude 193, *194*
Rapf, Matthew 228
Rapper, Irving 100, 115, 129–130, 166
Rathbone, Basil 71, 100
Rathbun, Walter ("Bunny") 151–152, 177
Reagan, Ronald 130, 151
The Red Banner 78, *79*
Red Headed Woman 105
Red Mountain 164
The Return of Captain Blood 178
Reynolds, Viola MacGlashan (JML's aunt) 10, 16, *16*, *18*, 24, 29, 50, 56, 57–58, 197–198, 246, 248
Reynolds, William A. (JML's uncle) 10, 24, 29, 55–56, 58
Riesner, Dean 41, 151–152
Roberts, Ben 237
Robertson, Stanley 238, 240, 258, 265
Robin Hood (TV series) 200
Roddenberry, Gene 236–238, 240
Rogers, Bill 11
Rogers St. John, Adela 11
Roman, Ruth 158–159
Romero, Cesar 166, 167, 207, 248
Romero Gonzalez, Virginia 240, 249, 258, 297

Sagal, Boris 287
St. Clair, Mal 38
St. Francis of Assisi 222
The Santa Fe Trail 33
Savalas, Telly 224
The Scarlet Hour 202
Schafer, Natalie 158
Schenck, Joseph 39, 78, 80
Schenck, Nicholas 39
Schiller, Wilton 170, 227–228, 231, 232, 249–250, 255, 256, 278, 281, 297, 302
Schratt, Katherine ("Kati") 77
Schuller, Rev. Robert 293–294
Scott, David 293
Scott, Lisabeth 163
Scott, Zachary 174
The Sea Beast 35
Serenade 195
Serling, Rod 250
Shanghai Express 167–168
SHARE 179, 241, 275, 277
Shatner, William 237, *239*, 251, 299
Shattuck, Ross 68
Shaw, George Bernard 78, 80, 98, 189
Shaw, Lou 278, 279, 281, 294–296
Sheen, Martin 243
Sheridan, Ann 109, 128, 187, 188
Simmons, Jean 204
Simon Locke MD 250, 251, 252–253, 255
Simon Locke/Police Surgeon 249–253, 255–256, 257
The Six Million Dollar Man 278
Sodom und Gomorra 79
The Soldier's Plaything 40
Solomon, Chaim 111
Solow, Herb 299
Sons of Liberty 111
Sothern, Ann 243–244
Stack, Robert 128
Star Trek 236, 237–240, *239*, 253, 293, 299, 301–302
Stern, Ethel 86, 90, 99, 222, 224, 240, 248
Stevens, Anitra *203*
Stewart, Jimmy 175, 176
Strange Interlude 105

Tarzan's Romance 21
Taylor, Elizabeth 161

Technicolor 108
Teresa, Mother 267–268
Thalberg, Irving 25, 37
The Thin Man (TV series) 190
The Third Degree 34, 37
This Is the Army 150–151, 152
This Is the Life (TV series) 282, *283*
Thompson, Fred 161
Timberline 106
Topper (TV series) 179, 190
Trevor, Claire 157, 159
Trey O'Hearts 22
Tuddawalli, Robert *214*
Tumbleweed 175–177
20000 Leagues Under the Sea 195–197

The Ultimate Computer 236
Under a Texas Moon 40
The Unsuspected 193–194, *194*
Ustinov, Peter *204*

The Vagabond King 203
Vera-Ellen 189
von Bernuth, Charles 257, 265, 292
von Bernuth, Eloise 257, 265, 292
von Bernuth, Oscar Max 106, 172
Von Braun, Werner 199
Vox Pop 146, 147, 149, 150

Walker, Card 196–197
Wallis, Brent 167
Wallis, Hal 5, *83*, *96*, 128, 161–163, *162*, 164–165, 168, 169–171, 208, 299, 300, 302
Wallis, Louise Fazenda 5, 161
Walsh, Bill 159, 196
Walt Disney Studios 195–196, 200–202
Walthall, Henry *26*
Warner, Irma 5
Warner, Jack L. 5, 69, 85, 94–95, 111, 114–115, 131, 138–140, 145–146, *162*, 171, 172, 190, 227, *228*, 303

Warner, Sam 95
Wayne, John 226
Webb, Jack 178–179, 191–192, 258
We're No Angels 203
Werner, Marti 86, 98, 135, 138
Werner, Mort 136–138, 302
When a Man Loves 35
Whiplash 25, 116, 205–206, 210–216, *214*, 220–222, 304
Wilding, Michael *203*
William, Warren 69, 116
Williams, John 248
Wilson, Carey 27
Windsor, Clair 26
Winfield, Joan *see* Lucas, Joan MacGillicuddy
The Wonderful World of Disney 196, 197, 200
Wong Howe, James *see* Howe, James Wong
Wood, Natalie 207
Woodward, Agnes *18*, 81
Woodward, Elizabeth (Aunt Lizzie) 18, *18*, 81
Woodward, Martha (Aunt Mattie) 18, 81
World Vision 258
Wynn, Keenan 157

Yankee Doodle Dandy 34, 138, *139*

Zanuck, Darryl 5, 14–15, 37–39, *38*, 45, 58–59, 63, 75, 78, 80–81, 91, 105, 124, 130, 131, 179, 200, 203–204, 244–245, 303
Zanuck, Richard 244–245
Zanuck, Virginia 5, 13–14, 58–59, 73, 75, 78, 81, 142, 203, 244–246
Zorro (TV series) 200–201
Zuckerman, Arnon 282–283, 284, 286–287

www.ingramcontent.com/pod-product-compliance
Ingram Content Group UK Ltd.
Pitfield, Milton Keynes, MK11 3LW, UK
UKHW041924140426
5217IPUK00014B/310